How to Do *Everything* with

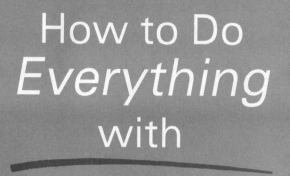

Google™

How to Do *Everything* with

Google™

Fritz Schneider
Nancy Blachman
Eric Fredricksen

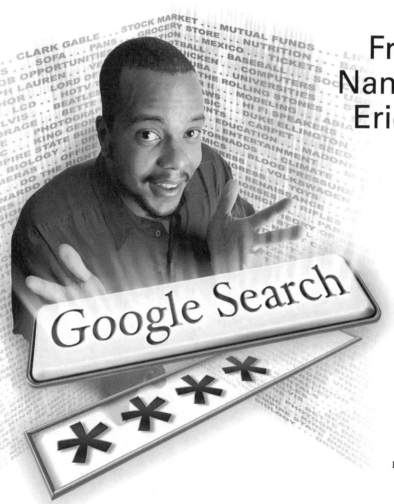

McGraw-Hill/Osborne

New York Chicago San Francisco Lisbon
London Madrid Mexico City Milan New Delhi
San Juan Seoul Singapore Sydney Toronto

The McGraw·Hill Companies

McGraw-Hill/Osborne
2100 Powell Street, 10th Floor
Emeryville, California 94608
U.S.A.

To arrange bulk purchase discounts for sales promotions, premiums, or fund-raisers, please contact **McGraw-Hill**/Osborne at the above address. For information on translations or book distributors outside the U.S.A., please see the International Contact Information page immediately following the index of this book.

How to Do Everything with Google™

1234567890 FGR FGR 019876543

ISBN 0-07-223174-2

Publisher:	Brandon A. Nordin
Vice President &	
Associate Publisher	Scott Rogers
Acquisitions Editor	Katie Conley
Project Editor	Julie M. Smith
Acquisitions Coordinator	Athena Honore
Technical Editor	Peter Norvig
Copy Editor	Linda Marousek
Proofreader	Susie Elkind
Indexer	Valerie Perry
Composition	Lucie Ericksen
Illustrators	Kathleen Fay Edwards, Melinda Moore Lytle
Series Design	Mickey Galicia
Cover Series Design	Dodie Shoemaker
Cover Illustration	Tom Willis

This book was composed with Corel VENTURA™ Publisher.

About the Authors

Fritz Schneider ping-ponged from San Diego, to New York, and back again in the course of his schooling, acquiring a B.S. in Computer Engineering at Columbia University, an M.S. in Computer Science at UCSD, and a boatload of Southwest frequent flyer miles. Before packing his bags and making steam for Google, he worked in web publishing, web privacy, and computer security. Fritz currently works as a Software Engineer in the Google mothership where, among other things, he is at the forefront of a heroic lobby asserting the obvious need for Google to open an Engineering office in Fiji. Until the lobby succeeds, he's content to live in San Francisco and dream of a world without war, and a city without parking enforcement.

Nancy Blachman regularly gives seminars and workshops on searching with Google and wrote an online tutorial and primer on using Google effectively, Google Guides, which is available at www.googleguide.com. She has written a half dozen tutorial and reference books on using mathematical software. She holds a B.Sc. in Applied Mathematics from the University of Birmingham, U.K., a M.S. in Operations Research from the University of California at Berkeley, and a M.S. in Computer Science from Stanford University, where she taught for eight years.

Eric Fredricksen was born in California, and somewhat later received his bachelor's degree in Mathematics from the University of California, despite the distractions of diverse arts, both noble and otherwise. Amidst stints at several companies working in cryptography, database software, accounting applications, and computer games, he received his master's degree, also illogically in Mathematics, from Stanford University. Late in the 20th century he overcame his fear of commuting to join Google, where he lead the development of the Google Toolbar. He lives blissfully married in San Francisco.

About the Technical Editor

Peter Norvig is the Director of Search Quality at Google Inc. He is also a Fellow and Councilor of the American Association for Artificial Intelligence and co-author of Artificial Intelligence: A Modern Approach, the leading textbook in the field. Additionally, he has written over fifty publications in various areas of Computer Science, concentrating on Artificial Intelligence, Natural Language Processing and Software Engineering. Dr. Norvig holds a B.S. in Applied Mathematics from Brown University and a Ph.D. in Computer Science from the University of California at Berkeley.

Contents at a Glance

Contents

Acknowledgments

This book couldn't have gotten off the ground without the confidence and support of lots of Googlers. VP of Engineering Wayne Rosing was of great help in the initial stages of the project. A number of people deserve thanks for going out of their ways to contribute advice, anecdotes, and encouragement. These people include Huican Zhu, Michael Schmitt, Naga Kataru, Andrew Fikes, Matt Cutts, Krishna Bharat, Lauren Baptist. Thanks also to Raymond Nasr, Cindy McCaffrey, Doug Edwards, and the rest of the staff in Corporate Marketing and Legal who shepherded us through this process.

We'd like to give particular thanks to our technical editor, Peter Norvig, for his helpful comments and corrective nudges.

Katie Conley and Julie Smith at McGraw-Hill/Osborne deserve recognition for keeping this whole herd of cats on track. Thanks for putting up with us!

Fritz Schneider: Several brave souls read over early versions of this book and provided helpful feedback: Nelson Blachman, Casey Brennan, Amy Jembrysek, and Phil Schneider. Thanks to them, as well as to other family and friends who endured my hermitude during this escapade: Em, Nic, my folks, Sharif, Tim, and Amy. Special thanks to Tammy Khaleel and Mary Parker for their hospitality. And finally, thanks to Thomas Powell for encouragement and confidence.

Nancy Blachman: First, I offer thanks to Jerry Peek for suggesting that I write a book about how to search with Google. I thank my wonderful co-authors, Fritz Schneider and Eric Fredricksen, without whom I could never have written this book. I also thank my agent, Neil Salkind at Studio B, for quickly taking care of all business matters so that we could focus on writing this book. I revised what I wrote incorporating the valuable comments and suggestions from many people to whom I am grateful. They include: Marian Bach, Joel Biatch, Henry Cejtin, Marie desJardins, Pauline Facciano, Philip Fire, Thomas Galloway, Ahuva Gelblum,

Johann George, Leora Gregory, Andrew Gumperz, Nancy Jamison, Doris Li, Liz Mabey, Jane Manning, Gwyn Firth Murray, Martha Newman, Steve Omohundro, Jerry Peek, Hamish Reid, Marlene Rozofsky Rogers, Malcolm Slaney, Paul Spinrad, Linda Walters, Rita Wespi, and Hanna Yap. I especially thank my father, Nelson Blachman, for asking questions that encouraged me to explore and learn more about how Google works and for reviewing numerous drafts. I thank Katie Conley, Julie Smith, and their colleagues at Osborne/McGraw-Hill for giving me the opportunity to share my knowledge and love of Google with you. I also thank my husband David desJardins, a software developer at Google, for suggesting topics to include, answering questions, and reviewing early drafts.

   Eric Fredricksen: I'd like to thank my wife Tracy for her support and indulgence throughout this project. I would also like to thank the friends and family I neglected while writing this book, and my coworkers and employer for their assistance. Last but not least, I'd like to thank the City of New York for its excellent subway system.

Introduction

About this Book

This book is for anyone who uses Google—or wants to learn to use Google—to find information online. It covers the range of Google's search offerings, from the popular task of searching for Web pages, to lesser-known services enabling you to find specialized content such as images, online news articles, products for sale, and discussion forums. Each of Google's features is explained at a basic level so as to accommodate novices, but includes substantial discussion that will interest intermediate users as well. For advanced users—professional web developers, long-time Internet users, and Google aficionados—some of the material will be review, but we believe there is plenty in this book that will help improve the way even seasoned veterans search with Google.

Approaching the issue from another angle, this book is for students, teachers, librarians, researchers, journalists, lawyers, activists, businesspeople, developers, the habitually curious, and anyone else searching Google on a weekly basis. It's for people who research as part of their job, as well as for those who are merely interested in seeing what they can find. And it's for people of all ages, not just in the United States, but all around the world.

The bottom line is that this is a book for people who want to use Google as an effective tool.

Why This Book is Helpful to Those Familiar with Google

When we started writing, fellow Googlers wished to know what someone already familiar with Google would learn from it. Friends and family members asked as well, so we thought this question was worth addressing.

Most people who use Google utilize only a small fraction of its features. Most aren't even aware of the *existence* of most of its features. This is good because it means Google often provides relevant results for most queries. But it's also bad because it means that in many situations, you might not be aware of how to find what you're looking for. Sometimes Google's results aren't exactly what you need and you might not be sure how to ask for more accurate results. Or you might spend valuable time trying to find certain kinds of information using only Google's most basic features when Google provides a better way to find it that is not only more precise, but faster as well. And there might be some information you go to offline sources for, but that is easily accessible with Google.

Simply entering search terms and hoping for the best *might* get you what you want. But you'll do far better if you know how to specify *exactly* what you want, and even the format in which you want it.

Knowledge is power. The more you know about Google—how it works, it's features, it's strengths, and it's weaknesses—the more powerful a tool it becomes at your fingertips.

Prerequisites

We assume that you, the reader, have a basic understanding of how to use the Web. In particular, that you're comfortable navigating around web pages using a browser such as Microsoft Internet Explorer, and that you're familiar with its essential features such as the back button and address bar (the space into which you type web site addresses). And of course we assume you want to learn more about searching with Google.

Getting the Most Out Of This Book

Generally speaking, the skills you should take away from this book fall into two broad categories. The first is knowledge you can apply almost every time you search. Such skills include forming effective queries, refining queries that don't give you what you want, and applying an understanding of Google's most useful tools. Mastering these skills is simply a matter of practice and experience. Once you've added them to your repertoire, they'll become a natural part of your everyday searches.

The second category encompasses a comprehensive awareness of what Google offers. By this we mean the knowledge of what you can and cannot find with Google, and the full extent of its capabilities. Such skills include some of the more esoteric search services Google provides as well as features that let you restrict the web pages Google searches according to some very specific criteria, for example by part of a site's URL (e.g., to search only sites ending with ".com"). You probably won't use all such features on a day-to-day basis. But chances are that when a search situation comes up that would previously have stymied you, applying one of these lesser-known tools can solve your problem. You might not be able to recall the exact details of each of these features, but you'll know they exist, where to look for them, and what to expect of them.

Inside Google: The Authors

We're not exactly what you'd call an impartial set of authors when it comes to Google; all three of us are closely connected to the search engine. Fritz Schneider and Eric Fredricksen work at Google as software engineers, and both have been there for several years. Nancy Blachman regularly gives seminars on searching with Google and has written an online tutorial and primer on using Google effectively, which is available at www.googleguide.com. She has been using Google since the Spring of 1999, when Google was less than one year old.

The advantage we have in writing this book is that we're insiders. As insiders, we're in a position to tell you about parts of Google that are often overlooked or seldom discovered, and to fill in our discussion with background information you'll probably find interesting, if not useful.

The disadvantage is that, from a journalistic point of view, we're biased. We're Googlers writing about Google, so obviously we have positive opinions about Google's services. However, when an aspect of Google is lacking in some respect, we've tried to state this clearly. Some features Google's users haven't found particularly useful we mention only briefly, or omit completely.

Learn the services Google has to offer, understand the tools we describe, and decide for yourself what is and is not useful for your particular set of tasks.

Special Elements

A number of special elements have been added to help you get the most out of this book.

- ■ **How to . . .**   These special boxes explain, in a nutshell, how to perform certain tasks or use the skills you've learned in this book.

- ■ **Did You Know?**   These special boxes provide additional information about topics related to Google.

- ■ **Notes**   These provide extra information or things you should know about Google.

Part I

Google
Web Search

Chapter 1

Welcome to Google

Though no one knows exactly how many pages there are on the Web, most estimates put the total at more than 10 billion. That's more web pages than there are people in the world, and more than 100 times the number of books in the U.S. Library of Congress. If you looked at web pages at a rate of one per second, never stopping to sleep or eat, it would take more than 300 years to see that many pages. Combined with the fact that millions of new web pages are added each week, and millions more changed, the only possible way to make use of this mass of data is to automate its organization.

Services like Google examine the vast amounts of information available on the Web and provide you with the capability to quickly find the pieces you need. Google can be used to discover information for which you might not otherwise know where to look. For example, you can find instructions on how to refinance your house or a discussion of Antarctic geography. It can also provide a shortcut to information you already know how to find. For example, if you wanted to find out about IBM Thinkpad laptop computers, you could go to **ibm.com** and click around the site until you found what you were after. But searching Google for **ibm thinkpad** immediately locates a number of IBM pages discussing Thinkpads, and does so more quickly and easily than browsing for them manually.

In this chapter, we introduce Google and its services and give you some background information that will be helpful in understanding what Google is and does. Once you get in the habit of searching for what you want, you'll probably find Google to be an indispensable tool for the task. It's almost always easier to search for something than rely on guesswork and luck when browsing for it.

Google

There are two primary approaches that make it easy for people to find what they're looking for amongst large amounts of data. The first is to enable them to describe what they're seeking, and use computers to locate needles that match the given description in the haystack of data. This approach is of course called *searching*, and the systems that provide this service in the online world are called *search engines*. You enter some words that you'd expect to find on a web page you're seeking (or, less often, words *describing* a page you're seeking) and a search engine sieves the Web for documents matching your description and shows you links to what it finds.

The second, major alternative, approach to searching is to categorize the data in a hierarchical fashion so people can navigate from general to more specific categories, and finally to individual pieces of data. For example, most online shopping sites organize their products this way. This approach is called a *directory*, and we'll have much more to say about directories in Chapter 11.

Google is primarily a search engine. You enter a set of words you'd like to find on the Web, and Google shows you pages matching those words. In search engine parlance, the words you enter to request information are called your *query*, and are often referred to as *search terms*. In this book, we call out search terms in boldfaced font, for example **piano composers**.

Google is not, however, *only* a search engine, as we'll discuss shortly.

The Google Interface

Before we talk about Google's interface, there's an important fact you should keep in mind. It's common for companies to change the appearance of their web pages in order to add new information, reorganize content, or simply to exhibit a fresh new look. Google is no exception. There's a good chance that Google will make adjustments to its interfaces between the time this book is published and the time you read it. Bear this in mind if the Google pages you see in your browser aren't exactly as they appear in this book. Regardless of how it appears, the way Google works isn't likely to change much. It's just that links and certain features might appear in different places than they do at the time of this writing. Now, on to Google's interface.

To bring up Google, point your browser to **www.google.com**. You'll see a web page like that shown in Figure 1-1. The most commonly used part of this page is the search box into which you enter queries. It's the text input box in the middle of the page. This page also contains links to more information about Google, and to some special features it provides.

An oft-overlooked but important part of this page is the row of tabs found under Google's logo (see Figure 1-1). These tabs are intended to appear as if you were looking at filing folders with their labels sticking up. Each tab represents a separate service Google offers, and the current service you're on is shown with a darker color. Click on a tab to take you to that service. Figure 1-2 shows the result of clicking the Images tab, whose interface is very similar to that of the web service.

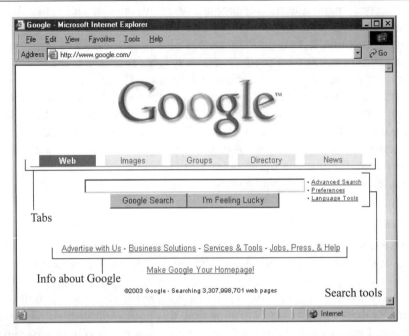

FIGURE 1-1 Google's home page

FIGURE 1-2 Google Images allows you to search for...you guessed it: images.

Google Doodles

Keep your eye on the logo on Google's home page; it changes. In celebration of holidays and special events, Google displays themed logos—Google Doodles—for the day. Figure 1-3 shows the Google Doodle for New Year's Day 2002. Figure 1-4 is the Doodle for American mystery filmmaker Alfred Hitchcock's birthday, shown on August 13, 2003.

Google Doodles aren't limited to major international or American holidays. Regional holidays such as Children's Day (Japan) and La Fête de la Musique (France) are celebrated, and occasionally even less well-known events such as Burning Man (Nevada, USA) as well. You can find a complete list of special Google logos at **http://www.google.com/holidaylogos.html**.

 *Click on a Google Doodle to find out more about the event it celebrates.*

The Google Doodler

Google has no Art Department per se; their much-loved doodles are the fruit of the labors of one humble man, Dennis Hwang. Though he's been favored with more than one news story for his doodling, Dennis' actual job at Google is web designer; his doodles are something he must fit into his schedule as best he can manage.

Each of Dennis' doodles finds its way to the desk of Google cofounder Sergey Brin, who has the final say on each of the doodles. Not cute enough? Too many bunnies? Then it's back to the drawing board for Dennis!

It was the antics of Sergey and his cofounder Larry Page in the very early days of Google that inaugurated the Google Doodle tradition. When the two left the fledgling search engine to fend for itself while they attended the 1999 Burning Man festival in the Nevada desert, they put up a special logo featuring the Burning Man himself to celebrate the event.

FIGURE 1-3   Google Doodles appear for many major international holidays.

| FIGURE 1-4 | Google picks a wide variety of events to celebrate, in this case Michelangelo's birthday. |

Google's Services

Primarily, people use Google to search for web pages. This is the default service when you go to **www.google.com**, as you can see from the fact that the web tab is highlighted in Figure 1-1. But this isn't the only service Google offers. In Figure 1-2, you can see that the Images tab is highlighted. This is another of Google's services; it provides you with the capability to search for images instead of web pages. In fact, each tab represents a separate service that Google offers, each of which enables you to find a specialized kind of online content.

Part I of this book (Chapters 1–7) is primarily about using Google Web Search: how to form queries, how to interpret results pages, and how to put Google's special search services features to good use. Part II (Chapters 8–14) is about other kinds of searches Google offers, and covers each of the services behind the tabs in more detail. Since Google's services all operate in a similar fashion, many techniques and concepts discussed in Part I are applicable to the specialized services discussed in Part II as well.

Note that you don't have to use the tabs to access these specialized services. Each service shown (and some that aren't shown!) is directly accessible by pointing your browser at a Google subdomain, for example **images.google.com**. Table 1-1 shows each service along with more information about it.

NOTE   *Google's smaller or less popular services aren't listed in Table 1-1. They are discussed where appropriate throughout the book, and in particular in Chapter 14.*

You can see from Table 1-1 that not all of Google's services are strictly search tools. Some, such as Groups and Froogle, allow you to search *or* browse content. This is why we said previously that Google is primarily—but not exclusively—a search engine.

Major Service	Site	Use	Chapter
Web	www.google.com	Find web pages and other information such as stock quotes, addresses, and maps.	1–7
News	news.google.com	Find and browse online news sources.	8
Groups	groups.google.com	Find, browse, and participate in online discussions.	9
Images	images.google.com	Finds images, graphics, and photos online.	10
Directory	directory.google.com	Browse web pages by category.	11
Answers	answers.google.com	For as little as US$2.50, obtain assistance from researchers with expertise in online searching.	12
Froogle	froogle.google.com	Find and browse products for sale online.	13

TABLE 1-1   Google's Major Offerings

NOTE   *When someone (including your authors) refers to a "google search," they usually mean a Google Web Search.*

Essential Google Facts

There are many reasons why Google is so popular. Among the most important reasons are the following facts about Google's services.

No Paid Placement

Some search engines have what is called *paid placement*. Paid placement means advertisers can pay the search engine to show ads as if they were search results. Some people (advertisers, mostly) argue that ads *can* be thought of as search results since they're typically targeted to a user's query. But most users expect that a search engine will show them the most relevant web pages for their search terms, not links purchased by online retailers.

Google does *not* sell placement in its results. When you perform a search, Google shows you the web pages it believes to be most relevant to your query. Ads are never mixed in with Google's results. Instead, Google shows ads separate from search results, in shaded boxes, and labels them as Sponsored Links.

The Google Friends Newsletter

If you'd like to stay up-to-date about the happenings with Google, consider signing up for the Google Friends newsletter. This newsletter is delivered via e-mail whenever Google feels it has sufficient new announcements or information to distribute. Typically, newsletters come out about six times per year, and include things such as the following:

- New product announcements
- Personal accounts of experience with Google
- Search tips
- Fun or interesting things you can find with Google
- Company news

You can sign up at **http://www.google.com/contact/newsletter.html**, or simply search for **google friends newsletter**. If you'd like to read the newsletter, but don't want to receive it by e-mail, you can find it archived on the Web at **http://www.google.com/googlefriends/archive.html**, or by searching for **google friends newsletter archive**.

Many people (the authors included) feel that this integrity with respect to searching is one of Google's most admirable characteristics. You can't buy your way into Google.

NOTE *While you can't buy your way into Google, some people have figured out how to cheat their way in, by trying to deceive Google as to the actual content of their page. For example, a page that appears to be devoted to men's health might, once loaded by your browser, change into a page filled with advertisements for Viagra and prescription drugs. We discuss this in a bit more detail in Chapter 4.*

Relevant Results

Google searches more than three billion pages every time you enter a query. It is surprisingly effective at selecting links that closely match your query from this vast number of pages. These facts, along with the absence of advertisements in the results, render Google one of the most effective search engines on the Web. In fact, because of the relevancy of Google's results, many people find it easier to return to favorite sites by searching for them on Google, rather than committing them to memory or bookmarking them in their browser.

Fast, Clean Interface

Google prides itself on providing users with an uncluttered searching interface. Google never uses pop-up advertisements (those that appear in a new browser window when you visit a site) and only permits subdued, text-based advertisements on its pages. This combination of factors, along with a lot of engineering know-how, makes Google searching very fast.

NOTE   *If you see pop-ups on Google, chances are that they're launched by the page you just left, or by a page in another browser window. It's also possible you might have adware on your computer, a small program that shows ads as you browse. Some adware even goes so far as to alter how you see the pages of popular sites (such as Google). Adware will sometimes replace the site's ads with those from the adware's affiliates. See **http://www.google.com/help/nopopupads.html** for more information.*

What Google Is Not

Now that you know a bit about what Google is and does, we'd like to discuss what Google *isn't*.

Google Is Not the Only Search Engine

The fact that Google is a tool is easy to overlook. It's not the *only* tool, nor is it necessarily the *best*; the *best* depends on your task. For example, Google doesn't let you specify the size of the file you're looking for. AllTheWeb (**www.allthe web .com**) does, so for that task there's no comparison.

Did you know?

Google's Privacy Policy

Many people are rightly concerned about the information collected about them by the websites they visit. The information a company collects and what it does with it are usually summed up in the company's *privacy policy*, an online note outlining their practices. Here we summarize the major features of Google's privacy policy at the time of this writing. However, this is no substitute for reading the policy itself, which you can find at **http://www.google.com/privacy.html**.

Google doesn't collect personally identifiable information about you except when you explicitly give it, for example when you sign up for a pay service such as Google Answers (Chapter 12). Like most search engines, Google *does* record each search that occurs. These records contain information automatically transmitted to every site you visit by your browser, and include your computer's current IP address, your language of preference, and the browser you're using. Google uses that information to improve its services and features, for tasks such as determining which result links users click on the most and tracking trends in its *userbase* (e.g., browser demographics, how people use the site, how often the average user does a search, etc.).

The information Google collects—be it personal information explicitly given or nonpersonal data automatically transmitted by the browser—is never shared with third parties except in aggregate. In other words, Google won't sell or give away information about individual users, but reserves the right to share data about its users as a whole. For example, Google might share information about how many people searched for "Pokemon" in a particular month, or the number of searches for "CSI" as opposed to "Friends." You can see more examples of this type of information on Google Zeitgeist (Chapter 14).

A notable exception to this rule is when Google is compelled to share information by law. In Google's words (at the time of this writing), "We will release specific personal information about you if required to do so in order to comply with any valid legal process such as a search warrant, subpoena, statute, or court order."

If you're serious about finding information online, don't limit yourself to just one source. Explore other search engines and directories, measure their strengths, and decide which is best for what task. Good starting points are **teoma.com**, **alltheweb.com**, and **searchenginewatch.com**. An interesting book on the parts of the Web you can't easily find with traditional search engines is *The Invisible Web* by Chris Sherman and Gary Price. A very good, more general (but somewhat dated) book about online research is *Find It Online*, by Alan Schlein.

Google Is Not a Sanctioning Body

As we've said, Google is a tool that helps you find things on the Web. Since tools don't make judgment calls about what you do with them, neither does Google. It strives to remain impartial to the content it makes searchable. Google doesn't endorse search results; it just reports them.

Google Is Not a Censor (When It Can Help It)

Just as Google doesn't sanction results, neither does it censor them. Google's policy is that it will remove pages from its search results under two conditions. The first is if specifically requested by the webmaster of the site. The second is if Google is required to by law. As is common practice, Google adheres to the law in international jurisdictions, so it's possible that some content may appear in results in one country, but not in another. For example, Germany has very strict laws prohibiting hate speech, so it's possible that some sites you might find from outside Germany are not searchable with Google from within Germany.

NOTE   *If you're adverse to adult content, we highly recommend you enable SafeSearch when using Google (see Chapter 7).*

A Brief History of Google

Sergry Brin and Larry Page were graduate students in Computer Science at Stanford University in 1996 when they began working on a project called BackRub. Their experimental search engine was named BackRub because it analyzed *back links*, or which pages link to a particular document.

Over the next couple of years, they improved BackRub and began to receive increased attention around campus and in academic communities. The attention came not just from the quality results their search engine provided, but from BackRub's voracious appetite for hard disks and the increasingly obvious fact that Larry Page had set up a server farm in his dorm room.

By 1998, Larry and Sergey badly needed to put their operation on more firm ground, that is, on ground that was not a dorm room or computer lab at Stanford. When they couldn't gain the support of the major search players of the day, they decided to find *angel investors* (individual investors) to fund their ideas. In a now-famous episode, one of Sun's founders, Andy Bechtolsheim, wrote out a check for $100,000 to "Google, Inc.," the fanciful company name they'd chosen. One tiny problem was that Google, Inc. didn't yet exist. The check sat uncashed for weeks while they quickly cobbled together a corporation and larger support base.

By late 1998, they'd gathered enough money to move the operation to a room in a house near Stanford in Menlo Park, California. They put their pursuit of Ph.D.s on the back burner, got **Google.com** up and running, and were answering 10 thousand queries per day from an index of 25 million pages! Less than six months later, they'd moved into an office in Palo Alto and were answering more than half a million queries per day. In the process, Larry and Sergey hired Susan Wojcicki, their landlord from their house in Menlo Park, away from Intel. She still works with them to this day as Google's Product Management Director.

By mid-1999, Google was experiencing ridiculously explosive growth, and was hiring like mad. It was serving more than 3 million queries per day, and the company had to move again to a much larger building in Mountain View to accommodate its new staff. One year later, Google was answering almost 20 million queries per day. Six month after that, 100 million queries per day. By late 2003, Google was serving over 200 million queries per day and had a staff of over 1,000 in 21 offices worldwide.

In what has become something of a tradition among Google employees, Larry and Sergey still have not completed their Ph.D.s at the time of this writing.

NOTE   *You can read more about Google's history at*
http://www.google.com/corporate/history.html.

Chapter 2

Craft Your Searches

How to...

- Enter a query
- Choose effective search terms
- Use Google's special search syntax to better specify what you want

In this chapter, we discuss the nuts and bolts of using Google and the craft of asking Google for precisely what you want. Your ability to find useful information with Google Web Search depends largely on your knowledge of how to ask for it. Contrary to many accounts, Google isn't omniscient; you'll want to tell Google what you want in a way that makes it most likely that you'll find what you're looking for. Part of getting what you want is choosing effective search terms, but you'll also need to know when to use Google's specialized search syntax, and how.

How to Enter a Query

If your browser isn't pointing to Google, enter **www.google.com** to visit Google's home page, shown in Figure 2-1.

You can enter a query in the search box in the middle of the page. A search box is also provided at the top of every results page (see Figure 2-2) so you don't have to go back to the Google home page to refine your query or enter a new one.

NOTE   *Because the Web is constantly changing, the results for the examples in this book and the results you see when you use Google might be different.*

Once you've entered something in the search box, press ENTER or click on the Google Search button. Doing so asks Google to search the Web for pages relevant to the terms you've entered. In response, it shows links to pages matching your query, as well as a snippet of text from each page with your search terms shown in boldface font.

Search Results pages like Figure 2-2 are packed with information and links relating to your query. In this example, Google Web Search results appear below news links and *sponsored links*, which is Googlespeak for "paid advertisements." Google never mixes ads into its search results. Instead, ads are shown in shaded squares or rectangles above or to the right of the results. We discuss the various parts of results pages in more detail in Chapter 4.

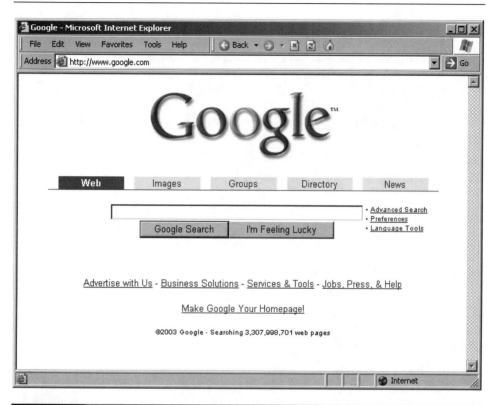

Enter queries in Google's Search box.

The results themselves are shown in order of relevancy: the pages Google believes most likely to be what you're looking for are shown first. Google considers a variety of factors to determine relevancy; for example, the popularity of a page and the presence of your search terms in prominent positions within the page, such as in the page's title. We discuss more about how Google orders its search results in Appendix A, How Google Works.

Go Directly to the First Result

Click the I'm Feeling Lucky button on Google's home page (Figure 2-1) to go directly to the first result. Instead of showing you a list of pages, Google sends you immediately to what it believes to be the most relevant page for the query, the first result. For example, if you enter the query **cirque du soleil** and click the I'm

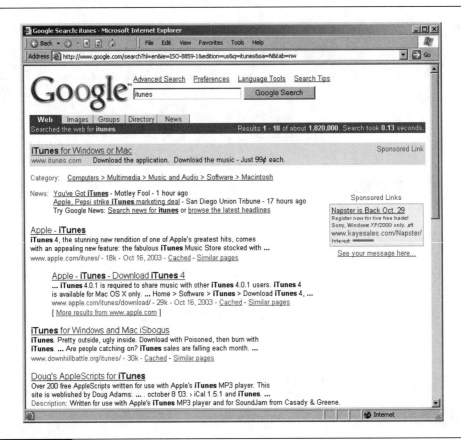

FIGURE 2-2   A Google Search results page includes a search box for viewing your current query and for entering another query.

Feeling Lucky button, you'll go to the Cirque du Soleil home page, shown in Figure 2-3.

> **NOTE**   *The I'm Feeling Lucky feature doesn't consider sponsored links (advertisements) when deciding where to take you.*

The I'm Feeling Lucky button can save you the time it takes to review your results and then click on the first one. It's best used when you're very confident the page you want is the best fit for your query, for example, if the page you're looking for is very popular. Most people find an I'm Feeling Lucky search is best used when you want to go to the home page of something or someone you know the name of. For example, it's a safe bet that an I'm Feeling Lucky search for **microsoft** will send you to **www.microsoft.com**.

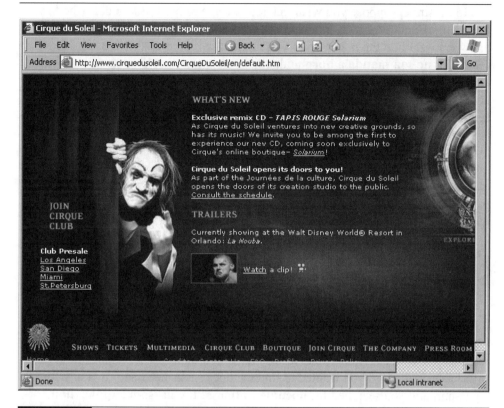

FIGURE 2-3   The result of an I'm Feeling Lucky search for "cirque du soleil"

Select Search Terms

When you use Google, the search terms you choose have a major impact on your ability to find what you want. How you craft your query determines both which pages will appear in the results and the order in which they'll appear. Selecting good search terms is the foundation upon which other searching skills are built. Here are the primary principles to keep in mind.

Use Words Likely to Appear on the Pages You Want

Google Web Search is based on analyzing the content of web pages and web page links, so the most important thing to remember is to search for words likely to appear on the pages you want in links to the pages. Effective searchers are good at predicting words that will appear in pages containing the information they're after.

To illustrate, suppose you wish to know the age of Nelson Mandela (the former President of South Africa). If you search for **nelson mandela** or **nelson mandela age** you might find the information you're after, but it's probably a better idea to search for **nelson mandela born** under the assumption that his date of birth will appear on some page in a sentence like, "Nelson Mandela was born on…." In fact, at the time of this writing, the first result for **nelson mandela born** includes the sentence, "Nelson Rolihlahla Mandela (born July 18, 1918)."

Since Google matches your query terms against words on the page, you should avoid using questions as queries. Doing so asks Google to find pages with the question on them, instead of pages containing the information you want. For example, the query **where can I find a marketing job in Sunnyvale?** will find pages containing these words, but it won't necessarily find pages answering your question. A better query might be **marketing jobs sunnyvale**.

NOTE *See the Common Word Exclusion section to learn how that feature mitigates this pitfall to some degree. To guarantee the best results, however, you should avoid using questions as queries, unless, you think it's likely you'd find your question on a web page along with its answer.*

A subtle pitfall of Google Web Search is using search terms describing the information you seek, rather than terms that would themselves be part of the information. Suppose you wanted to find the documents necessary to apply for a passport and you searched for **documentation of the passport application process**. This query is problematic because it includes the term "documentation." Google finds pages containing your search terms, so this query returns pages on which the word "documentation" can be found. Because information on the Web is rarely labeled this nicely, there are probably many potentially useful pages this query won't turn up (and many useless pages it will). A better query might be **passport application process**.

In general, you should avoid search terms describing the form in which you want information. Queries beginning with "articles about," "discussion of," "documentation of," and "pages about" are all examples of these kinds of searches. There are times when using such terms is appropriate, but in general, you should stick to search terms that are likely to appear on the pages you want.

The bottom line is to avoid using terms that, though they might be associated with your topic, wouldn't necessarily be found on a page containing the desired information.

Pose Answerable Queries

It's a good idea to use precise, unambiguous terms and to avoid common ones. For example, if you need information about the development of young children, a search for **babies** is far too ambiguous. Instead, try **baby development, baby milestones**, or **baby development milestones**.

An excellent way to determine whether your query is likely to give you useful results is to apply what we call the *answerability test*. This test is simply to think about whether the query contains enough specific information for Google to know exactly what you're seeking. For example, it's hard to tell what a user searching for **orange** might want. Information about Orange County, California? The city Orange, California? The color orange? The fruit? Orange brand mobile phones? Orange juice? This query is not very answerable and thus less likely to return results relevant to the meaning the user had in mind.

A query that passes the answerability test is likely to return good results because it provides Google with enough information to be answered unambiguously. A consequence is that if you're searching for something that could return many different types of results, you should add a term that distinguishes your query among them. For example, if you wanted to search for information about the Detroit Lions football team, you might search for **lions football** instead of just **lions**.

NOTE   *The query **lions football** isn't quite the same kind of query as **baby development**. The first contains two keywords you might not expect to be adjacent, whereas the second is a phrase you would expect to find with both terms adjacent in the page text. We'll have more to say about a better way to find phrases in the "Quotes" section.*

If you're having trouble coming up with more specific terms to add, think about what you know about the topic. Consider using the answer to the question "What kind?" You can also add information about who, what, where, when, why, or how.

Be Brief

Google limits your query to a maximum of 10 words, but for best results, use a few precise search terms rather than a larger number of terms.

The query **quit smoking program** is much better than **program to treat tobacco cigarette smoking addiction**. One of these terms might not be present in a page that would be of interest to you.

Search Behavior

Google treats search terms in ways that might not be obvious to the average user. An awareness of how Google behaves with respect to certain aspects of your query will help you avoid crafting ineffective queries. It might also help you understand why a particular query you've used doesn't return the results you expect.

Implicit AND

The most important element of Google's search behavior is its so-called *implicit AND* rule. This means that when you enter multiple search terms, Google assumes you want pages matching *all* of the search terms. Google calls this implicit (or implied) AND because it interprets a search for **baseball card dealer** as a search for pages containing the word "baseball" *and* the word "card" *and* the word "dealer." To get this behavior in other search engines, you might use a query like **baseball AND card AND dealer**, or in some way indicate that you want to match all terms, not just any term.

NOTE   *If you don't want this behavior, Google provides an OR operator (discussed in the "Search Operators" section), which allows you to state your wish to find pages containing any (instead of all) of the search terms.*

Because of implicit AND, you can "narrow" the focus of queries that are too broad by adding more query terms. Consider the search results for **phoenix** in Figure 2-4. There is information about a browser named Firebird; Phoenix, Arizona; a company called Phoenix Technologies; and a Massachusetts magazine. These results are too broad if you're interested in information about Phoenix, Arizona, so adding the term **arizona** to the query can help focus on what you need. It will find pages containing "phoenix" that also contain the word "arizona." Figure 2-5 shows the results for **phoenix arizona**. Sure enough, these results are all specifically about the desert city.

Common Word Exclusion

Not all words are equal in the eyes of Google. Common words such as "an," "the," "how", and "where" are ignored as search terms, as are most words consisting of only a single letter or digit. Figure 2-6 shows search results for **to be or not to be**.

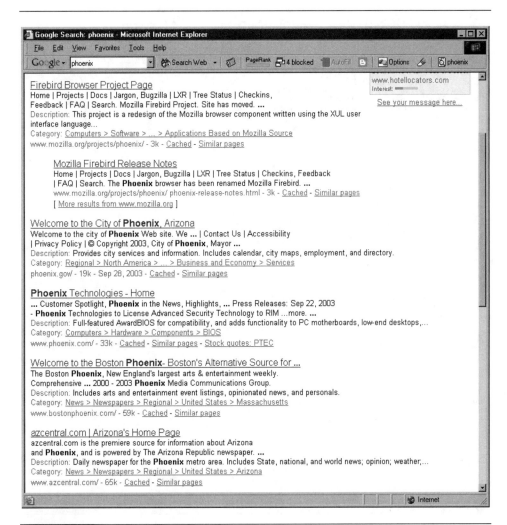

FIGURE 2-4   A search for *phoenix* turns up pages related to different uses of "phoenix."

Notice the subtle indication Google gives that the common words have been ignored. You can see that it ignored every word in the query except "not."

NOTE   *Google provides a way to include these "stop words" in your search terms if you really want to. See the "Using Quotes" section for more details.*

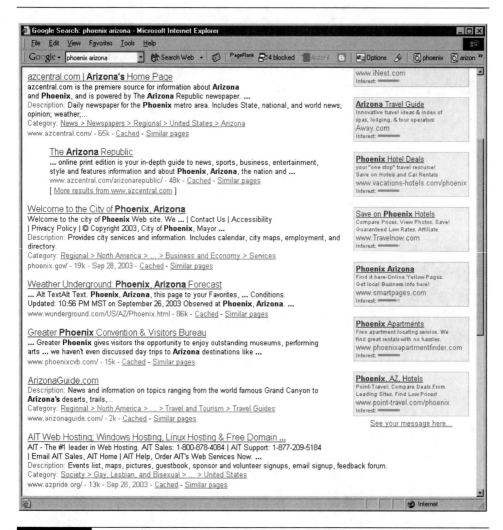

FIGURE 2-5   A search for *phoenix arizona* focuses on one particular way to use "phoenix."

This behavior, referred to as *common word exclusion*, was introduced because these words are found on virtually every page on the Web. As a result, these words most often do little to help focus a query. By searching for them, Google would increase the time it takes to return results with little benefit.

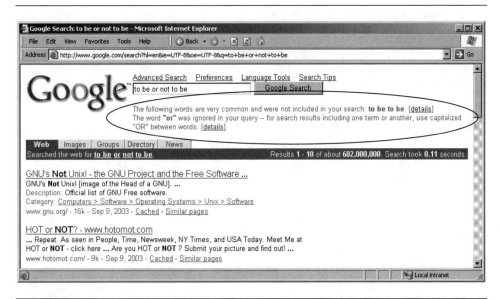

FIGURE 2-6 Google ignores very common words in search terms.

Common word exclusion is another reason not to pose queries to Google in the form of a question: most of the words that structure the question (for example, "who," "what," "when," "where," "why," and "how") are ignored! If you pose your query in the form of a question, you often end up searching for only the nouns and adjectives. For example, the query **who is the tallest man on earth?** is the same query as **tallest man earth**.

There is an exception to this rule. If a search consists of only normally excluded common words and nothing else, then, in this case, Google does perform a search for the word or words. For example, a search for **the** *has billions of results.*

Case Insensitivity

Google does not distinguish between capital and lowercase letters in search terms. So the query **King Lear** gives the same results as **king lear** and **KiNG LEAR**. This behavior rarely presents a problem because there are very few cases where a search term could mean something different depending upon how it is capitalized.

In fact, case insensitivity usually *improves* your search results because it finds all pages containing the term regardless of how the author chose to capitalize it. Otherwise, a search such as **weightwatchers** would not match pages containing "WeightWatchers" or "Weightwatchers." Note that, unlike some other behaviors, there is no way to avoid Google Search's case insensitivity.

Punctuation Exclusion

Because punctuation is typically not as important as the text around it, Google ignores most punctuation in search terms. Searching for **dr. seuss** is the same as searching for **dr seuss**.

There are two exceptions. When an apostrophe (single quote) or a hyphen appears within a search term (as opposed to in front of or following it), it is not ignored. Apostrophes are matched as you would expect, so **we're** and **were** are distinct terms, but the treatment of hyphenated words is less obvious. Because hyphenated words are often spelled different ways, Google searches for variations on any hyphenated terms you enter. It searches for the term as you entered it, the term with the hyphen omitted, and separately for the two parts of the term that the hyphen separates. For example, the query **part-time** searches for **part-time**, **parttime**, and **part time**. If you're not sure whether your word should be hyphenated, go ahead and use a hyphen anyway.

Search Term Order and Proximity

Word order affects multiterm queries: pages containing your search terms in the same order as they appear in your query are favored. As a consequence, you should enter search terms in the order they might be found in a sentence. Hence, a search for **archbishop of new york** promotes pages about the Archbishop of New York over the new Archbishop of York, England, as found by the query **new archbishop of york**.

Google will also somewhat favor pages containing your search terms nearby each other. So a search for **snake grass** is good for finding information about a plant of that name, while **snake in the grass** tends to emphasize pages about sneaky people. Note here that although, as we've seen, Google doesn't try to find the words "in" and "the" in the page, they still affect the search by spacing out the terms it does pay attention to. See the "Wildcards" section for a little further explanation of this phenomenon.

A summary of Google Web Search behavior is shown in Table 2-1.

Behavior	Description
implicit AND	Google finds pages containing *all* the search terms by default.
common word exclusion	Commonly used words unlikely to improve search results are ignored by default.
case insensitivity	Google doesn't distinguish between upper- and lowercase words.
punctuation	Google ignores most punctuation in your query except for operators. It treats apostrophes as significant. When you use a hyphen, it finds the term hyphenated, with the hyphen replaced by a space, or with the hyphen deleted.
word location	Google promotes pages containing terms ordered similarly to how the search terms are ordered.

TABLE 2-1   How Google Treats Parts of a Query

Search Operators

An *operator* is something you can add to a query that has special meaning to Google. Used in conjunction with search terms, operators modify how Google works. For example, an operator might tell Google that instead of looking for all the pages including a particular search term, you wish to find all the pages that do *not* include it.

Quotes

Enclosing multiple search terms in double quotes finds pages where the terms appear together, in the same order. For example, **"billy the kid"** searches for pages containing that phase. The query **billy the kid** finds pages in which "billy" and "kid" appear, but doesn't require that they're adjacent. Punctuation and capitalization are ignored as usual, but common words are *not* excluded from quoted search terms. Google finds the words in the quoted phrase exactly as you entered them.

NOTE *Phrases must be enclosed in double quotes (as in "..."). Using single quotes (as in '...') doesn't work.*

Using Quotes

Quoted phrases are probably the most used (and most useful) type of special search syntax. They are helpful any time you are interested in a specific phrase, such as an actual quotation (**"happy campers you will always be"**), song lyrics ("**i hear the train a comin'**"), a title ("**how the west was won**"), or name ("**larry page**").

Quoting is most necessary when the words are relatively common or have multiple meanings, and the phrase is relatively uncommon. For example, **apocalypse now** finds pages about the movie by that name quite easily without quotes, but if you were trying to find a less known phrase, such as the song containing some lyrics you remember, quote marks can be crucial. For example, "**girl, I'm leaving you tomorrow**", when queried for as a phrase, is enough to identify the lyrics of a song, as we see in Figure 2-7, much more easily than the same search would without the quote marks.

As we've said, common words that would normally be excluded from a search are automatically included when inside a quoted phrase. Perhaps the best example of a phrase that really needs to be quoted to be found is the famous line from Shakespeare's *Hamlet*, "to be or not to be." Most of these words would normally

FIGURE 2-7   Searching with quotes around one line of song lyrics often works well.

be ignored in a search, and in any case they are common. (In practice, to find Hamlet's soliloquy containing these words, you're better off searching for **hamlet "to be or not to be,"** since the phrase is famous enough to be used in many other contexts).

One powerful way to use quotes is to find very specific information. If you can guess a phrase that will appear on pages containing the information you want, you can find the information very quickly. Suppose you wanted to learn how to change your car's oil. You could search for **oil change**, but you will probably have better luck finding a step-by-step explanation by searching for **"how to change your oil"**. This phrase is a likely title for the page you want.

In the "Select Search Terms" section, we said that you should avoid asking Google questions. Instead, consider querying for part of the *answer* to your question. If you wanted to know the average rainfall in the Amazon basin, search for **"the average rainfall in the amazon basin is"**. To find recommended mystery books you might search for **"best mystery books"** in hopes of finding pages containing lists for these books.

Some people use the quoting feature to detect plagiarism. They copy a few unique and specific phrases from a paper into the Google Search box, surround them with quotes, and see if any results are similar to their students' work. Do a Google Web Search for **"ways to detect plagiarism"** and **"how to detect plagiarism"** to find more techniques!

As with all of Google's features, you're best off trying the simplest thing first, and only bother to think about what you're doing if that doesn't work. Usually, it does, so why worry about it? If the results are unsatisfactory and you think quoting a phrase will help, you can always add the quotes later.

Wildcards

There might be cases where you know only part of a phrase you wish to find. Perhaps you know a few words in the chorus of a song or part of a book title. For these situations, Google provides a wildcard operator * (asterisk) that matches *any* word. Google treats the * as a placeholder for some word you don't know. For example, in Figure 2-8, **"I * new york"** tells Google to find pages containing a phrase that starts with "I", followed by any word, followed by "new york." It would find pages containing "I love new york", as well as "I luv new york," "I hate new york," and so forth.

NOTE   *Google uses * for its wildcard operator because there is historical precedent for using "*" to mean "anything" in various computer programs.*

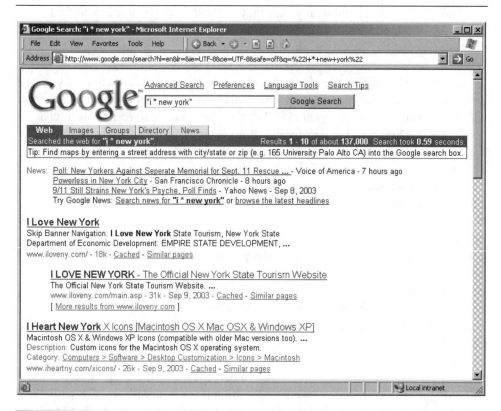

FIGURE 2-8   Use asterisks within a quoted phrase to complete the phrase.

You can use multiple wildcards in one quote. **"On * * * the south surrendered"** finds pages containing "on" and "the south surrendered" separated by three words. Similarly, **"a * work of * genius"** matches the book title "A Heartbreaking Work of Staggering Genius."

The OR Operator

Google's implicit AND behavior means that by default Google finds pages that include *all* your search terms. You can use the OR operator to tell Google that instead you wish to find pages including *any* of your search terms. For example, **auto OR automobile OR car** will turn up pages containing any of these three terms. Figure 2-9 illustrates the concept.

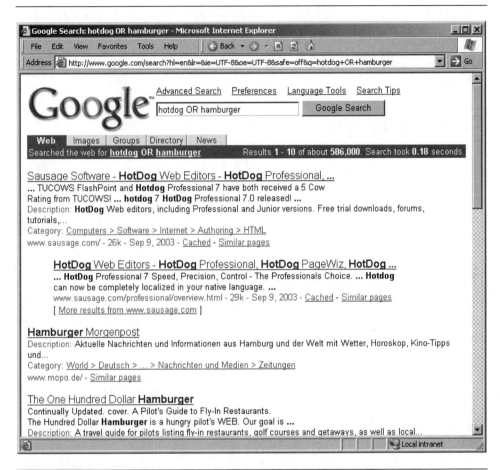

FIGURE 2-9   The OR search in action: hotdog vs. hamburger

Be sure to use "OR" and not "or" because Google treats the first as an operator, but the second as a normal search term. While Google isn't case sensitive with regard to search terms, operators *are* case sensitive.

The OR operator applies to the search terms immediately adjacent to it. The query **home loan OR mortgage** finds pages containing the term "home" as well as either "loan" or "mortgage" (or both). Google doesn't provide a way to specify an exclusive OR, that is, a way to specify pages with one term or another but not both.

Because Google doesn't automatically find synonyms of your search terms, the OR operator is useful for including specific variations on words in a single search.

For example, you could search for **tv program OR show** to ensure you find pages referring to either. It is also useful for including both singular and plural forms in the same search, for example, **giant panda OR pandas habitat**. The OR operator also lets you easily accommodate regional spelling differences (for instance **color OR colour**).

The Inclusion Operator (+)

Placing a + before a term (with no space between) instructs Google to require the word be present in the page for the page to be returned as a result. The inclusion operator is most often used to tell Google to search for common words it would otherwise exclude. For example, suppose you were searching for job listings in Los Angeles, you might wish to search for **+LA jobs**, since "la" (which means "the" in Spanish and Italian) is normally excluded.

The Exclusion Operator (–)

Many users find the exclusion operator to be one of the most useful. When placed at the beginning of search term (with no space between), it instructs Google to find pages that do *not* contain the given term. For example, **lions –football** finds pages containing "lions" that do not contain "football."

You can use the exclusion operator multiple times in a query, but it cannot be used alone. Because of implicit AND, a search for **salsa –dance –class** finds pages containing "salsa" that do not contain "dance" and do not contain "class." However it doesn't make much sense to search for just **–class**. Applying the answerability test (as discussed in the Pose Answerable Queries section), what could someone searching for **–class** conceivably be looking for?

Some words have multiple meanings or are used in many different contexts. You can use the exclusion operator to eliminate results that have the meaning you don't want. In the previous example we eliminated pages containing "salsa" that made reference to "dance" or "class." Presumably what would be left would be sites about the Mexican condiment.

To illustrate, consider the results in Figure 2-10 for the search **virus**. The word "virus" can apply to a computer or a biological virus, but the results in Figure 2-10 are exclusively related to computers. By adding **–computer**, you can eliminate all (or at least most) of the pages about computer viruses. Figure 2-11 shows the results for **virus –computer**. Notice how they are very different from Figure 2-10; they show information related to other uses of the word "virus", in

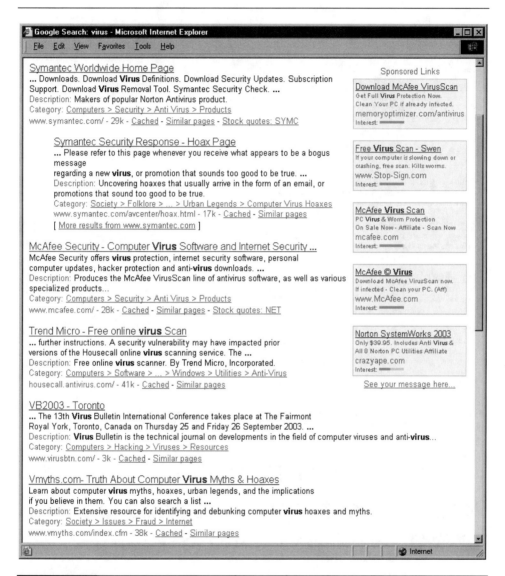

FIGURE 2-10   Most of the top results for **virus** are related to computers.

biology, entertainment, and (satirical) religion. Excluding words likely to be found on pages you know you don't want makes your query more answerable. Searching for **virus –computer** or **virus –disease** makes it more clear what you're looking for. Because of this, you'll find the exclusion operator is very useful for query refinement.

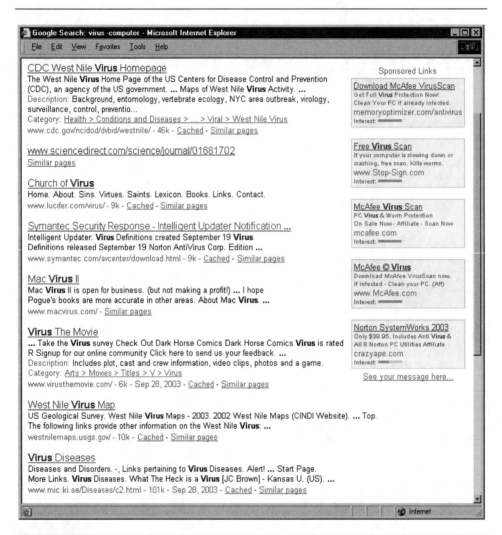

The top results for **virus −computer** are related to biology and entertainment.

When pages you want are being crowded out by pages pertaining to a different meaning of your search terms, it may occur to you then to exclude a word connected to that other meaning. If you want to focus your query more precisely, consider using the exclusion operator instead of adding more specific search terms. Sometimes exclusion works better than adding terms, as with the previous phoenix example, because instead of adding words that *might* appear in pages you want, you're excluding words you *know* you don't want.

> *You can remember that "−" is the exclusion operator by thinking of it as subtraction. By beginning a term with − you are removing or subtracting pages containing the term from the search results.*

The Synonym Operator (~)

Place the synonym operator at the beginning of a search term (with no space in between) to make Google search for the term as well as its synonyms. A search for ~**auto loan** would find pages about auto loans whether they referred to "automobile" loans, "car" loans, or "truck" loans. A query for **health ~data** would find pages referring to health "information" and "statistics" as well as "data." And ~**run** might bring up pages matching "run," "runner's," "running," and "marathon."

> *In math, the "~" symbol means "approximately." This might make the ~ operator easier to remember. It tells Google you're interested in pages containing words that are approximately like the term it's applied to.*

The synonym operator works best when applied to general terms as well as things to which people refer in different ways. Applying it to abbreviations, slang, concepts, and adjectives is likely to improve your search results. Unsurprisingly, applying it to terms without well-defined synonyms doesn't have much impact. For example, a search for ~**giraffe** won't be much different from a search for **giraffe**.

You might find that Google has a funny notion of synonyms. For example, the boldfaced words in the search results for ~**cheap** shown in Figure 2-12 indicate that Google considers "buy" to be a synonym. Google determines synonyms based on usage of the Web, so its idea of related words can be pretty different from what you might find in a thesaurus. This can work either for or against the success of a particular search, depending on the situation.

FIGURE 2-12   Google's notion of synonyms comes from usage on the Web.

NOTE   *You can use OR to achieve an effect similar to that of the ~ operator. However, if you use OR for this purpose, it's you, rather than Google, that has to come up with the synonyms. Use OR when you want to search for a specific few synonyms. Use ~ when you want to search for all synonyms.*

Table 2-2 shows a summary of the Google Web Search operators.

Notation	What it means	Example
term1 term2	Find pages containing both term1 and term2	**marco polo**
term1 OR term2	Find pages containing either term1 or term2 (or both)	**tahiti OR hawaii**
+term	Pages found must contain term	**+the knack**
−term	Do not find pages containing term	**twins −minnesota**
~term	Find pages containing term as well as any of term's synonyms	**orange ~soda**
"term1 term2"	Find pages containing the terms in that order	**"i have a dream"**
"term1 * term2"	Find pages containing the phrase with * replaced by any one word	**"crosby stills * and young"**

TABLE 2-2   Google Web Search Operators

Common Misconceptions

Usually, Google Web Search works effectively "right out of the box"; however, it pays to know how to craft effective searches. While some users are just unaware of the tools available to them, others bring misconceptions from other search tools, which can be a source of frustration for them. In this section, we point out operators and techniques that Google *doesn't* support, and what equivalent techniques, if any, can be substituted.

One difference between Google and many other search engines is that Google's support of logical (also known as *Boolean*) operators is very bare bones. Some engines enable you to group search terms together to specify what you want as a logical clause using AND, OR, NOT, and parentheses. Google supports OR, but because of its "implicit AND" behavior, there's no need for an AND operator. The keyword NOT is supported to the extent that the exclusion operator "−" can be substituted. Google ignores parentheses in search terms, so it's not possible to specify searches using complex logic.

For example, a logical, unsupported query like **(pie OR cake) AND NOT (meat OR fish)** (see Figure 2-13) has as its Google equivalent **pie OR cake −meat −fish**. Whereas the simply expressed, but also unsupported, query **(june**

FIGURE 2-13 Google doesn't understand complex logical searches.

AND july) OR (august AND september) really has no appealing Google equivalent. The best you can do would be **june OR august july OR august june OR september july OR september**. (Satisfying yourself that this is so is left as an exercise for the reader! The point is, though, that logically complex queries aren't easily performed on Google.)

Finally, as stated previously, Google doesn't attempt to be a question-answering expert system. A query like **where did thomas jefferson live?** (see Figure 2-14) doesn't work as well as **thomas jefferson home**.

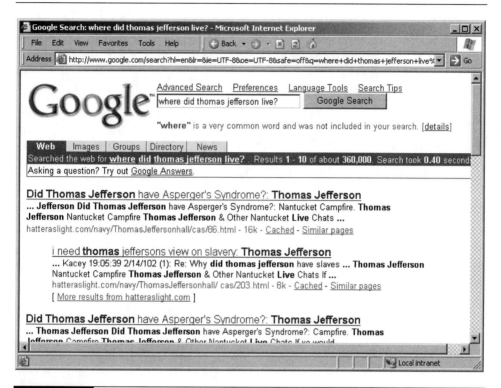

FIGURE 2-14 "If only I had a nickel for every time someone asked me this…"

Chapter 3

Find Specialized Information

How to...

- Use shortcuts to find specific kinds of information
- Carry out computations and conversions with Google

In Chapter 2, we discussed crafting searches to find web pages of interest. But web pages aren't the only kinds of information you can find with Google. In this chapter, we show you how to find smaller, more specific kinds of information. For example, you can use Google Web Search to locate phone numbers, maps, stock information, and even answers to mathematical calculations. You don't have to visit web pages returned as search results to find these data. Google provides them automatically when it believes it knows the specific kind of information you're searching for.

Correct Spelling

If you're not sure how to spell something that you want to query for, don't worry, try a phonitick speling or a guess. In just his first few months on the job, engineer Noam Shazeer developed a spelling correction (suggestion) system for Google. The system automatically checks whether you are using the most appropriate spelling of each word in your query.

This is a fantastic feature if your spelling is poor, your typing is poor, or you're just too lazy to spell correctly. In a classroom, these might be considered negative traits, but not on Google! The spelling corrector is happy to pick up the slack for you.

If Google thinks you misspelled a search term, it proposes a correction. Figure 3-1 shows the search results for the (incorrectly spelled) query **geneology**. Notice the correction offered near the top of the page. Click this link to search Google for the spell-corrected term.

Spelling correction isn't limited to single search terms. Google suggests corrections for any terms it believes might be misspelled. Figure 3-2 shows the results for the query **mispelled words**. Google shows suggestions for terms that might be misspelled in boldfaced and italic font.

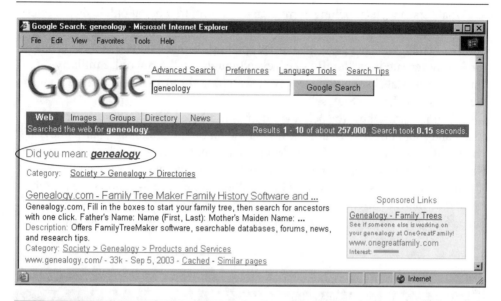

FIGURE 3-1   Google's spelling correction suggestions appear near the top of search results.

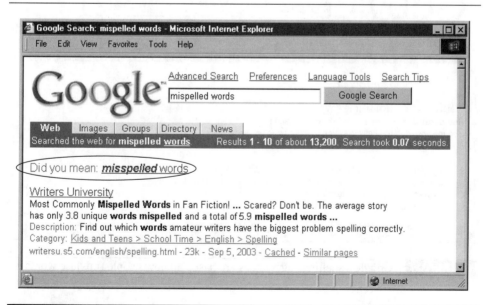

FIGURE 3-2   Spelling correction also applies to multiterm queries.

What sets Google's spelling correction apart from traditional online dictionaries is its awareness of popular phrases and proper names. If you search for **anna kournakova**, it suggests the correct spelling, "Anna Kournikova." A search for **family tee** suggests "family tree," even though "tee" is a word. Similarly, "untied" and "stats" are both words; yet, searching for **untied stats** brings up the suggestion "United States?"

If you're unsure how to spell a word or phrase, searching Google for it can be easier and more effective than looking it up in an online dictionary, particularly if you use the Google Toolbar (see Chapter 6). It can, however, also be less accurate. Because Google spelling correction works by examining word usage on the Web, if enough people misspell a word, Google does too. Figure 3-3 shows the search results for **beurocratic**. Google suggests "beaurocratic" as the correct spelling, but, according to the dictionary, the word is spelled "bureaucratic." Google's

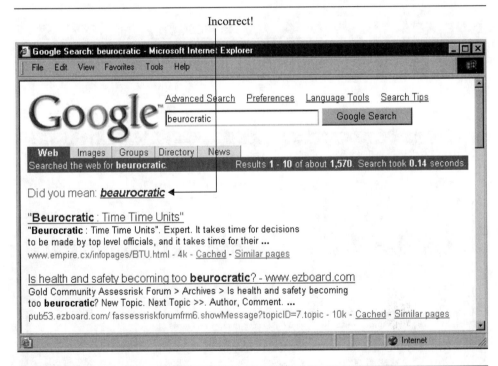

FIGURE 3-3   Google's spelling suggestions are based on how people (mis)use words on the Web.

Opps, I did it agan

Britney Spears has always been a darling of Google users, and she has figured high in query popularity since its early days. Britney also happens to have a name that's relatively difficult to remember how to spell. People searching for her try spellings of her name ranging from "Brinty" to "Brightney," by way of "Dritney", "Brandi" and "Briottany". Visit **http://www.google.com/jobs/ britney.html** to see hundreds more. It's also an amusing game to try to find the worst spelling you can of "Britney Spears" (or some other query) that the spelling corrector can still understand.

suggestions are usually correct, but keep in mind the fact that it can be fooled by popular misuse.

CAUTION *Also, be aware that the spelling correction system isn't able to distinguish between a variant spelling and a word or name that is spelled similarly, especially without the context of other search terms. For example, when searching for Mistrale (a small San Francisco Bay Area design firm) by entering the query* **mistrale***, Google will ask "Did you mean: mistral." Before clicking on what Google suggests, check that it's what you intended.*

NOTE *Many people argue that the "correct" spelling of a word is defined not by the dictionary, by how the majority of people spell it. This is interesting to think about, but not likely to excuse "creative" spelling in school or the workplace!*

Word Definitions

When your query matches a word that can be found on **dictionary.com**, Google provides a subtle, yet useful link to its definition in the blue search status bar. Figure 3-4 shows search results for **obfuscate**. Click the link for "obfuscate" in the results status bar to look it up on dictionary.com.

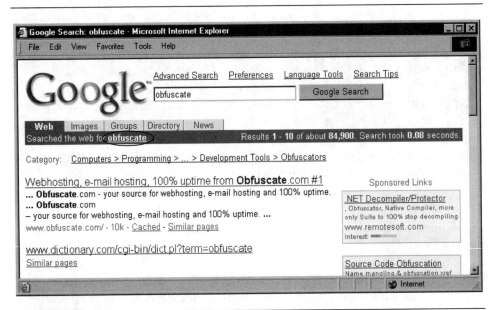

Phone Numbers and Addresses

When you search for a business or personal name along with a location, Google
finds the address and phone number for you in online white pages. This feature
can be very helpful if you only have white pages for your immediate area, and
need to contact a business or residence located further away.

You can use a comma to separate the business or residence name from the
location, and commas in the location as you might when addressing postal mail.
For example, a search for **william clinton, new york, ny** finds former U.S.
President Bill Clinton's office in Manhattan. Using commas isn't required, but
it helps us remember what valid ways there are to enter an address query, so we
use them anyway.

As you can see in Figure 3-5, phone number and address information displays
below the status bar, above the search results. A link to the address location is
also provided, and will be discussed in the Street Maps and Directions section
of this chapter.

Table 3-1 shows the name and location formats Google recognizes. In addition
to these formats, you can also separate the first and last name with a comma, for
example **alan, turing, 94111**.

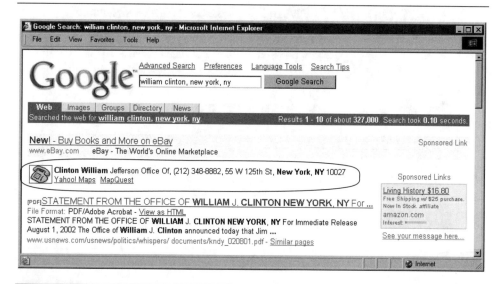

Address and phone number information appears above search results.

NOTE *Google only provides phone number and address information for land lines in the United States. Cell phones and international addresses aren't available.*

Reverse Lookups

You can also do reverse phone number lookups with Google. Searching for a phone number like **650-930-3500** or **(650) 930-3500** gives you the address information of the business or residence to which the number is registered (see Figure 3-6).

Query Format	Example
Business name, city, state	Google, Mountain View, CA
Business name, zip code	Google, 94043
Last name, city, state	Turing, San Francisco, CA
Last name, zip code	Turing, 94111
First name (or initial) last name, city, state	Alan Turing, San Francisco, CA
First name (or initial) last name, city	Alan Turing, San Francisco
First name (or initial) last name, state	Alan Turing, CA
First name (or initial) last name, zip code	Alan Turing, 94111
First name (or initial) last name, area code	A Turing, 650

TABLE 3-1 Use one of these formats to look up an address or phone number.

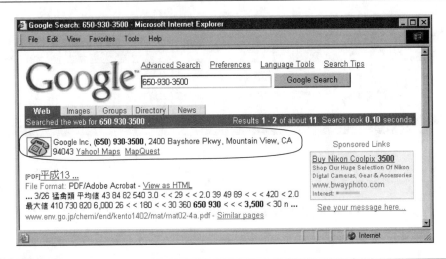

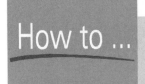 **Remove Your Listing**

The fact that Google provides address and phone number listings makes some people uncomfortable. An e-mail that circulates from time to time claims that this feature represents a "Big Brother" move on Google's part, and that by providing this information Google violates the privacy of residents.

This information has been available offline in libraries for a long time, but what most people don't realize is that it has been widely available *online* for a long time as well, since before Google even existed. Services like **anywho.com**, **reversephonedirectory.com**, **whitepages.com**, and Yahoo! People Search (**people.yahoo.com**) provide this information, and some even go so far as offering e-mail addresses and past residential history.

You can remove your information from Google's index by filling out the form at **http://www.google.com/help/pbremoval.html** (or just search for **remove address google**). But you should be aware that doing so doesn't remove your information from any of the services previously mentioned, nor from others we didn't mention. To truly make your address and phone number inaccessible online, you will need to visit the large number of white pages-like services available on the Web, and remove yourself from each. Perhaps a better solution is to get an unlisted phone number, or only use a cell phone.

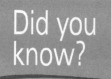

3

How to Keep Your Privacy Online

You can learn more about on- and offline privacy by visiting the websites of activist organizations. Two of the authors' favorites are the Privacy Rights Clearinghouse (**www.privacyrights.org**) and **privacy.org**. Organizations that focus primarily on electronic privacy include the Electronic Frontier Foundation (**www.eff.org**) and the Center for Democracy and Technology (**www.cdt.org**).

Street Maps and Directions

When Google recognizes your query as a location, it provides links to an online map of that area. Figure 3-7 shows the results for **710 ashbury street, san francisco, ca**. Click on the link to Yahoo! Maps or MapQuest to see a street map for the address (see Figure 3-8).

FIGURE 3-7   Google provides links to street maps.

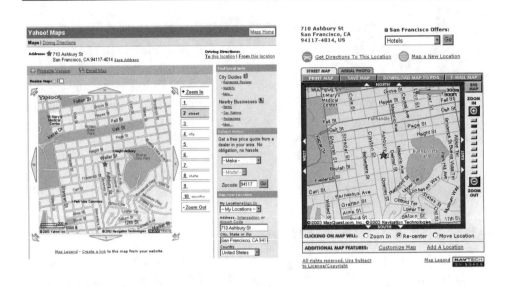

FIGURE 3-8 Yahoo! Maps and MapQuest show a street map of the location.

Both of these services enable you to get driving directions to or from the given location. To get directions with Yahoo! Maps, use the To This Location or From This Location links it provides:

On MapQuest, use the Get Directions To This Location link:

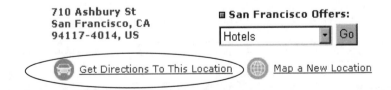

The result is a nice set of directions you can print out and take with you when driving. You can also download the directions into a PDA (Personal Digital Assistant).

Table 3-2 shows ways to search for a location in order to find a map. For the Street Address, you can use an actual street address (e.g., **1116 25th st, san diego**), a street name (e.g., **haight street, san francisco**), or an intersection (e.g., **haight street and ashbury street, san francisco**).

If you don't search for an actual street address, the link to the maps will appear a bit differently. Searching for San Diego produces this result:

Show map of **San Diego CA** on Yahoo! Maps - MapQuest

Stock Quotes

Searching for an NYSE, NASDAQ, AMEX, or mutual fund ticker symbol returns a link to financial information about that stock. Figure 3-9 shows search results for **aapl**, the ticker symbol for Apple Computer Inc. Click the link to go to the Yahoo! Finance page for Apple, which contains historical stock data, detailed analysis, and current headlines that might affect the stock price.

> NOTE *If you don't know a company's symbol, try the query **stock symbol** to get a list of sites where you can look them up.*

When you enter multiple tickers in one query, Google provides a link to a page containing information about all the given stocks. For example, the result for **aapl yhoo msft brka** is the following:

Show stock quotes for
AAPL (Apple Computer Inc.) - YHOO (Yahoo Inc.) -
MSFT (Microsoft Corporation) - BRKA (Berkshire Hathaway Inc.)

Query Format	Example
city	San Diego
city, state	San Diego, CA
street address, zip code	1116 25th St, 92102
street address, city	1116 25th St, San Diego
street address, city, state	1116 25th St, San Diego, CA
street address, city, state, zip code	1116 25th St, San Diego, CA, 92102

TABLE 3-2 Find maps by entering a location in one of these formats.

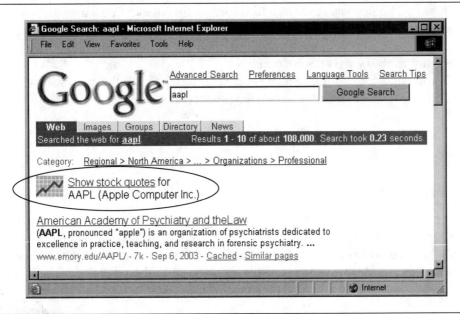

FIGURE 3-9   When you search for a stock ticker symbol, a link to Yahoo! Finance appears.

NOTE   *Entering one or more ticker symbols on Google's home page and using the I'm Feeling Lucky button (see Chapter 2) will not take you to a page with stock or mutual fund information. Instead, it will take you to the top web page that matches the query terms, which may or may not be useful.*

Calculator

Google provides an easy way to solve math problems, from the simplest arithmetic to the most esoteric unit conversions. All you do is type a mathematical expression directly into the Google search box and press ENTER or the Google Search button to search for it as you would any other query. But, instead of showing you web pages, Google gives you the answer. Figure 3-10 shows the result for **7907 + 3307**.

Although we'll highlight some of the Calculator's major features, it has too many to be remembered by most people. The best way to use the Calculator is to simply type in your equation (as best seems reasonable to you) and see if it answers. More often than not, it will!

3

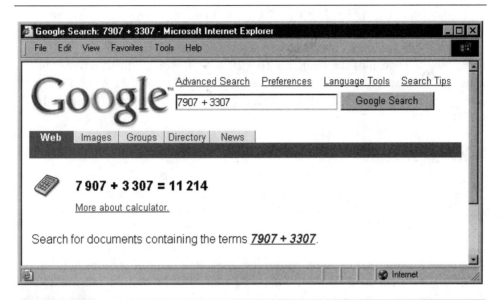

FIGURE 3-10   Searching Google for a mathematical expression shows you the answer.

Basic Arithmetic

The Google Calculator feature supports all the basic arithmetic operators shown in Table 3-3. You can use as many terms and operators in your expression as you'd like, for example **2 + 37 + 32 - 99 + 3 * 107**. Spaces between terms aren't significant, so **2 + 37 + 32 - 99 + 3 * 107** is the same as **2+37+32-99+3*107**. Parentheses can be used to indicate *associativity* (order of operation). For example,

Operator	Meaning	Example
+	addition	23 + 17
-	subtraction	1024 - 256
*	multiplication	43 * 22
/	division	1200 / 16
^ or **	exponentiation	2^20 or 2 ** 20
% of	percentage of	15% of 39.54

TABLE 3-3   Basic arithmetic operators the Calculator supports

you might search for **(99 + 84 + 80 + 91) / 4** to find the average of 99, 84, 80, and 91.

The Calculator feature works just as well if you enter your query in English. For example, instead of searching for **10 * 10 + 7 ^ 4**, you could search for **ten times ten plus seven to the fourth power**. Figure 3-11 shows the result for this query. You can also use **half**, **twice**, **thrice**. For example, you might query **half of 250,570**.

Advanced Math

 *If you're not into math, feel free to skim this section or skip to the section titled Units of Measure and Conversions. If you are into math, computer science, or the physical sciences, you're in for a treat!*

The Calculator feature supports the comprehensive set of functions listed in Table 3-4. When using these functions, use parentheses liberally to indicate clearly the value on which the function should be evaluated. Get yourself into the habit of using parentheses even with simpler computations. It will keep you from making mistakes when you enter more complicated expressions.

FIGURE 3-11   You can enter queries with numbers or write the expression in English.

3

Operator	Meaning	Example
!	factorial	5!
choose	combinations without replacement (n!)/((k!)(n-k)!)	10 choose 3
sqrt	square root	sqrt 81
log	logarithm (base 10)	log 100
lg	logarithm (base 2)	lg 1024
ln	natural logarithm (log base *e*)	ln 20
exp	*e*-to-the	exp 1
sin, cos, tan, csc, sec, ctn	trigonometric functions (radians)	sin (0) + ctn (3)
arcsin, arccos, arctan, arccsc, arcsec, arcctn	inverse trigonometric functions (radians)	arccos(1) + arctan(1)
sinh, cosh, tanh	hyperbolic trigonometric functions	sinh(2) + cosh(2)
mod	modulo (remainder)	10 mod 4
reciprocal of	one over	reciprocal of 10

TABLE 3-4   Some advanced mathematical functions the Calculator supports

The Google Calculator is amazingly versatile. Some of its features include the following:

■ The ability to specify units of measurement for trigonometric functions. The default is radians (units of pi over 180, i.e., half the unit circle), but you can use degrees by placing **degrees** after a number, for example **sin(90 degrees)** or **minutes** and **seconds** in a similar fashion.

■ Awareness of commonly used constants such as pi, *e*, phi (the golden ratio), and Euler's constant. Write them as you would expect, for example **sin(2 * pi)** or **ln(e)**. When in doubt, write out the constant's name, for example **2 * euler's constant**.

■ Understanding of scientific notation, for example **10e6 * 27e3**.

■ Ability to use complex numbers. The calculator gives the correct answer for **(4 + 3i) * (2 + 4i)** and returns "3.14159265*i*" as the answer for **ln(-1)**.

■ Capability to work in bases other than 10. To specify number in binary (base 2), add "0b" (zero bee) to the front of the number, for example **0b101001 * 0b11001**. Octal (base 8) is denoted with "0o" (zero oh), for example **0o31337 + 0o43021**. Hexadecimal (base 16) uses "0x" (zero ex) and numbers 0-9 and letters a-f (or A-F). For example, **0x10a4fb8 * 0xad1b93* 0xdeadbeef**.

If you're doing lots of math with the Calculator, it's important to realize that it uses *floating-point arithmetic* for very large (or very small) numbers. This means that there can be loss of precision for extreme values, so calculations might not be exactly what you expect. For example, **tan(90 degrees)** results in "1.663317787 x 10^16." If you've worked with large (or small) numbers on calculators or computers before, this won't come as much of a surprise. But if you haven't, welcome to the world of modern scientific computation. This is a common limitation of how machines do math.

Physical Constants

The Calculator is aware of so many *physical constants* (numeric values for properties of the universe we live in), we don't have space to list them all here. But to give you some idea, here's a sample:

- Boltzmann constant
- atomic mass constant
- permeability of free space
- magnetic flux quantum
- Faraday constant
- mass of a proton
- speed of sound
- mass of each planet
- radius of each planet

You can use the common abbreviation for many constants, for example **c** for the speed of light and **h** for Plank's constant. You can also use notation as a physicist might, with an underscore (_) representing "sub." For example, the mass of the earth is typically written "m sub earth," so you can use **m_earth** in an equation. You might therefore query **(G * m_earth) / (r_earth ^ 2)**.

If you're not sure what the symbol for a constant is or how it might otherwise be written, simply write the constant you want using English words. For example, you could use **10 * avagadro's number** or **the molar gas constant times 55**.

Units of Measure and Conversions

One of the most useful features of the Calculator is its ability to convert from one unit of measurement to another. How to perform a conversion is best illustrated by example. Figure 3-12 shows the result for the query **55 miles per hour in kilometers per day**. The basic idea is to use a query like "*x someunits in otherunits*" that states a quantity of some measurement, and the units to which it should be converted.

As you can see in Figure 3-12, you can specify units in English. You can also use the common abbreviation, for example **oz.** for ounces. It's important to end abbreviations with a period because otherwise the calculator won't necessarily recognize them. For this reason, it's usually a better idea to write out the measurement in English than risk having your abbreviation overlooked.

The Calculator is aware of most units of measure you are likely to need, and then some. Some of the units it includes are the following:

- Mass (e.g., kilograms, grains, pounds, carats, etc.)

- Length (e.g., meters, miles, feet, hands, angstroms, cubits, furlongs, etc.)

- Volume (e.g., gallons, liters, bushels, teaspoons, etc.)

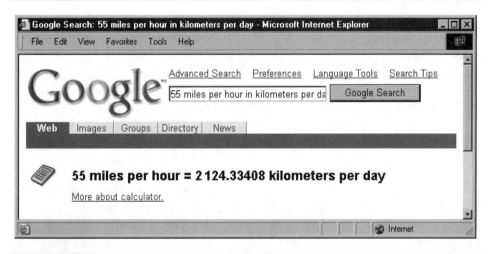

FIGURE 3-12   The Calculator can convert to and from almost any unit imaginable.

- Area (e.g., square kilometers, acres, hectares, etc.)

- Time (e.g., days, seconds, centuries, sidereal years, fortnights, etc.)

- Electricity (e.g., volts, amps, ohms, henrys, etc.)

- Energy (e.g., calories, kilowatts, British thermal units, etc.)

- Information (bits and bytes)

- Raw units (e.g., dozens, percents, gross, etc.)

- Numbering systems (hexadecimal, decimal, octal, and binary)

Entering just the name of a unit shows you its measurement with respect to a more well-known unit of measure. For example, querying for **cubit** reveals that it is equivalent to 45.72 centimeters.

Try some of these examples to get the feeling for how conversions work:

55 degrees celsius in fahrenheit

four score and seven years in seconds

20 miles per hour in furlongs per fortnight

3 bushels in teaspoons

5 megabits in bytes

1 acre in square feet

130 pounds in stones

26 miles over five hours in meters per second

25 in binary

The beauty of the Calculator is that you can use all of its features—mathematical expressions, physical constants, and units of measure—in combination. For example, you can use unlike units in an equation and let Google do the conversions for you. You might write **2 meters + 3 feet** or **3 meters times 15 feet in square yards**. Or, as a more advanced example, to see if the Earth is denser than water you might write **m_earth / (4/3 * pi * r_earth^3) in g/cm^3.**

   As we said at the beginning of this section, the key to using the Calculator
is just trying things out and seeing if they work. We've covered a lot of what the
Calculator can do, but we haven't covered everything. For example, try experimenting
with math on Roman numerals!

 The Calculator is even rumored to hold the answer to life, the universe, and everything. Just ask!

3

Chapter 4

Understand Search Results

How to…

- ■ Recognize the major parts of results pages

- ■ Utilize the features available on results pages

- ■ Distinguish ads from search results

- ■ Evaluate your search results

When you perform a Google Web Search, results are shown on the *search results page*. In contrast to Google's simple home page, the typical results page is filled with information and links to even more pages. Hopefully, what you're looking for is linked to among all these data. A good understanding of how to read the search results page can help you find what you're looking for.

The Anatomy of a Results Page

Figure 4-1 shows a typical search results page. The top part of the page, plus the very bottom, show information about the current search and present tools you can use to alter or refine the search. The majority of the page is taken up by a number of web search results, each one of which links to a web page matching your search criteria, and shows information about that page. Above the results there may sometimes be bonus information and links relating to your search, such as spelling corrections, maps, or other kinds of information (as discussed in Chapter 3). The shaded areas above and/or to the right of the search results are advertisements, which Google always labels as Sponsored Links and places on a shaded background.

We now look at features found in each section of the results page and point out ways they can be of value to you.

Search Tools and Information

Located at the top of the page (see Figure 4-2) are a number of search tools, collected around a Google Search box. It's a sort of control center for the current search; this area of the page is useful for modifying, refining, or following up on the search.

Bonus info   Ads

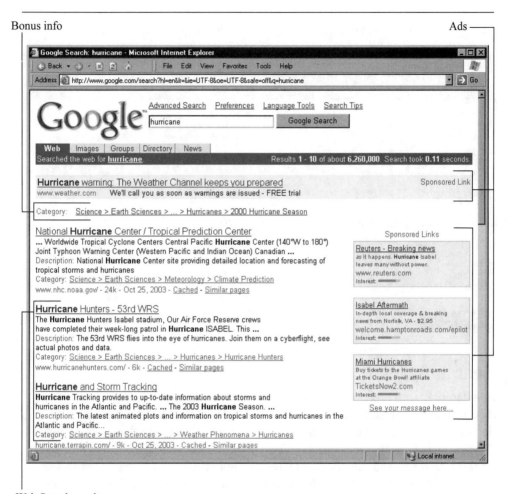

Web Search results

FIGURE 4-1   A typical search results page

Some of these screen elements are also repeated on the bottom of the page as a convenience for when you've scrolled to the bottom and not found what you're seeking. After you've rejected the last result, you'll have tools at hand to change your search without scrolling back to the top of the page.

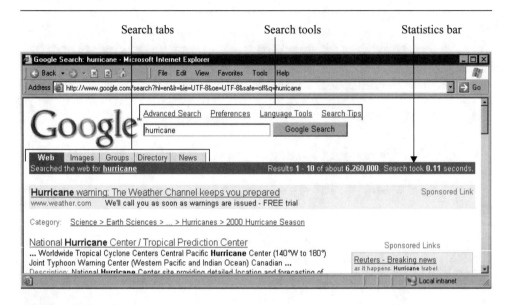

FIGURE 4-2 Google includes links to advanced search tools and tips.

Search Boxes

The familiar search box from Google's home page reappears at the top (and bottom) of every results page, which is useful if you wish to revise your query or initiate a new search. The search boxes are initially filled with the query entered for the current results page, making it easy to refine the search. You can edit what's in the search box and run another search. If the query uses any special operators (for example, if you used the advanced search form discussed in Chapter 5), these will appear in the search box as well.

Near the search box at the bottom of the results page (Figure 4-3) is a Search Within Results link. Click on this link for Google to run a new search only among the pages found from your previous query. Because of implicit AND (Chapter 2), this is identical to simply adding more search terms to the ones already present, so no need to bother with the Search within results link if you understand how Google Search functions; simply add more terms to the search box instead.

Links to Tools and Tips

Above the search box at the top of the result page are links to pages that provide more advanced control over how you use Google (see Figure 4-2). Google strives

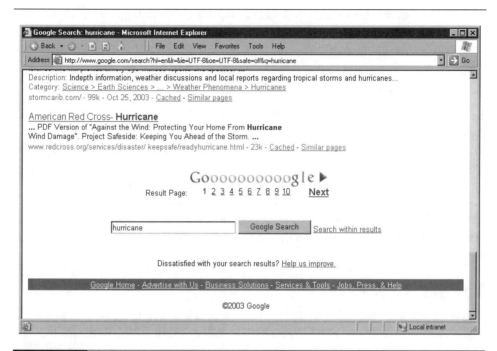

FIGURE 4-3   The search box is shown at the top and bottom of the results page.

to make searching intuitive enough that you'll probably not need these links often, but it's good to be aware of them in case you do.

- **The Advanced Search link**   Connects to Google's Advanced Search page. This feature provides various tools you can use to select or exclude pages with more precision than a simple list of terms. The Advanced Search page is discussed in Chapter 5.

- **The Preferences link**   Connects to Google's Search Preferences page, where you can customize the way you search by configuring your Google global preferences. The Preferences page is discussed in Chapter 7.

- **The Language Tools link**   Connects to Google's Language Tools page. As the World Wide Web has become more ubiquitous, more and more web pages are available from countries outside the United States and in languages other than English. With Google's Language Tools, you can locate pages in a specific country or in specific languages, and translate text or a web page to or from different languages. Learn more about Google's language tools in Chapter 5.

- **The Search Tips link**   Navigates to Google's main help page, which in turn links to all sorts of information about Google's site, services, and about the company itself.

Search Tabs

Below the search box are the search tabs (Figure 4-4), which switch between result pages of Google's various search services. For example, click the Groups tab to see the results of your search on Google Groups. Each of the tab services is described in detail in Chapters 8 to 13.

You can think of the tabs as switching between the different pages of the search you already completed, and that's what it feels like. In reality, Google performs a new search on a different service each time you click a different tab. But the search is usually completed so swiftly that the delay, while noticeable on slower connections, is not bothersome.

The Statistics Bar

The bold Statistics bar is located at the bottom of the search tools area and is separated from the result area below it. We see an example of the Statistics bar in Figure 4-5.

The statistics bar displays the following:

- **A description of your search, including the query terms used**   If a query term is underlined, you can click on it to see its definition (see Chapter 3).

- **The number of results on the current results page and an estimate of the total number of results (see Figure 4-5)**   For the sake of efficiency, Google only estimates the number of results; it would take considerably more time to compute this number exactly.

- **How much time it took Google to answer the query**   It's usually well under one second.

FIGURE 4-4   The search tabs page between Google's main search services

FIGURE 4-5   Statistics about your search appear in the aptly named Statistics bar.

Although the number of results reported is only approximate, you can use it to estimate popularity—is **madonna** more popular than **shakira**—or as a way of gauging spelling or usage: is it "turnabout is fair play" or "turn about is fair play"? But be careful; these are just estimates. Sometimes, the Web is just wrong: there are more results for "a real trooper" than "a real trouper" even though the later is the correct idiom.

Web Search Results

The real meat of the search result page is, of course, the series of (usually ten) *web search results*. Each result displayed on the search results page contains a link to the page that was found for the query, plus some extra information to help you decide if that's the page you want. Figure 4-6 shows an example result listing.

Search results are ordered by their relevance to your query, with the result Google considers most relevant listed first. So, you're more likely to find what you're seeking quickly by checking the results in the order that they appear. Google measures relevance by considering a combination of over a hundred

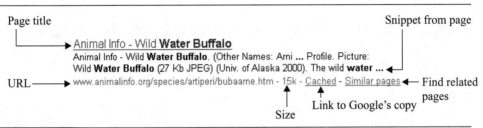

FIGURE 4-6   One result for the query **water buffalo**

factors, all based on two types of information: how important the page is in general (as measured primarily by Google's PageRank algorithm, see the Appendix), and how the search terms you use appear within the page (e.g., how often, where, and near what?).

These results are what Google Web Search is really all about! Let's look in detail at what can appear in each result listing.

The Result Link

The title of each web page found is displayed as a link to the actual page. If the title of the page is not available for some reason, the URL of the page is displayed instead. In cases where you're looking for a whole page (rather than some specific fact within a page), the title is usually the best clue as to the general topic and type of information on the page. Hopefully, these are summed up in a few words in the page title. Consequently, when you're looking for a page on a particular subject, the title is most valuable measure of which result is of interest.

In the following 11 sections, we describe the other items that can appear in a result listing, which can be of great use to identify applicable results in other situations. For example, when you're looking for a specific fact that will likely appear somewhere on a page, the snippet will usually be of more use to you than the title.

Snippets

Each search result usually includes one or two short excerpts from the page's text, known as *snippets*, shown below the result link. In the snippet, your search terms are shown in context and appear in boldface type.

The snippet is often as useful as the page title in discovering whether the page is what you're looking for. Snippets can provide you with the following:

■ The actual information you are seeking, so that you don't even need to visit the result page at all,

■ An idea of what you might expect to find on the linked page (and whether its what you're after), and

■ Ideas for terms to use in your subsequent searches.

For example, to find the writer Anne Lamott's 2003 UC Berkeley commencement speech, enter the query **Anne Lamott commencement speech**, the result page for which is shown in Figure 4-7. By reading the snippets and title of the first two results, you can surmise that both results probably lead to the text of the speech.

Another example is shown in Figure 4-8, where we've tried to learn the wingspan of the Lappet-Faced Vulture. We searched for **wingspan lappet-faced vulture**. In this case, there's no need to even visit the page; the answer is there (2.6 meters or 9 feet) in the snippet.

FIGURE 4-7   The title and snippets often indicate whether a result contains the information you seek.

FIGURE 4-8   The Lappet-Faced Vulture is evidently a large bird.

It's not uncommon to find the information you're after waiting for you in the snippet. A common example is searching for the names of companies or people to get their addresses, e-mails, or phone numbers. These things often appear right in the snippet, saving you a trip to the page where this information is found.

 If you don't see a term highlighted in the snippet, it could be because your term isn't on the page, but has been associated with the page in some other way. For example, it might appear in the URL (web address), or in the text of a link to the page.

Sometimes Google is unable to display a snippet for a result. The reason is that it doesn't have a cached copy of the page (see the Cached Version of the Result section), so it doesn't know the precise text on the page.

Technical Information

The URL, or web address, of the result is displayed below the snippet. It can be useful to determine the sort of page that was found as well as the credibility of the result. For example, the host shown in the URL might be a site you know does or does not have the kind of information you want. In the result of Figure 4-9, you can see that clicking on the result link will take you to **http://www.djuma.co.za/ djuma/bird_lappetvul.htm**.

Just after the URL, also in green, is the size of the text portion of the web page. We say "the text portion of the page" here because the size given doesn't account for images or other resources that may have to be downloaded to display the page.

In Figure 4-9, "5k" means that the text portion of the web page is 5 *kilobytes*. One kilobyte is 1,024 bytes, and a *byte* is essentially one letter, number, or other character. Since, in general, the average size of a word is six characters, each 1k of text is about 170 words. Since this particular page has 5k characters, it's probably about 850 words long. This isn't always information you need to know, but it can be nice to know whether a page is relatively large, or relatively small. For example, you might be connected to the Internet over a slow line, and unwilling to download large pages.

If Google didn't crawl the page, it won't know the size, so no size will be displayed in the listing. See the following section for circumstances that might cause this to happen.

Cached Version of the Result

As Google "crawls" the Web looking for pages to add to its search engine (see Appendix A), it takes a snapshot of each page it examines and caches (stores) this copy. The cached version is what Google uses to judge if a page is a good match for your query, and is updated on a regular basis.

Practically every search result includes a Cached link; clicking on it takes you to Google's cached version of that web page instead of the current version of the

Lappet-faced Vulture
Lappetfaced Vulture Torgos tracheliotus. They can be ... Africa. They are the largest vultures in the area with a 2.6m **wingspan**. They are ...
www.djuma.co.za/djuma/bird_lappetvul.htm - 5k - Cached - Similar pages

FIGURE 4-9   Below the snippet is technical information about the result.

page on the original site. In other words, you load the copy of the page that Google stores, which may or may not be the same as the page at present on the Web. This is useful if the original page is unavailable because of Internet congestion, the server being down, or if the page has been removed.

As a bonus feature, on the cached page your search terms are highlighted in different colors, making it easier to find the information you seek within the page. Suppose you wished to find the contents of the publication *The Mathematical Scientist*. Figure 4-10 shows the search results for **"the mathematical scientist" contents**. The first result is the journal's web page. Clicking its Cached link takes you to Google's copy. You can see in Figure 4-11 how the highlighted search terms make it easy to find the sections of the page relevant to the query. The header at the top of the page serves as a reminder that what you see isn't necessarily the most recent version of the page.

Aside from enabling you to see pages that would otherwise be unavailable, Google's cached copy can also save you time. Because Google's servers are

FIGURE 4-10   Search results typically include a link to Google's cached version of a page.

Google's header information

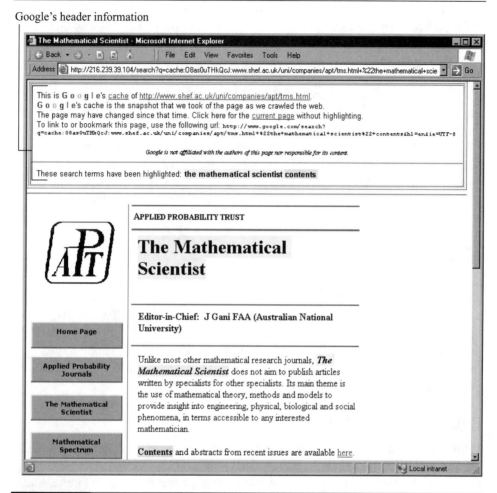

FIGURE 4-11   Search terms are highlighted on the cached version.

typically faster than other servers on the Web, you can often access the cached copy faster than you could the real page.

The Cached link is also useful for retrieving an older version of a page that has since been updated; the page may have been edited and the information you wanted might be gone. If Google returns a result that appears to have little to do with your query or the snippet that was displayed, it could be because the page changed very recently. In this case, try looking at the cached version.

Of course, Google can only show cached versions of pages it has a copy of, and there are many pages that Google either didn't download or has discarded for one reason or another. Usually, this is because Google never got around to downloading the page, but knows of it because pages it did download link to it. But it can also be because the site has asked Google not to download the page or to remove it from its cache after the fact. When one of these conditions applies and Google lacks a cached version of the page, the Cached link, as well as the snippet and page size, will be absent from the result listing.

Be aware that a cached page that contains JavaScript might not work as intended. Such technologies are often used to implement the checking of data entered into forms and navigational enhancements such as fancy pull-down menus. If the page doesn't appear to be working properly, you will have to load it normally.

NOTE *All links in the cached copy of the page are to the original site.*

The Similar Pages Link

Sometimes you like a page you've found and want to see more like it. Click on the Similar Pages link, as shown in Figure 4-12, when you want to find more resources of the same kind or competing sites. As discussed in Chapter 5, you can also find similar pages from the Page-Specific Search section of the Advanced Search page.

Categories and Description

When a result page is listed in Google's Directory (Chapter 11), you'll see the Directory category to which the page belongs named below the snippet. Click the link to see the entire Google Web Directory category mentioned (see Figure 4-13). This is sometimes more useful to you than the individual page in the result, especially when the page itself doesn't turn out to be exactly what you're after. Web Directory categories which relate to your search in general (as opposed to matching a particular result) often appear above the search result listing.

The Translate This Page Link

If a page isn't in a language you know, Google can make a *machine translation* of a page for you. That is, Google can translate the page by computer. Machine translation is difficult to do well, and the results can be…unusual, and not nearly

FIGURE 4-12   The Similar Pages link for consumerreports.org finds like organizations.

as clear as human translation. However, since the machine translations that Google offers are easier to understand than a language you don't know, they can usually give you the gist of what's being said.

Results that link to pages in a language Google can translate into your interface language may include a Translate This Page link, as in Figure 4-14. Your interface language is determined by your preferences settings (which are discussed in

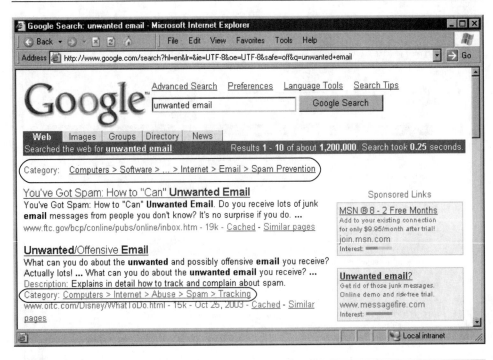

FIGURE 4-13   When you want more resources on a topic, consider clicking on the category links included with some search results.

Chapter 7) with a reasonable default, which depends on the part of the world you're in and your browser. The interface language is the language in which Google displays messages, buttons, and tips on Google's home page and results page. Currently, English speakers can get translations from French, German, Italian, Portuguese, and Spanish. Speakers of French, German, Italian, Portuguese, and Spanish can translate pages in English into their respective interface languages as well.

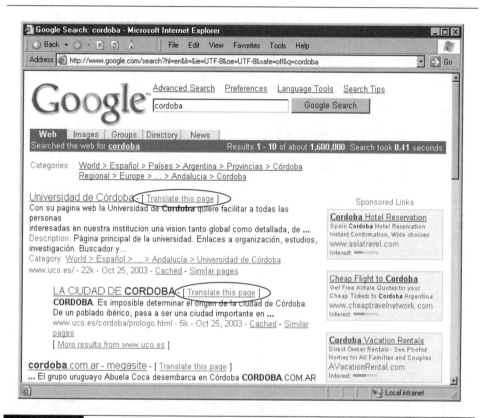

FIGURE 4-14   Results include a Translate This Page link when Google finds a page in a language different from your language of choice.

File Type Conversion

Sometimes Google finds documents that aren't web pages. For example, it could find a document in Microsoft Word format or Adobe PDF (Portable Document Format) format. Google provides the ability to convert such files to either HTML (the language in which web pages are written) or text.

File type conversion is useful if you can't view the page in its native format—for instance, if you don't have the appropriate software installed on your computer, or if you want faster access to the file (because other document formats can be very large, and thus slow to download). When a converted version of the document is available, Google shows you View As HTML (Figure 4-15) or View As Text links. Click on one of these links to see the converted page.

FIGURE 4-15   Non-HTML files can be viewed in their original format, or as either HTML or text.

Naturally, the conversion to HTML or text is performed by a computer program, not a human. These automatic conversions are typically far less artfully composed than the original, but are usually quite readable.

Of the many file formats that Google searches, some of the more common ones are the following:

- Adobe Portable Document Format (.pdf), which can be viewed using Adobe Acrobat

- Adobe PostScript (.ps), a printer language commonly used for academic papers

- Microsoft Excel (.xls), a spreadsheet format

- Microsoft PowerPoint (.ppt), a popular format for slideshow presentations

- Microsoft Word (.doc), the most common word processor format

- Hypertext Markup Language (.html, .htm), the primary language of the Web

- Plain text (.txt), without any special program-specific markup

See Chapter 5 if you want to learn how to search for documents of a particular format.

Many Results from a Single Site

When Google finds multiple results from the same website, it lists just two results, with the most relevant result first and a second result from that same site indented below it. A link labeled More results from... appears next to the result; click this link to see *all* the results from that site. As an example, take a look at Figure 4-16, which shows a search for **peace**.

Treating results from the same site specially like this is a good thing. If all the hits on the **peacecorps.com** site were included in the example shown, thousands of results from that site might crowd out all other peace-loving sites from the first result page. The indented results make it obvious that there are multiple hits on the same site, so it strikes a good balance for diversity in the results. But remember to hit the More results from link when you need it!

Go Beyond the First Page of Results

When, as is often the case, more than one page of results is available, you can view subsequent pages by clicking either a page number or a letter *o* in the whimsical Goooogle, which appears below the last search result on the result page, as shown in Figure 4-17.

If you find yourself paging forward through results a lot, you can also change the number of results displayed on each page to as many as 100, using the Google Search Preferences page, which is described in Chapter 7.

When looking at your search results, it's sometimes hard to know whether it's worthwhile to look past the first page. Typically, you should do so when the results on the first page are pretty much on target, but aren't exactly what you're looking for. On the other hand, if the titles and snippets of the results on the first page don't look relevant, it's probably a better idea to refine your query. Helpful ways to refine your query are discussed in Chapers 2 and 5, and most often involve rerunning your search with more specific search terms, using the exclusion

FIGURE 4-16 A search for **peace** has many hits on peacecorps.com.

operator (–) on words you see in results you don't want, using quotes, or using the synonym operator (~).

Keep in mind that studies have indicated that few results past the first 25 are worthwhile, so if you reach the bottom of the third page of results without turning up what you're looking for, it's probably high time to refine your query.

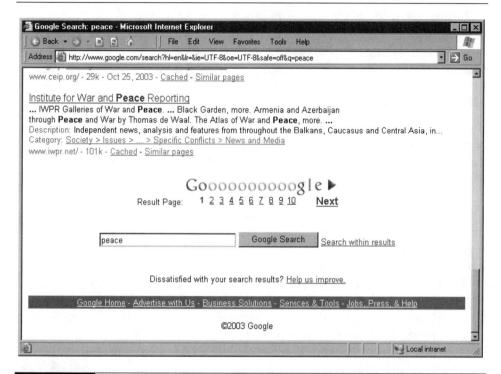

FIGURE 4-17   Click on a page number or an *o* to see another results page.

As an example, let's take an arbitrary tour of history and try to discover who the last person to be crowned King of Prussia was. We start with a reasonable attempt, and search for **last king of prussia**. Unfortunately, King of Prussia is the name of a town in Pennsylvania, and looking through the titles and snippets on the results page, that subject clearly saturates the results. To counteract this, we'll try eliminating these pages by excluding mention of the state, with the search **last king of prussia –pa –pennsylvania**. This gets us closer to our goal; the town is mostly out of the picture, but there are still horses by that name, and pages that seem somewhat, but not completely, relevant to what we're after. Including the word "royal" in our search is enough to give it a nudge toward the subject we're after, and Wilhelm II emerges as the likely answer, without even the need to visit any of the pages.

One obvious case where you would want to examine every result page is if you wished to compile an exhaustive list of every page that matches some (hopefully narrow) criteria. For example, suppose you wished to find everything the Web had to say about Rajah Brooke's Birdwing butterfly (*trogonoptera brookiana albescens*), you might do a phrase search on its name and comb through every single result.

Omitted Results

Sometimes Google finds many identical or nearly identical pages in several places on the Web. This happens with content that many people want to make available, for example: form letters, popular stories, manuals for computer programs, and archives of old posts to mailing lists.

In such cases, Google lists only one version in the search results, but includes a message after the last search result telling you that very similar results have been omitted. This message contains a link that offers to "repeat the search with the omitted results included." Click this link to do just that: repeat the search without filtering out pages that are very similar.

By way of a contrived example, Figure 4-18 shows the link on the third and last page of results for the ill-fated query **solid gold tupperware chafing dish**. There are some more results that can be displayed, but they are probably duplicates or near-duplicates of the ones already listed.

This link is sometimes alluring when you fail to find what you wanted in the first try. Unless you are looking for some very specific page that would be expected to have many almost identical brethren, or are interested in finding as many copies of the same content as you can for some reason, the link is a fool's paradise. Over time, you'll probably learn to almost never click it and revise your query instead.

Other Kinds of Search Results

Remember to keep an eye on the area above your search results, where you're likely to see all sorts of "bonus" information related to your search terms. Such tidbits stray outside of the confines of web search, and may include spelling suggestions, calculations of mathematical expressions, or links to news articles, street maps, phone numbers and addresses, or stock information, all pertaining to the search you performed. Once you know what to expect to see in this area, you'll find yourself using Google Search for purposes having nothing to do with conventional Web Search. See Chapter 3 for more details on specialized searches.

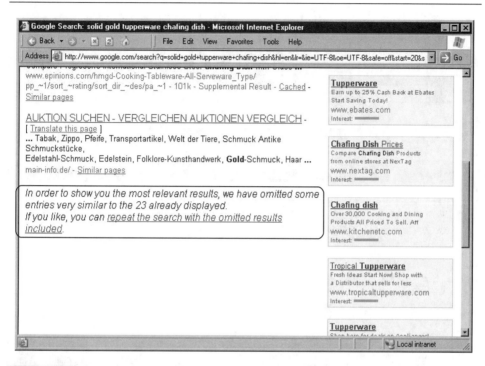

FIGURE 4-18 Google provides a link to display results that are very similar to those already listed.

Sponsored Links (Paid Advertisements)

The results pages for many (perhaps most) searches on Google include some sponsored links, that is, paid advertisements, matched to the search you performed. Google displays advertisements on results pages in two areas: above the search results, and to the right of them. The ads are clearly identified and kept separate from search results; you can distinguish ads by their pastel-colored backgrounds and the box drawn around them (and they are also labeled Sponsored Links).

At most, two sponsored links appear above Google's Search results, and up to eight may appear down the right side. Ads contain a title, a short description, and a URL. Ads along the right side of the results page also include Interest Bars indicating how often people click on the ad when it's shown. Figure 4-19 shows an example of ads on a result page.

Google ads

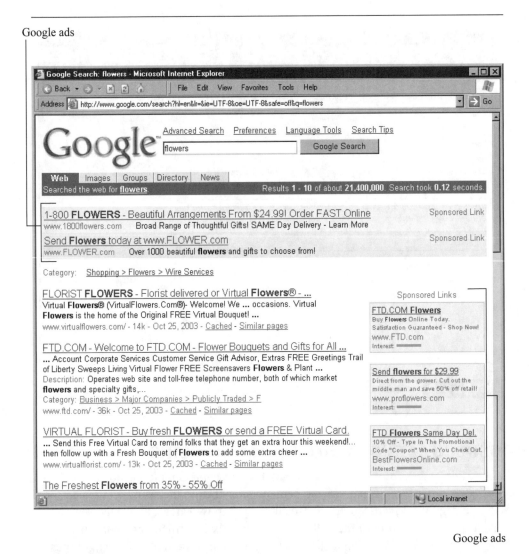

Google ads

FIGURE 4-19 Google's ads appear above and/or to the right of the search results.

Unfortunately, some search engines freely mix ads with their true search results, a practice referred to as *paid placement*. Many people feel that paid placement is a deceptive practice since a user can't distinguish an independently determined result from an advertisement. Google keeps the two strictly separate; it does not have paid placement. Among the web search results, no one can pay

Google to increase the ranking of their page, so if a web page appears in Google Web Search results, it's because Google thought it was a good result for your search, not because someone paid Google to do so.

Another practice among other search engines is *paid inclusion*, whereby sites must pay to be indexed by the engine in the first place, without any guarantee about where they will appear within search results. This is less obviously bad for the user; the sites simply pay to ensure that the search engine will devote some of their resources to crawling their site. But on the other hand, as a user, you simply want the best content on the Web, whether they've paid to be indexed or not, so paid inclusion does hurt quality to some degree. Consequently, Google does not have paid inclusion either.

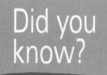

Where Ads Come From?

Advertisers decide which queries their ad should match, and then Google decides on their *placement*: which advertiser's ads to show for each query, and in what order. Placement is determined by an auction. The auction, of course, takes place in just milliseconds, inside of a computer. Advertisers bid on how much they'd pay each time a user clicks on the ad. According to the auction rules, ads with higher bids and higher *click-through rates* (how often users click on the ad) get higher placement among the ads that have been matched to your query.

It is in the interest of everyone (the user, Google, and the advertiser) to make sure ads appear only where they are useful. Therefore, Google insists on certain quality controls over ads. Most importantly, ads are required to be relevant to your query terms as measured by users' reaction to them; in fact, if the click-through rate of an ad falls below a certain level (indicating the ad isn't very relevant to the query), then the ad is disabled.

In a further effort to promote a positive user experience, Google enforces quality controls over the page an ad displays a link to. These rules are, again, good for everyone (Google, its users, and its advertisers) because if users are accustomed to a positive experience when following links from Google, then they will be more willing to follow Google ad links in the future.

So, to ensure a good experience for users with respect to ads, rules of the following sorts are enforced over advertisers:

- Ads must be relevant to your search; people must click on them a certain percentage of the time.

- Ads must not be deceptive about what sort of page they link to.

- Ads must be simple, readable text messages, without attention-grabbing characteristics like *OBNOXIOUS* FORMATTING AND **PUNCTUATION**!!!!

- The page an ad links to must be user-friendly, without pop-ups, or other annoying features.

It is also worth noting that Google refuses ads from certain classes of advertisers. Google refuses ads for firearms, drugs, tobacco products, hate speech, or anything illegal. Google does show ads for pornography, but only to users who have not activated SafeSearch (see Chapter 7), and only on result pages for searches that were apparently looking for pornography in the first place.

NOTE   *No customer is too small for Google. For more information, visit **http://www.google.com/ads**. For tips on advertising, visit **http://www.google.com/ads/tips.html**. For what to do if you find a (banned!) pop-up on a page advertised on Google, visit **http://www.google.com/help/ nopopupads.html**.*

Evaluate What You Find

You don't have to be a computer whiz to become proficient at finding what you want with Google. However, there are several skills you should definitely master if you want to be a great searcher. The most obvious requirement is a firm understanding of what you can find with Google. Chapters 2 and 3 discussed what you can find with Google Web Search, and the second part of this book is primarily dedicated to finding specialized information online such as news, images, and products for sale. Throughout this book, we also discuss another important aspect of searching: the tools you can use (such as operators and special links) to specify more precisely what it is that you're looking for. The final major component is equally as important, but is often overlooked—evaluation of results.

Great searchers know how to quickly evaluate the results Google shows them. They don't have to waste time clicking on lots of links until they happen to find the information they want. Instead, an experienced searcher will examine the titles, snippets, and URLs of results and determine whether any of them are worth clicking, and if not, how to retarget the search to find what they're after.

Credibility

On the Web, people can express whatever opinion they feel, invent any nonsense they please, and copy, falsify, or omit information intentionally or accidentally, whatever the original source. While it's a fact that most of the information on the Web is forthrightly expressed, there is also no shortage of misinformation, and you should be circumspect about what you're willing to trust.

Google's web result ranking system, PageRank (Appendix A), does, to some extent, tend to show more credible and trusted results over less informed or lunatic ravings (though without any guarantees). Well-respected information is likely to be linked to by well-respected sites, and this linking causes pages bearing better information to be listed higher (first) within search results. However, the system is not foolproof.

Many people publish pages to get you to buy something or believe a particular point of view, or just to mislead you for the fun of it. Google makes no specific effort to discover or eliminate unreliable and erroneous material. It's up to you to cultivate the habit of healthy skepticism. The ultimate arbiter of authenticity is inevitably your own judgment, so it pays to keep a skeptical eye on anything you read.

Consider the following as you evaluate the credibility of a result:

- Is the host for the content known to you? You might rightly be skeptical of taking financial advice from **www.low-cost-viagra.com**.

- Does the title look relevant? If you're looking for medical information about rashes, a page titled The Professor's Mighty Cream of Healing is probably not such a good candidate.

- Does the snippet look interesting? In particular, is the snippet nonsensical or does it make outrageous claims? DOES IT CONTAIN OVERPOWERING CAPITALISATION AND PUNCTUATION!!!???!!!

When visiting a page, you also want to consider the author and his/her bias, evidence given to support claims, and how up-to-date the page appears to be. You can also glean information about a page's credibility by seeing who links to it. Try a Links query as discussed in Chapter 5. For more tips, search for **hints evaluate credibility**, though of course this begs the question of the credibility of the sites discussing credibility!

You can also make use of Google to test answers that you find, the idea being that although there's a lot of erroneous information on the Web, the weight of the evidence usually points in the right direction. For example, to find out who wrote "fools rush in where angels fear to tread," search for the phrase (with quotation marks). The answer appears to be Alexander Pope. Another search for **"fools rush in where angels fear to tread" alexander pope** yields enough results from enough respectable sources to confirm that this is probably correct. (Be careful when using this technique. For almost any quotation, there is someone on the Web who will claim that Mark Twain said it!)

 *Readers seriously interested in evaluating the credibility of the information on the web might wish to check out the book Web of Deception: Misinformation on the Internet, by Steve Forbes (edited by Anne Mintz, with contributions from ten additional authors).*

Types of Results

There are many general types of pages you might encounter in your search results. We point out a couple of the most common here, but as you learn from your searches, you'll be able to quickly identify many more.

Spam

Pages sometimes make their way into search results by showing Google deceptive content. The goal is almost always to make money by showing ads to the hapless web surfer who clicks on the result, and sometimes to sell a product that may or may not be related to the query. Such results are generally known as *spam*. They're much like the unsolicited bulk e-mail you receive in your inbox, except that they manage to worm their way into Google's results instead of your e-mail.

Sometimes it's obvious from the title, snippet, or URL when these pages aren't related to your query. For example, the following result for the query **web history** is probably not going to contain information about the history of the World Wide Web:

search the **web**
Click Here to Enter.
www.todayseek.com/ - 2k - Sep 22, 2003 - Cached - Similar pages

Sometimes spammy sites are a little more clever, and attempt to "overload" the snippet that Google generates with keywords that appear to be related to your

4

search terms. The middle result in Figure 4-20 for the query **bicycle history** attempts this deception. It's unlikely that a site with real information about the history of the bike would include such a nonsensical passage, so you can typically skip results such as these.

Other spammers aren't so obvious. At first glance, this site's title and snippet might appear to be legitimate, but, upon closer examination, turn out to be suspicious. Consider the following result for **remove wine stain**:

how to **remove** a red **wine stain**
how to **remove** a red **wine stain** - Shop for how to **remove** a red **wine stain** at **Wine**-Beer-Depot.com! **wine**-beer-depot.com your ...
www.wine-beer-depot.com/wine-9/ how_to_remove_a_red_wine_stain.html - 13k - Cached - Similar pages

The result appears normal, but the URL and the curious phrase about "shopping for how to remove a wine stain" might be enough to dissuade you from clicking.

The worst kind of spam is that which looks completely normal, but takes you to an unexpected page not at all related to your query when clicked. Sometimes, even the closest scrutiny can't tell them apart, so your best defense is a pop-up blocker like that offered by the Google Toolbar and lightning-fast back-button reflexes. Be particularly careful on queries that are most likely to be spammed: those related to porn, prescription drugs, products for sale, file sharing, and anything illegal or of questionable ethical value.

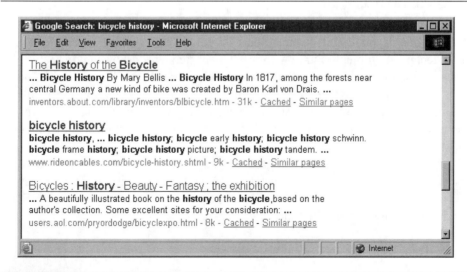

FIGURE 4-20   Guess which of these results is probably spam.

 *You can report spammy results to Google at **http://www.google.com/ contact/spamreport.html**, or by searching for **google spam report**.*

Commercial Results

Commercial results are easy to recognize. If you look at the title, snippet, and URL and feel that it *could* be a site that's selling something, it probably is. Lots of legitimate for-sale sites appear in search results, and they shouldn't be confused with spam. The difference between spam and legitimate sites is that spam is deceptive. It tries to get you to click it by tricking you into thinking it offers something you might want, when in fact it does not.

Even if a site looks like it might be spam, it might not be. Consider the following result for **clocks**:

Alarm **Clocks** - Alarm Clock Radio - Clock Radios
... Home | Alarm **Clocks** |Alarm Clock Radios | CD Alarm Clock Radios | Alarm Clock Phones Shopping Cart | Site Map | Contact Us | Privacy Policy | Links For ...
www.thealarmclockshop.com/ - 12k - Cached - Similar pages

The series of what appear to be spammy keywords in the snippet are actually legitimate text found on the page. They compose the menu at the bottom of the page used to navigate to products this site has for sale. So be sure a site really is deceptive before reporting it to Google as spam.

Message Boards

Certain types of information are more likely to be found in online discussion forums (bulletin boards, mailing lists, etc.) than on regular web pages. For example, talk about technical problems and how to solve them frequently shows up in search results in the form of message board posts or mailing list archives. Figure 4-21 shows the results for **nero problem** (Nero is the popular CD creation software produced by Ahead Software, **www.nero.com**). *All* of the search results shown are messages from web-based discussion boards. Figure 4-22 shows one of these pages.

It's important to be able to recognize message board posts in your results because there are times when you want them, and times you don't. They're easy to recognize once you become aware of them. Some features common to results that are discussion forums are the following:

- Conversational title and/or snippet

- The word *thread* or *board* in the title, snippet, or URL (a *thread* is a topic of conversation in an online forum)

Cues in the URL

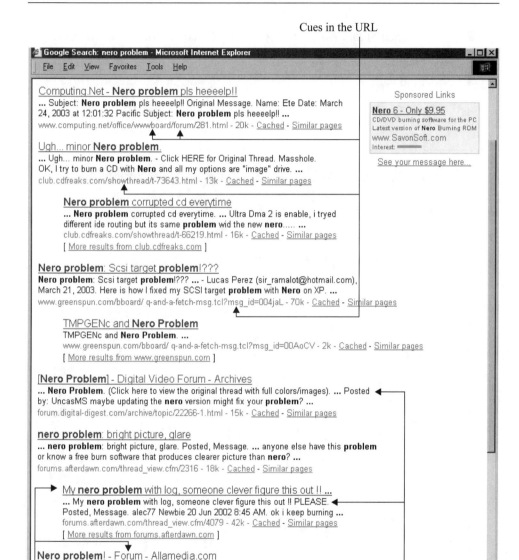

Cues in the title

Cues in the snippet

FIGURE 4-21   Message board posts frequently appear in results for queries likely to be discussed in an interactive manner.

- Message numbers or IDs in the URL

- The presence of *Subject:*, *Date:*, *Original Message:*, or e-mail addresses in snippets

- Direct indications in the title (*Forum* or *Archives* or *Message Board*)

- Presence of link text in the snippet, for example, "Click HERE to respond"

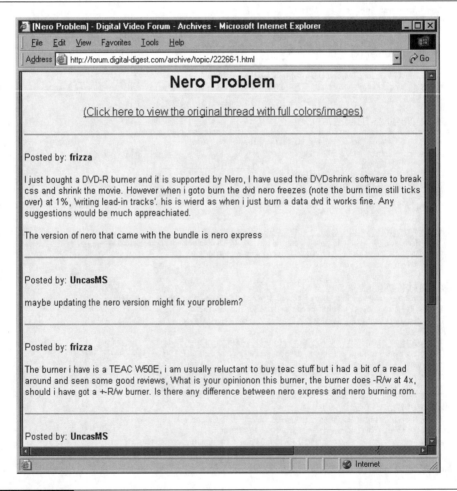

FIGURE 4-22 Message boards are great for finding problem-solving advice.

Login Pages

You can pick login pages out of search results pretty easily. They usually contain reference to signing in, forgotten passwords, or the term LOGIN itself. For example:

> **Salon** Premium
> **Salon**.com, ... Forgot your password? If you prefer to **login** via a secure connection, click here. NOT A SUBSCRIBER? Find out more or register now. **LOGIN**. Username: ...
> premium.salon.com/acc/login.jsp - 11k - Sep 26, 2003 - Cached - Similar pages

Errors

Sometimes snippets for sites are misleading or just plain useless. Consider the following result for **hotmail**:

> Sign-in Access Error
> **Hotmail**. Sign-in Access Error. JavaScript required. The browser that you are using does not support JavaScript, or you may have disabled JavaScript. Help. ...
> Description: Free web-based e-mail. 2MB e-mail storage, signatures, stationery, HTML compatible.
> Category: Computers > Internet > E-mail > Free > Web-Based > H > Hotmail
> www.hotmail.com/ - 10k - Sep 26, 2003 - Cached - Similar pages

This is definitely the site you want if you wish to log into Hotmail, but the snippet seems to imply that the page is broken. It isn't, however; the Hotmail site requires users to log in, using JavaScript. Of course, Google's crawler (the system for scanning the web, called the GoogleBot, which is described in the Appendix) can't log in, and it therefore presents itself as not being capable of running JavaScript. In response, the Hotmail site returns an error page with the title "Sign-in Access Error".

Since chances are your browser supports JavaScript, if you follow the link to the Hotmail site, you'll see a page whose title is "Please sign in" instead of an error page. The mismatch in technology between the GoogleBot and a typical Web browser brought about this misleading situation.

This kind of error can be lumped into a larger category of results whose snippets or titles indicate errors, but which are probably just fine. Such pages contain phrases like the following:

- JavaScript required

- Script error

- An error has occurred

- Server is temporarily unavailable

- Page is temporarily unavailable

- ■ Frames required

- ■ No frames

The problems indicated by these kinds of snippets are usually transitory, or even illusory. That is, they happen only for a short period of time, and perhaps even only for Google. They don't necessarily indicate that the page is *currently* broken, or that there would be an error if *you* clicked the result. They just mean that the page was broken for the Google crawler the last time it visited the page.

The bottom line is that the snippets for these kinds of results are annoying, but the site is still probably worth clicking on because it's likely the problem has already gone away (or wouldn't exist for you in the first place).

Moved Pages

Another kind of result you might see is one indicating that the page has moved (see Figure 4-23). The snippets of these results usually include phrases such as: Redirect, Page Moved, and Site Moved.

Despite the appearance of the snippet, these pages are also worth visiting. While the information that used to be there isn't any longer, more often than not they include a link to its new location, or even redirect you there automatically. (Google is able to follow most such redirects during its crawl, pointing to the new location and thus eliminating this kind of result. But some webmasters don't know how or are unable to configure their site to redirect so as to allow this, leading to snippets like the one in Figure 4-23.)

NOTE   *If the URL of the new location is visible in the snippet, you can always copy it and paste it into the browser's address bar.*

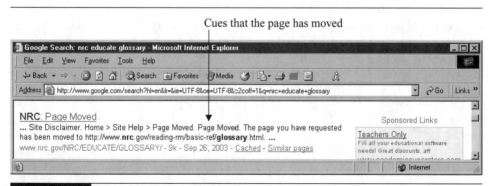

FIGURE 4-23   Result snippets occasionally indicate that a site has moved.

Chapter 5

Advanced Web Search

How to...

- Search more precisely using the Advanced Search page

- Use advanced searching via advanced operators

- Search for information about a specific page

- Translate pages and text

- Refine your query

Google search is usually as simple as typing a few words and hitting the Search button. From time to time, however, your target may be a bit more elusive, and Google's power must be more tightly directed on the problem. This chapter discusses Google's advanced search capabilities, syntax and tools, as well as advice on how to use them to make Google work better for you.

Use the Advanced Search Form

When a basic search comes up dry, consider specifying what you want more precisely using the Advanced Search form. You can find the Advanced Search page by clicking on the Advanced Search link located to the right of or above the search box (or just enter the URL **http://www.google.com/advanced_search**). The Advanced Search form is shown in Figure 5-1.

Don't be put off by the name Advanced Search; it's easy to use, and it allows you to select or exclude pages in a variety of useful ways. You'll generally leave most of it blank and just fill in the fields you need.

Advanced Operators

You can employ most of the functionality available on the Advanced Search page in a regular Google Search box query by using *advanced operators*, i.e., using words that have special meaning to Google. The Advanced Search page offers a convenient way to use these operators without having to remember them. Of course, if you happen to know them, you can use them directly and save a trip to the Advanced Search page. You can learn operator syntax for advanced searches you often repeat simply by observing special notation that appears in the search box of the results page, as a result of using the Advanced Search form.

As we discuss the elements of the Advanced Search page, we'll also list the special syntax that can be used in the normal search box, if any. Later, we'll touch

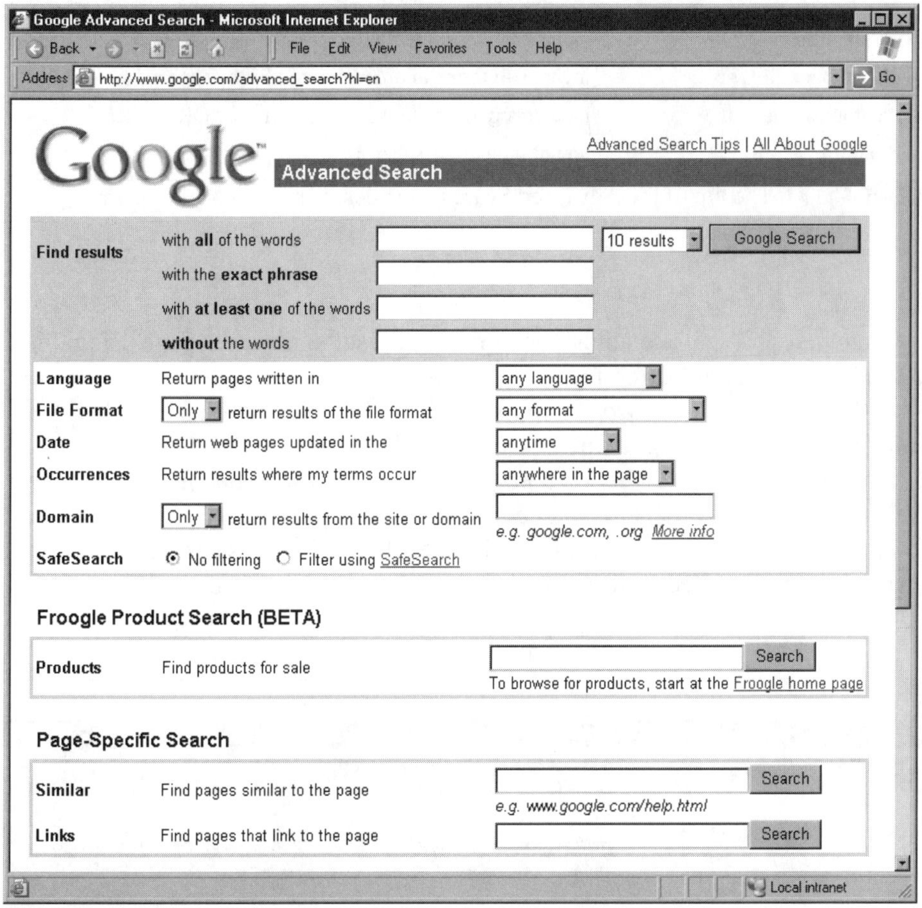

FIGURE 5-1 Search more precisely using the Advanced Search form.

on any operators we've missed, summarize them all, and show how they can be used to go beyond what you can do using the Advanced Search form.

Group or Exclude Terms

The top portion of the Advanced Search form is an easy way to write basic restricted queries without having to remember the special notation (quotes, the "–" exclusion operator, the OR operator, etc.) described in Chapter 2. Table 5-1 summarizes the types of searches on this portion of the page, and equivalent notation that you can use from the normal Google Search box.

Find results	Matches pages that...	Special notation
with **all** of the words	include all search terms	britney spears
with the **exact phrase**	include all terms in order	"britney spears"
with **at least one** of the words	include any of the terms	britney OR aguilera
without the words	do not include these terms	spears –britney

TABLE 5-1   The top of the Advanced Search page determines how query terms combine.

Note that you can also adjust the number of results listed per page using this part of the Advanced Search form. For example: *What is an appropriate gratuity when purchasing take-out (to-go) food?* Here we find recommendations by searching for **tipping "take out"**, (see Figure 5-2).

Another example may be: *Find pages that will help someone learn cribbage.* We expect that such a page would certainly contain the word cribbage, and also some word signifying a tutorial, so we look for that or various similar words. See Figure 5-3 for the filled-in form.

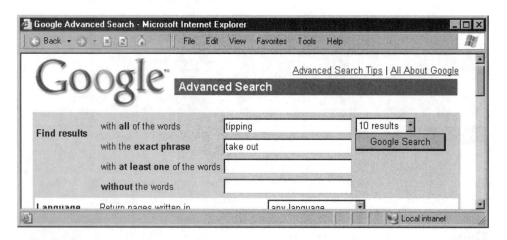

FIGURE 5-2   How much should I tip when I pick up food to go?

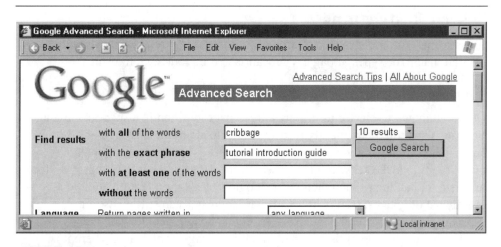

FIGURE 5-3   A hunt for tutorials about cribbage

A final example: *Marlon Brando was in some western with Karl Malden called the "Jacks" or "Kings" of something or other, or something like that. It wasn't one of the ones he's most famous for. What movie was that?* Figure 5-4 shows that question expressed in the language of the Advanced Search form.

(By the way, the answer is *One-Eyed Jacks* ([1961]).)

FIGURE 5-4   Tell me, Google, what movie am I thinking of?

Search Restrictions

The next part of the Advanced Search page, seen in Figure 5-5, lets you put restrictions on the types of pages you want listed in your search results.

Language

Use the Language selector to limit results to pages written in a specific language. You can also more permanently restrict results to a certain language or set of languages by adjusting your Google preferences, as we'll see in Chapter 7. It might seem to make sense to always search for pages in languages that you understand, but due to such factors as Google's translation feature and the prevalence of images, results in unfamiliar languages can still be useful, especially when no useful page exists in any language you know.

The language selector is repeated in the Language Tools page, where it is accompanied by several other language-related tools. The Language Tools page is discussed later in this chapter, where you will find examples that make use of the Language selector that apply equally to the one in the Advanced Search page.

File Format

Use the File Format selector to restrict your results to a particular type of file, or exclude a file format from your results. The choices include a number of editing, publishing, and presentation formats, which are listed in Table 5-2.

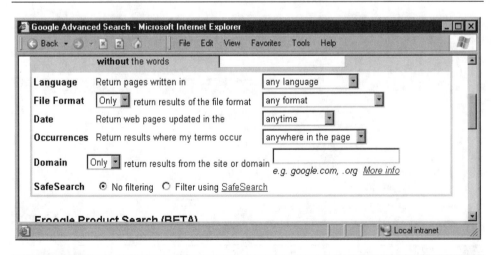

FIGURE 5-5   Place limits on the types of pages listed in your search results.

File type	Extension	Description
Adobe Acrobat PDF	.pdf	Adobe Portable Document Format, the Web's most common publishing format for product manuals and documents of all kinds
Adobe PostScript	.ps	A printing format often used for academic papers
Microsoft Word	.doc	A common word processor format
Microsoft Excel	.xls	A spreadsheet format
Microsoft PowerPoint	.ppt	A format for presentations and slides
Rich Text Format	.rtf	An interchange format used to exchange documents between Microsoft Word and other formats

TABLE 5-2   Common File Type Restrictions on the Advanced Search Page

You can use the special syntax "filetype:" directly in queries to restrict a search to a particular file type, by specifying the file extension for the format. For example, online versions of product-owners manuals tend to be .pdf files. Supposing you owned a Honda HR215SXA lawnmower, had lost the owners manual, and wanted to know what grade of motor oil it requires, a search for **hr215sxa filetype:pdf** turns up an online version of the owners manual. (The answer is SAE 10W-30, in case you're curious.)

The **filetype:** operator also gives you access to more file types than are available from the Advanced Search page; see Table 5-3 for a list of the most common ones and their most common extensions. Although there are still more file types that Google attempts to index, they are extremely rare; in fact, except for HTML and plain text, those that are in Table 5-3 are already pretty obscure. (Remember that Google automatically searches all file types if you don't specify one.)

Google can convert all file types it understands to either HTML or text. If you can't view the page in the native format—for instance, if you don't have Adobe Acrobat installed on your computer—or if you want faster access to the file, click on either the View As HTML or View As Text link (see Figure 5-6).

File type	Extension	Description
HTML, Hypertext Markup Language	.htm, .html	The primary format of the Web
Lotus 1-2-3	.wk1	A spreadsheet format
Lotus WordPro	.lwp	A word processor format
MacWrite	.mw	A Macintosh word processor format
Microsoft Works	.wps	A word processor format
Microsoft Write	.wri	A word processor format
Plain text	.txt	Ordinary text with no special formatting

TABLE 5-3   Other File Formats You Can Use with the **File Type**: Operator

Convert file format

FIGURE 5-6   Files that Google caches can be viewed as HTML or text.

Date

Use the Date selector to restrict your results to pages updated in the past three, six, or twelve months. Note that any change in the page counts as an update; for example, when someone corrects the spelling of a word, the entire page is considered updated even though very little may have changed. For example: *Is it a good idea to get a flu shot this year?* Obviously, such information is timely. Use the search terms **flu shots** and, if winter is approaching, set the Date selector to Past 3 Months.

5

> **NOTE**   *Another good way to find recent results is by including the year in your query, e.g.,* **flu shots 2004***. This works well in many kinds of searches, for example, in finding information on this year's model of a car, or this year's version of a conference, or other annual event.*

Occurrences

Use the Occurrences selector to specify where your search terms must occur on the page. You can insist on matching only words in the following areas:

- **In the title**   The text that is displayed in search results as the link to the page, and in the title bar of your browser when you visit the page

- **In the text**   The textual content of the page

- **In the URL**   The web page address, such as **http://www.apple.com/store/**

- **In links to the page**   In the text of other pages where they link to the page in question—for example, if a page had a link labeled "information about toothaches" to **http://dentistry.com/**, then a search for **toothaches** restricted to occurrences in links might turn up **dentisry.com**

By default, of course, a search applies to all of these areas: anywhere on the page or in links to the page.

Another example may be: *Locate IRS tax form 1040.* We'll suppose that the title of the page with the form 1040 will include the words "form 1040," so we fill out the search form as in Figure 5-7.

Occurrence Location Operators   Each of these options for occurrence has an advanced operator equivalent; in fact, advanced operators can give tighter control over the search than the Advanced Search form allows by letting you combine searches for terms in different locations in a single search. These operators are listed in Table 5-4.

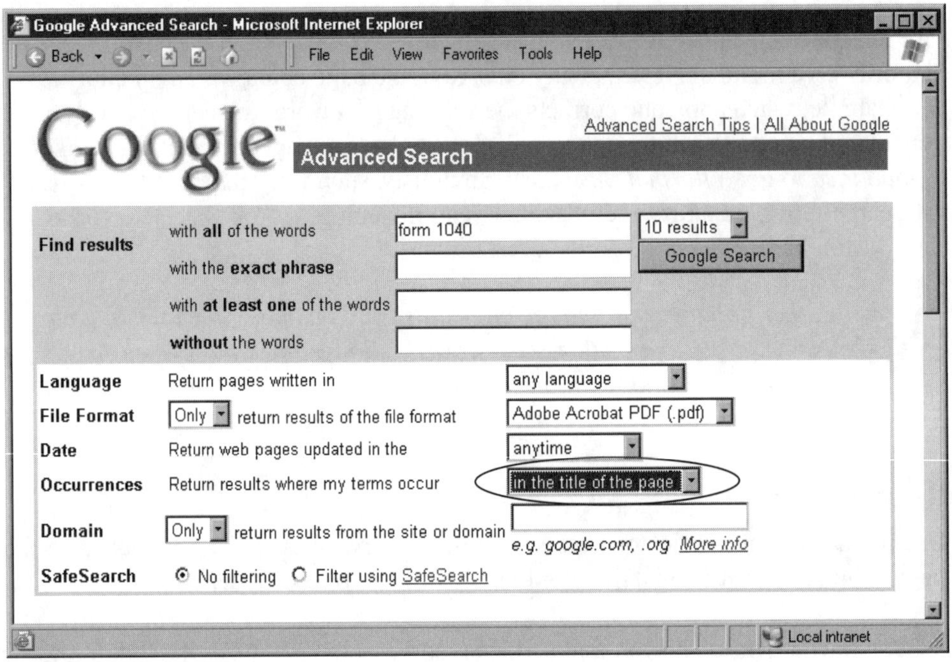

FIGURE 5-7   Using Advanced Search to get ready for federal tax time.

For example: *Locate IRS tax form 1040 from the main Google Search box.* The operator syntax for the search shown in Figure 5-7 is **allintitle: form 1040**.

For example: *Look for pages about surfing, the sport, not about "surfing the World Wide Web."* Search for pages with "surfing" in the title that never mention the Internet: **intitle:surfing –intext:internet**.

Operator	Meaning
allintitle:	All query terms must appear in the page's title
intitle:*term*	The single term must appear in the page's title
allinurl:	All query terms must appear in the page's URL
inurl:*term*	The single term must appear in the page's URL
allintext:	All query terms must appear in the page's text
intext:*term*	The single term must appear in the page's text
allinanchor:	All query terms must appear in links to the page
inanchor:*term*	The single term must appear in links to the page

TABLE 5-4   Restrict Search Based on Where Query Words Appear.

For example: *Find pages about plagiarism that deal with detecting it.* We suppose that pages about plagiarism will mention "plagiarism" in the title. Ideas about detecting plagiarism might be just one section in the larger document, so we'll look for that word anywhere. Using the search terms **intitle:plagiarism detect** should do the trick.

Example: *Find pages* about *Google that don't belong* to *Google.* Searching for **intitle:google –inurl:google** works pretty well. Of course, one result is **http://www.deja.com/**, which is an alias for **http://groups.google.com/**, since Google purchased Deja.com in early 2001 (see Chapter 9). Another interesting result of this search is "elgooG," a "mirror" of Google at **http://www.alltooflat.com/geeky/elgoog/**.

5

Domains

Use the Domains text box to search only on a specific website (e.g., **www.eff.org**) or domain (e.g., .org), or to exclude that site or domain completely from your search. This feature is most commonly used to find things within a particular site's pages. In fact, many sites include search boxes that are powered by Google through an equivalent feature, as seen in Figure 5-8.

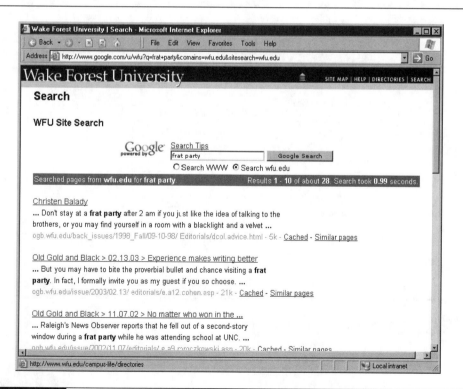

FIGURE 5-8   Wake Forest University borrows Google's search on its own site.

To search on a particular site, simply enter the host name for the site in the Domains box. The *host name* in a URL can be found after the http:// (or ftp:// or https://) until the first /. For example, the host name in the URL **http://www.google.com/search** is **www.google.com**.

Searching a site using Google is a very effective technique. You can use it to search a site that doesn't offer built-in search features as part of its interface. Even if a site does provide a search box, using a domain-restricted Google Search is often more effective. For example: *Find recipes for lasagna*. Figure 5-9 shows a search for **lasagna** on the recipe site Epicurious. More examples that use this technique appear later in this section.

You can also restrict a search to a domain, essentially a subset of the Internet. The *domain* is the last part of the host name, for example, .com or .org. It can also be a regional code, such as *.it* for sites in Italy, or .au for sites in Australia, or .ca.us for sites in the California domain (most of which are run by the state government,

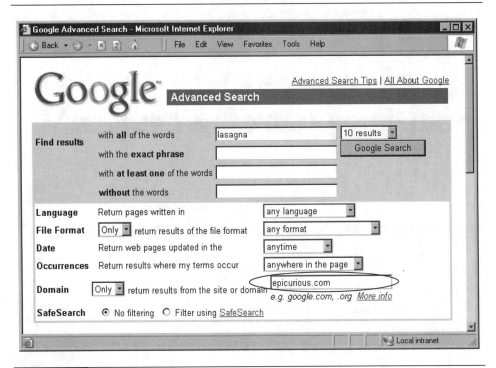

Finding articles about lasagna on a site with recipes

for example the websites of public secondary schools). For the most part, though, American sites use three-letter domains such as *.com*, *.gov*, or *.edu*; this is an artifact of the Internet's origins as the U.S.-only ArpaNet. Most international websites tend to do the same.

Domains can indicate a category or a political location. Here are some common domains:

Example Domain	Type of Site
.com	commercial business site
.net	networks, Internet service providers, organizations
.org	U.S. nonprofit organizations and others
.edu	educational site (usually a university or college)
.gov	U.S. government/non-military site
.mil	U.S. military sites or agencies
.de	Sites in Germany
.fr	Sites in France
.jp	Sites in Japan
.uk	Sites in the United Kingdom
.ca.us	Sites in California
.tx.us	Sites in Texas

Simply fill in a domain in the Advanced Search form to restrict a search to a particular country's sites or to just nonprofit organizations, for instance. For example: *Find information on volunteering for a nonprofit organization* (Figure 5-10).

From the normal search page, you can use the **site:** operator to restrict a search to a site or domain, bypassing the Advanced Search page. For example, **site:edu world history** will locate information on world history on academic sites.

Another example: *Find admissions information at London School of Economics' site.* Enter **www.lse.ac.uk** in the domain field of the Advanced Search page, and the term **admissions** in the query terms box. Or, just search for **site:www.lse.ac.uk admissions**. Either way, the result is the same, as displayed in Figure 5-11.

Furthermore: *Find information about the security of Microsoft Windows outside of Microsoft's site.* You can use many of the advanced operators in conjunction with the exclusion operator (–). In this case, we search for **windows security –site:microsoft.com**.

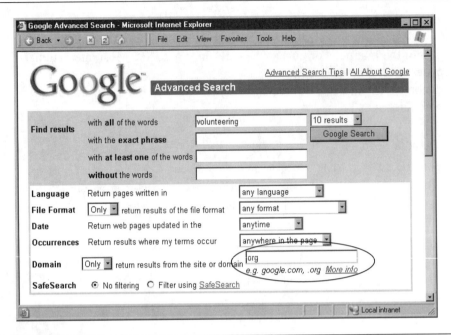

FIGURE 5-10   Search for volunteering for an organization.

FIGURE 5-11   How to get into the London School of Economics

NOTE *In fact, the **site:** operator (and the Domain text box) is not restricted to only domains or entire sites. You can restrict a search to any host name suffix. So you can limit a search to the following:*

- **www.lse.ac.uk:**   The London School of Economics' main website

- **lse.ac.uk:**   Any site operated by the London School of Economics, which, for example, also encompasses **cep.lse.ac.uk**, their Centre for Economic Performance

- **ac.uk:**   Academic sites in the United Kingdom

- **uk:**   Any site in the United Kingdom domain

NOTE *You can only use portions of the host name starting from the right. It doesn't make sense to specify **site:www**, for example.*

SafeSearch

Use the SafeSearch selector to specify whether to filter out sites that contain pornography or explicit sexual content from search results. Be aware that Google's automated filtering doesn't guarantee that you won't be shown offensive content; unlike some similar systems, SafeSearch doesn't attempt to filter out illegal, hateful, tasteless or any otherwise possibly objectionable material, besides adult content.

SafeSearch does sometimes make mistakes. In the interest of avoiding any embarrassment, it is more likely to exclude a page that isn't porn than it is to allow a page that is porn. If you are relatively unperturbed by such content, it is better to switch SafeSearch filtering off, even if you don't ever want adult content. And even without SafeSearch filtering, Google avoids showing adult results prominently on searches that don't appear to be seeking adult content.

Find Information on Specific Pages

Farther down the Advanced Search form is a section dedicated to page-specific tools (see Figure 5-12). These provide a means to search Google for information about a particular page. (You can more easily search for information on the page you're currently visiting by using the Google Toolbar's Page Info menu. The Google Toolbar is described in Chapter 6.)

Unlike the other fields in the Advanced Search form, the page-specific searches can't be combined with other query terms; consequently, each has its own search button.

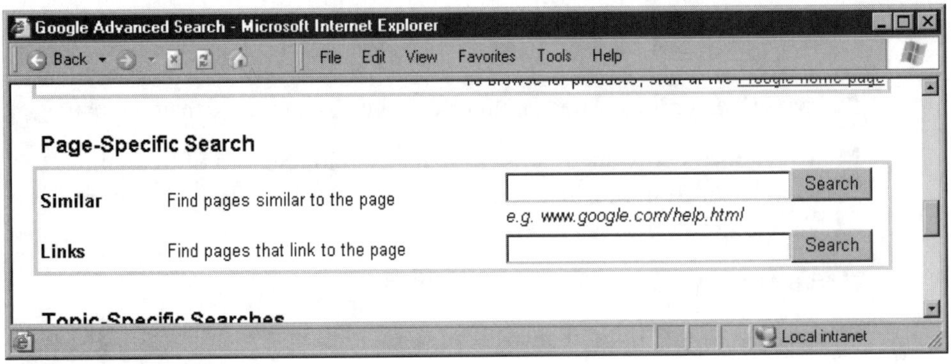

FIGURE 5-12   The Page Specific Search section

Search for Similar Pages

Use the page-specific Similar search box when you'd like to find pages that are along the same lines as a particular page without having to invent search terms. If you are looking for product information, this feature can find information on competitors so that you can make direct comparisons. For example: *Find pages similar to Consumer Reports' web page*. Enter **http://consumerreports.org/** in the similar page-specific search box and then click on the associated Search button (or press ENTER). The results are shown in Figure 5-13.

The usefulness of the Similar Pages feature can vary widely from page to page. You'll probably find that it works better on home pages and well-known pages—or more accurately, on pages with a high PageRank. (The Google Toolbar's PageRank display is about the only way to determine the rank of a page; see Chapter 6.)

You can bypass the Advanced Search page when finding similar pages using the **related:** operator. For example, to find pages similar to the *New York Times'* home page, just do a normal search for **related:nytimes.com**.

Find Who Links to a Website

Hypertext, the system of web pages linking to one another, is one of the most essential features of the Web. But links are unidirectional—you can follow links from one page to another, but you can't tell just from looking at a page who links *to* that page. Google, however, crawls practically the whole Web, keeps track of the links it sees to each page, and makes this information available to you.

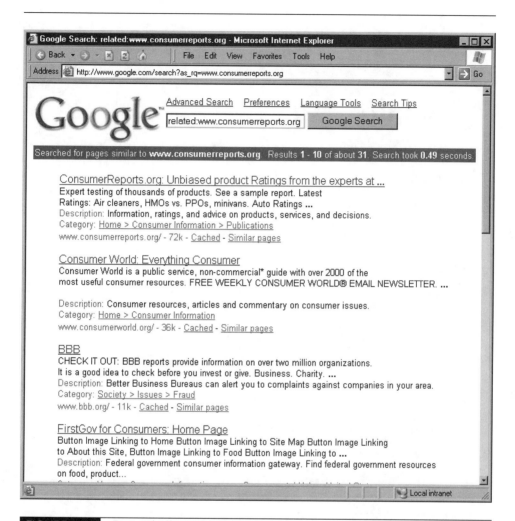

FIGURE 5-13   Pages similar to the Consumer Reports' web page

To find out who links to a page, fill in a web address (URL) in the Links page-specific search. As an example, let's find who links to the Doctors without Borders website **http://www.doctorswithoutborders.com**. See Figure 5-14.

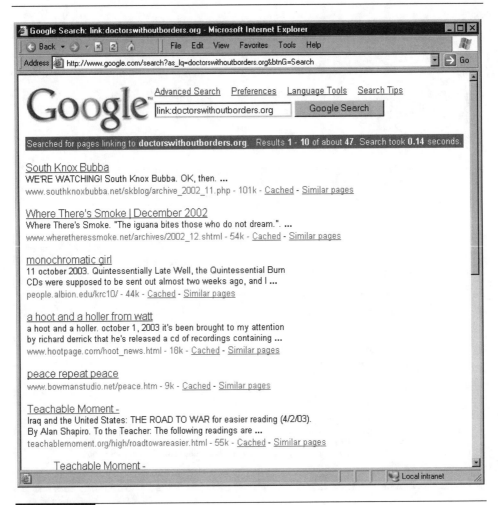

FIGURE 5-14   Find what sites link to a page.

Why bother? The most common users of backward links searches are webmasters who are curious to know who links to their site. They may also be curious to find out who links to competitors' sites; perhaps those sites would be willing to link to them, too.

A more ordinary use of this feature is to find a table of contents for a page you find in Google. For example, suppose you find the second page of a multipage article, which lacks a link back to the first page. A Links search can help you find the first page.

Yet another use of this feature is as a way of judging reliability. If you're not sure of the trustworthiness of a page, looking at the links to the page may help you decide.

Again, there is a shortcut. You can simply type **link:*page*** in the regular Google Search box to get backward links for a page.

Access All Information About a Page

Instead of going to the Advanced Search form, you can access all of Google's information about a web page more conveniently simply by performing a normal Google Search on its address; Figure 5-15 shows the result of searching for **cia.gov**.

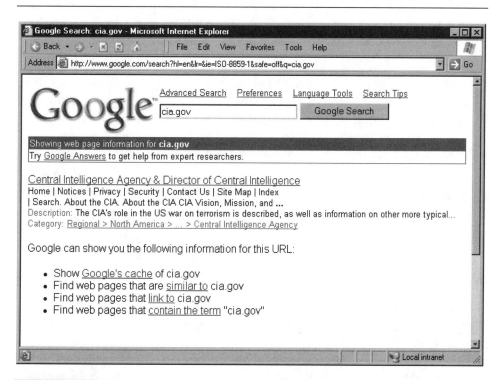

FIGURE 5-15   Spying on cia.gov

Google returns a number of links related to the site, including links to the other page-specific information we've already discussed in this section. There's also a link you can use to do a normal keyword search on the web address; that is, find pages that mention the site instead of the special page information listing shown in Figure 5-15.

Finally, there are links to both the actual page and to Google's cached copy of the page. This shows the snapshot of the page that Google has in its cache, which you can also access by clicking on the Cached link in a normal results page; this is discussed in Chapter 4, where you can learn more about Google's cached pages. Searching for **cache:***url* is another way to access the cached version of a page, and you can also include search terms to highlight on the page (e.g., **cache:britneyspears.ac/ physics/dos/dos.htm energy states**).

NOTE *If you're a fan of the highlighting you see on cached pages and you use Internet Explorer, you should know that the Google Toolbar (described in Chapter 6) lets you highlight terms similarly on any page—a very useful feature. Just enter the terms you wish to highlight in the Toolbar search box and hit the Highlight button instead of the Search button.*

Another way is to access the page information by using the **info:** operator. For example, searching for **info:cia.gov** is equivalent to searching for just **cia.gov.** As things stand (at the time of this writing), there's no reason to take the trouble, but if Google changes the way they handle searches for URLs in the future, the behavior of the **info:** searches are likely to remain the same as described here.

Search by Topic

The bottom part of the Advanced Search page, shown in Figure 5-16, contains links to topic-specific search services.

These searches allow you to locate pages within a fixed set of specific topics, which include various computer systems (for example, Figure 5-17), U.S. government pages, and many universities. The special search restrictions typically work better than just including an extra keyword (say, macintosh) in your search; they use more complex (though still keyword-based) techniques to determine whether a page belongs to the set than just that.

Why does Google provide topic-searches for these topics and not others? Early on in Google history, some engineers created these specialized search engines to serve their own interests. They've remained part of the site though Google has turned its attention to other types of search services and features.

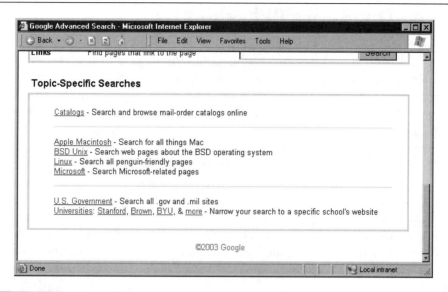

FIGURE 5-16   Special search services narrow your search to a topic.

FIGURE 5-17   A topic-specific search for the "fsck" program for BSD Unix. (The cute little devil is the BSD Unix mascot.)

Advanced Operators Rehashed

As we've seen throughout this chapter, you can specify most of the Advanced Search options in a regular search box using advanced operators. Advanced operators offer quicker access to the special features available on the Advanced Search page, and are more flexible. On the other hand, they require that you remember them, and not all of the Advanced Search page functionality is replicated in operators; most users find that making use of the Advanced Search page, instead of using advanced operators directly, fulfills their specialized search needs.

There are just a few advanced operators that we haven't already covered in this chapter, so in this section, we'll clean up a few loose ends in that department, and then summarize the syntax of all the operators. As previously mentioned, to discover, or rediscover, advanced operators on your own, search using the Advanced Search form and look at the search box on the results page. Your query may now include special notation or special operators corresponding to the special search operation.

define:

To get a list of "web definitions" for a word or phrase, use the **define:** operator. Web definitions aren't limited to dictionary definitions; instead they are drawn from glossary pages all over the Web. For example, try **define: geek**, **define: google** or **define: old ironsides**. The **define:** operator is the same as the Google Glossary feature on labs.google.com, which is discussed in Chapter 14.

stocks:

Use the **stocks:** operator to access financial information for public companies by ticker symbol. The financial page includes tabs so that you can switch between the listings on Yahoo Finance, The Motley Fool, and so on.

For example, search for **stocks: pg** brings up financial information for Procter & Gamble. You can also list multiple stocks on one page by specifying multiple ticker symbols, e.g., **stocks: hpq ibm** gets listings for both Hewlett Packard and IBM on the same page.

As we saw in Chapter 3, you can also simply search for the ticker symbol without the **stocks:** operator to get a link to the stock listing on a regular results page. You can also search for the company name; the result listing for the company site will typically include a stock quote link so that you don't need to remember the ticker symbol. This is handy: financial sites rarely have as good a tool as this to search for the ticker symbol for a company.

phonebook:

Prefixing a query with the **phonebook:** operator locates phone book listings. The search must include both a name and a location, separated by commas, or it will fail. You must also make sure the **phonebook:** operator appears first. To restrict the search just to residential, or just to business listings, you can instead use the operators **rphonebook:** or **bphonebook:**, respectively. These operators are a more explicit and fine-grained way to perform the phone book lookups we saw in Chapter 3.

In Figure 5-18, we see just some of the listings for the search **phonebook: white house, dc**.

5

FIGURE 5-18   There are many phone book listings for the White House.

Summary of the Advanced Operators

Table 5-5 lists the syntax and operators that Google supports, in alphabetical order. The list includes some that Google hasn't documented. For example, there's no online help on **phonebook:**, **intext:**, **inanchor:**, and **daterange:**. Be advised that such undocumented features may possibly change their function or be eliminated completely.

Operator	Meaning	Notes & examples
"..."	All query terms must appear in order as given	**"bloom upon the mountain"**
+	Normally ignored term must appear on the page	**+the end**
–	Item must not appear on the page	**aa –airlines**
~	Look for synonyms of the term	**~vehicle accidents**
OR	One of the terms must appear on the page	**harpo OR groucho OR zeppo OR gummo**
allinanchor:	All query terms must appear in links to the page	**allinanchor: best search engine**
allintext:	All query terms must appear in the text of the page	**allintext: net profit**
allintitle:	All query terms must appear in the title of the page	**allintitle: bank comparison**
allinurl:	All query terms must appear in the URL of the page	**allinurl: 2001 nasa**
bphonebook:	Show business white pages listings	**bphonebook: roto rooter, albuquerque**
cache:	Show Google's cached snapshot of the web page	**cache:www.ishkur.com/ features/music/**
define	Show web definitions (for a word or phrase)	**define:white gold**
ext:	Undocumented alias for "filetype:"	**ext:xls national gdp**
filetype:	Restrict to files of the specified type	**filetype:xls national gdp**
id:	Undocumented alias for "info:"	**id:www.adobe.com/products/ acrobat/**
inanchor:	The term must appear in links to the page	**inanchor:evil**
info:	Search for information about a specific page	**info:www.adobe.com/products/ acrobat/**

TABLE 5-5   Summary of Special Syntax and Operators

Operator	Meaning	Notes & examples
intext:	The term must appear in the text of the page	**hair intext:net**
intitle:	The term must appear in the title of the page	**intitle:1040ez**
inurl:	The term must appear in the URL of the page	**mars mission inurl:2001**
link:	Search for pages that link to a specific page	**link:toolbar.google.com/**
phonebook:	Show all white pages listings	**phonebook: high school, beverly hills**
related:	Search for pages similar to a specific page	**related:www.acehardware.com/**
rphonebook:	Show residential white pages listings	**rphonebook: alan ralsky, west bloomfield**
site:	Restrict search to a specific site or domain	**riaa site:chillingeffects.org**
recall election source:new_york_times		
stocks:	Get stock quotes and financial info for a ticker symbol	**stocks:fred**

TABLE 5-5   Summary of Special Syntax and Operators *(continued)*

Language Tools

As the Web has become more ubiquitous, more and more web pages become available in more and more languages. Pages in a language you don't understand aren't entirely useful, so Google provides a Translate This Page link on search results it knows how to translate into the interface language, as discussed in Chapter 4, and also provides a Language Tools page, pictured in Figure 5-19, which we delve into here.

To visit the Language Tools page, **http://www.google.com/language_tools**, click the Language Tools link above or to the right of the Google Search box. The Language Tools page allows you to:

■ Search for pages written in specific languages

■ Search for pages located in specific countries

■ Use Google in another language, e.g., set Google's home page, messages, and buttons to display in a specific language

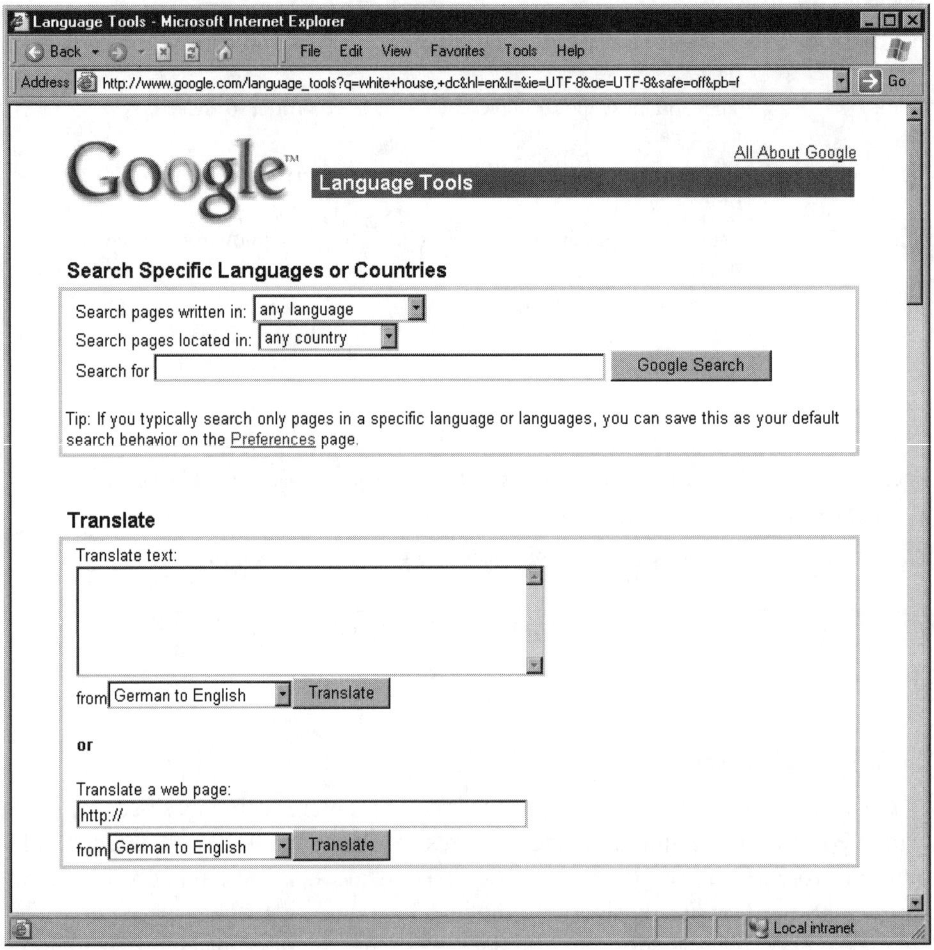

FIGURE 5-19   The Language Tools page

■ Visit Google's site in a specific country, e.g., **google.ch** in Switzerland

■ Translate text or translate a web page

Currently, you can translate pages written in French, German, Italian, Portuguese, and Spanish to English, or vice versa (for example, see Figure 5-20).

The set of possible languages in which you can display messages, buttons, and tips (your interface language as specified on Google's Preferences page) is much larger than the set of languages you can translate to or from English, and includes many relatively obscure languages, such as Basque, Georgian and Zulu, and even artificial languages, such as Klingon, Pig Latin, and Elmer Fudd (for example, see Figure 5-21).

For example: *Find out about famous statues that you can see when visiting Naples, Italy.* First, we find the Italian words for "statue in Naples" (see Figure 5-22).

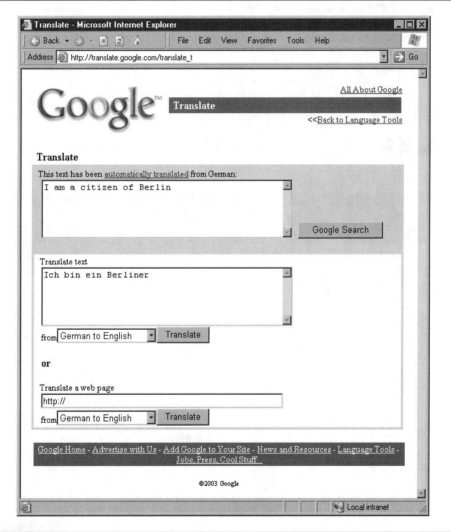

FIGURE 5-20   Translate using Google's Language Tools.

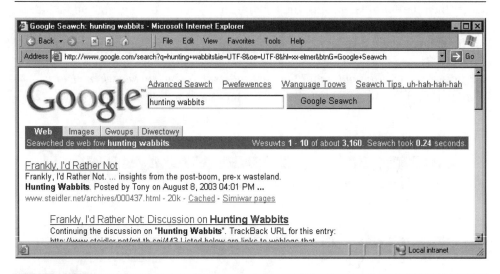

FIGURE 5-21　Google has been twanswated to Ewmew Fudd; no one knows why.

FIGURE 5-22　Google can translate from English to Italian, among other combinations.

Second, search for the terms by hitting the Google Search button on the page. If neccessary, you can add **"site:it"** to restrict the search only to Italian sites. It's not neccessary here, but we'll do it anyway to illustrate the point (Figure 5-23).

Finally, use the Translate This Page link in the result to get a vaguely understandable answer to the original inquiry (Figure 5-24).

As discussed in Chapter 4 Google uses machine (computer) translation, which tends not to be as clear as human translation, but it can give you the gist of what's being said.

FIGURE 5-23   Search within a country's domain.

FIGURE 5-24   This page appears to tell us something about the Neapolitan statue pictured.

Refine a Query

An important prerequisite for getting the most out of Google is learning the art of refining your query: altering search terms to do a better job of returning the pages you're seeking. For elusive information, it can take even expert web researchers several tries to find what they're after.

When a search completes without offering up the page you want in the first ten or so results, rather than simply combing through pages of results (or giving up completely), you can get ideas for subsequent searches by reviewing the effect of your search to try and diagnose why you missed your target.

Often, you may see that many results pertain to a different meaning of one of your search terms. For example, there may be a company or product named for the generic term you use, as in the case for a search for (the bird) **eagle**. Company, product, and mascot names crowd out pages that pertain to the animal itself.

There are several ways we've seen to remedy the situation. One is to supply other words that are likely to appear on the sort of page you're after. In our example, we might add "bird" or "beak" to our search. Another strategy might be to try to eliminate competing concepts, using the exclusion operator; we could search for **eagle –football** instead. The word "eagle" is used in too many ways for that to work here. But when a word only has a couple different common usages, it can be very effective; **engine –search** avoids lots of pages about Google and its competitors so that most results that remain are about machines that convert energy into motion.

Changing a search term to something more or less specific is also a good way to tune results. A search for **apple laptop** turns up results that mostly pertain to their PowerBook. If their more affordable iBook is the actual focus of the search, then of course **apple ibook** gives better results. By the same token, a search that is unnecessarily specific can miss your target.

Sometimes, it's hard to find specific words that relate only to the topic of interest. Narrowing the search by quoting an exact phrase you expect to appear verbatim in the text can make a big difference. But using a phrase can get you into trouble as well. Even though **"dizzy gillespie died at age"** might seem a likely way to find out how old the jazz great was when he passed away, unless some article uses that exact phrase, the search will come up empty. In general, you'll want to try most searches without quote marks; that works much better in this case. Searches for exact quotations are somewhat of an exception to this, but omitting the quotes allows more room for errors. Suppose you are looking for Clint Eastwood's "do you feel lucky?" speech from the movie *Dirty Harry*, so you try what you think is a phrase from that speech, **"ask yourself punk, do you feel lucky?"** While there are results, they are all misquotations, without the quote marks we find the real line, "You've got to ask yourself one question, do I feel lucky. Well, do ya punk?"

If you realize ahead of time that you are unclear on some part of a phrase, you can generalize the phrase search using the wildcard operator (*). What was that first line of Jimi Hendrix's *Purple Haze*? "Purple haze something something"? Search for **"purple haze * in my *"** to get the answer: "Purple Haze all in my brain." And if you have a rough idea of what that something is, you can make a guess in hopes the tireless spelling corrector can handle the task. The search **"semper fidelus"** turns up a suggestion for the correctly spelled motto of the U.S. Marines "semper fidelis" (always faithful).

In a like manner, limiting to a domain like .edu, .org or .gov is a good way to find pages published by American universities, nonprofit organizations, or government agencies, respectively. A search for **oil industry** brings up mostly corporate pages, but adding **site:org** reaches pages with an environmentalist slant (Figure 5-25).

Narrowing to a specific language can help as well. A "hamburger" is a food item in English, but a resident of Hamburg in German. Use the Language Tools page to search only for pages in a particular language. If you're searching for resources that are likely to appear in a foreign language (preferably one you know, or that Google will be able to translate for you), it might make sense to translate the search terms into the target language, search for those terms, and translate the result. For example, if you're in Toulouse, France looking for a bakery, you can use the Language Tools page to translate "bakery" to "boulangerie," then search for **boulangerie toulouse**. As you may observe in Figure 5-26, all results have a Translate This Page link.

FIGURE 5-25   Nonprofit organizations' take on the oil industry.

FIGURE 5-26   Bakeries in France, it seems

Also note that all of the sites in Figure 5-26, **www.commerces-a-vendre.com**, **www.planet-artisans.com**, etc., though very local to France, are in the .com domain, not the .fr French locale. Nevertheless, if a search is very regional, especially if governmental, it may be worth narrowing the search to a specific country or other regional domain. For example, a search for **national parks site:ca** might be a good tool to start planning a summer trip to Canada. Likewise, **helena site:mt.us** is a good way to locate the home page for the City of Helena, Montana and other official pages, since local governmental pages are generally on regional domains (Figure 5-27).

Of much more frequent value is the **site:** operator for full host names; for example, searching for information about Mars on NASA's site is as simple as typing **mars site:nasa.gov**. You can use the **site:** operator with *subdomains* also, meaning that both **site:www.irs.gov** and **site:jobs.irs.gov** are valid.

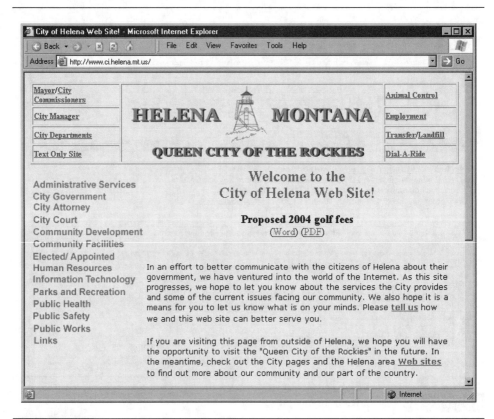

FIGURE 5-27   Helena, Montana's official site is found on the .mt.us domain.

Other portions of the URL can also be accounted for in a search using the **inurl:** operator. For example, CNN.com organizes their site to have 2002 weather information within **http://www.cnn.com/2002/WEATHER/**, so the search **storms site:www.cnn.com inurl:2002/weather** is an effective way to narrow a search on CNN.com for news about rainstorms to just the weather section and the year 2002 (Figure 5-28).

The **inurl:** operator is also of use for limiting a search to a site when the site spans many host names. A search for **travel site:yahoo.com** finds some of Yahoo's travel offerings, but if you'd like to get an idea of the many internationalized travel pages on Yahoo (Yahoo Japan, Yahoo France, etc.), **travel inurl:yahoo** works pretty well.

Trying to kill too many birds with one stone will miss good resources. Instead of searching for related topics with a single query, divide the query into several

FIGURE 5-28   Combining advanced operators can narrowly focus a search.

parts. If you're looking for advice on job hunting, you'll find more sites by searching for tips on each aspect separately than you will by searching for sites that describe all the aspects of a job search. For example, **job application cover letter interview salary negotiation** will miss much that is valuable. Instead, search for **job application** and **job cover letter** separately, and so on.

Even when looking for just one thing, over-specifying the search can be a hazard. Although the search **"akira kurosawa" "seven samurai" black and white film** finds lots of information about Akira Kurosawa's black and white film, *The Seven Samurai*, just **kurosawa "seven samurai"** does too, and with many times more relevant results. Obviously, the more specific query found plenty of results too, but there's no reason to eliminate relevant pages from the running just because they lack some of the words you speculate might appear; the pages you miss might well suit your needs better.

Table 5-6 presents a summary of ways for narrowing or refocusing a search in which the pages you're interested in are crowded out by others you don't want, as well as tips for broadening a search that has missed the pages you wanted.

Too many results? Focus the search by...	Too few results? Broaden the search by...
adding a word or phrase	removing a word or phrase
require words to appear as a phrase by enclosing them in double quotes	specifying words instead of phrases
using a more specific term	using more general terms
identifying ineffective terms and removing them	including synonyms or variant word forms or using a more common version of the word's spelling
limiting to a domain or site	searching the entire Web
limiting to a date range	removing a date range
limiting where terms occur	removing redundant terms or splitting into multiple queries
restricting type of file	searching any type of file
limiting pages in a particular language	translating your search terms into other languages and searching for the translated terms or searching pages in any language
limiting pages to a particular country	searching the entire Web

TABLE 5-6   Tips for Focusing Searches

Chapter 6

Make Searching Easier with Google Tools

How to...

- Configure your web browser in order to search Google more easily

- Install search tools in your browser

Searching with Google couldn't be much easier...but it could be a *little* easier, and this chapter talks about some tools that help you access Google features with less effort. If you search somewhat often, say more than a few times per day, you might be surprised to find how big a difference even seemingly small improvements make. These tools also bring some of Google's secondary services within easy enough reach that you might begin to use them, whereas you might not have bothered before. Give some of these tools a try; simple as they sound, soon you may wonder how you lived without them.

Because Microsoft Internet Explorer (IE) is by far the most widely used browser on the Web today (it accounts for about 90 percent of accesses to **google.com**), it is the primary focus of our discussion in this chapter. Of course IE is not the *only* browser out there. Some people prefer Opera, Mozilla, Safari or Firebird (a faster, leaner version of Mozilla). If you're one of these people, you may wish to just skim some of the following sections.

Make Google Your Home Page

The browser's *home page* is the default page it loads when it first starts up. If you use Google a lot, it's handy to have **google.com** right there when you open a new browser window. And there's another good reason to make Google your home page—speed. Google's front page is small and fast. If your home page is a big, messy portal page with ad banners on it, it can take several seconds after you open your browser before you get a chance to type the URL you really want.

To make Google your home page, click the Make Google Your Homepage! link, shown in Figure 6-1. If you've disabled JavaScript in your browser, you will have to make Google your home page manually, and it's a handy thing to know how to do, because you might have some other page you'd rather start on. (For

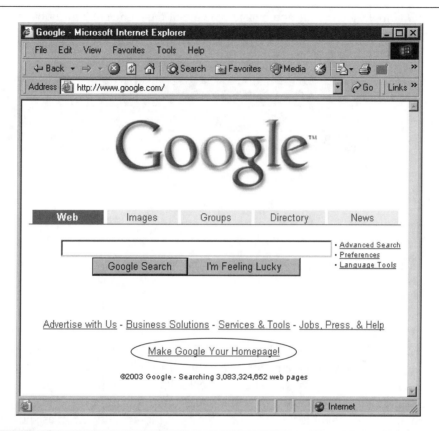

| FIGURE 6-1 | Link is provided when your browser enables your home page to be automatically set. |

example, Google News is great choice for news hounds!) To do so with Internet Explorer, use the Home Page field in the Internet Options dialog box of the Tools menu. For other browsers, simply conduct an I'm Feeling Lucky search for **make google your homepage**, and follow the simple instructions Google provides.

NOTE   *Google doesn't show the Make Google Your Homepage! link if your browser doesn't support this feature.*

With Google set as your home page, you are at most one click away from Google, no matter what page you're viewing. To go to Google, just hit the browser's home button,

Home button

or press ALT-HOME (the HOME button is usually found near the PAGE UP and PAGE DOWN buttons).

The Google Toolbar

Avid users of Google type searches into the Google Search box much more often than they type a URL into their address bar. So why not have a search box that's as accessible as the address bar? The Google Toolbar arms Internet Explorer with just that, plus a bunch of handy tools that make your browser better. The Google Toolbar stakes out a spot just below the Internet Explorer address bar, as shown in Figure 6-2, providing instant access to Google searches. It also provides useful tools, such as a pop-up window blocker and a form-filler, which is a utility that saves you time by automatically inserting data into web pages at your command. We won't discuss all the features it offers, but we will highlight some of the most useful.

Install the Google Toolbar

We describe the installation procedure as of the time of this writing. The appearance and content of some steps might change.

To install the Google Toolbar, follow the instructions found on **toolbar .google.com**. After you select your language of choice, press the Download Google Toolbar button, and agree to Google's terms of service, you'll need to select whether you'd like to install with or without Advanced Features. The

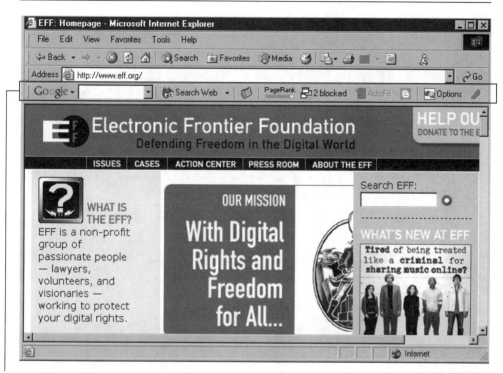

Google Toolbar

FIGURE 6-2   The Google Toolbar lets you search Google from any page.

interface with which you make this choice is shown in Figure 6-3. This is an important choice from a privacy perspective. Advanced Features provides you with the PageRank meter in the Toolbar,

which displays Google's measure of the popularity of the site you're viewing (see the Appendix). The Toolbar asks Google "how much" PageRank to display in the meter for each site you visit. In order to ask for PageRank data, it sends Google the site's URL. It doesn't send Google information about *you*, it just requests PageRank data and specifies the site. But for privacy reasons, some users prefer not to enable this feature. To disable the feature, choose the Disable Advanced Features option, shown in Figure 6-3. (You can change this setting after installing.)

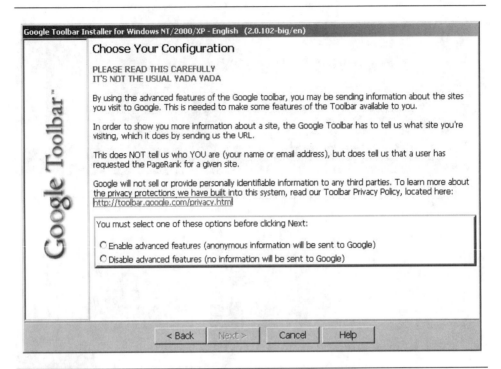

Choose Your Configuration

PLEASE READ THIS CAREFULLY
IT'S NOT THE USUAL YADA YADA

By using the advanced features of the Google toolbar, you may be sending information about the sites you visit to Google. This is needed to make some features of the Toolbar available to you.

In order to show you more information about a site, the Google Toolbar has to tell us what site you're visiting, which it does by sending us the URL.

This does NOT tell us who YOU are (your name or email address), but does tell us that a user has requested the PageRank for a given site.

Google will not sell or provide personally identifiable information to any third parties. To learn more about the privacy protections we have built into this system, read our Toolbar Privacy Policy, located here: http://toolbar.google.com/privacy.html

You must select one of these options before clicking Next:

○ Enable advanced features (anonymous information will be sent to Google)
○ Disable advanced features (no information will be sent to Google)

< Back   Next >   Cancel   Help

FIGURE 6-3   Choosing Advanced Features has privacy implications.

 *The privacy policy for the Google Toolbar is found at **http:// toolbar.google.com/privacy.html**. It states that Google does not sell or provide personally identifiable information to third parties.*

Search with the Google Toolbar

A major benefit of the Google Toolbar is the ability to search from any page you're on, without having to first go to the Google home page. Simply type your query into the search box and press ENTER, or click the Search Web button.

For maximum convenience, press ALT-G to place your cursor in the Toolbar's search box, which saves you from even having to move your hand to your mouse before entering a query. Just press ALT-G, type your query, and hit ENTER.

By default, the Toolbar performs a Google Web Search. To search other Google services, click the small triangle to the right of the Search Web button and select a service to use from the menu, as shown in Figure 6-4.

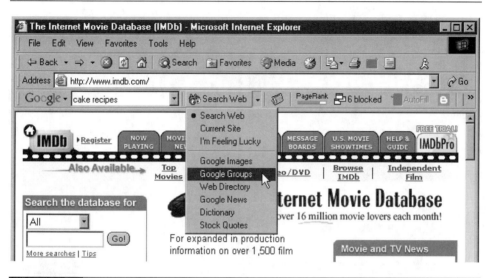

FIGURE 6-4   Search other Google services using the Search Web menu.

Find and Highlight Words

Google Search helps you find pages containing your search terms, but the Google Toolbar can take you one step further, to help you locate terms within the pages you find. Query terms remain in the search box after you've performed a search. They enable the highlighting and word-finding features, which assist with the location of search terms in a page. These features are found at the right-hand end of the Toolbar.

   Click the Highlight button to highlight the query terms in the page shown in Figure 6-5. Note that highlighting remains active until you press the Highlight button again. That is, the Toolbar will continue to highlight your search terms in any pages you visit until you deactivate highlighting.

The rightmost buttons on the Toolbar reflect your search terms. Press one of these buttons to go to the portion of the page containing the term. For example, if the term "recipe" is found at the bottom of the page, the Toolbar scrolls the browser's view downward so the term is visible, and then selects the word.

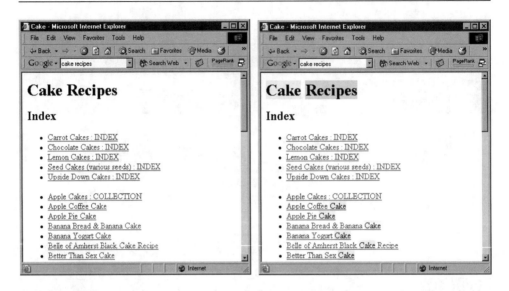

FIGURE 6-5 Locate search terms in the page using highlighting.

Highlighting and searching work even if you haven't done a Google search. On any page, you can type terms into the Google Toolbar Search box and then, without first running a search, hit the Highlight button to highlight these terms in the document, or hit a term button to search for the next occurrence of the term.

 *If you wish to search backwards in the document (e.g., find the term above your current position on the page), hold down* SHIFT *when you click the button.*

Search History

The Toolbar remembers the last few Google searches you've performed and keeps them in a list beneath the search box. To repeat a recent search, click the small down arrow next to the search box and select the search terms you're after.

To clear this list of recent searches, use the Toolbar control menu, or Google menu, located on the extreme left end of the Toolbar (where the Google logo is). Just click the Google logo and select Clear Search History.

NOTE *The Google menu is also where you'd go to uninstall the Toolbar, if you decide you want to get rid of it!*

Pop-up Window Blocker

A *pop-up window* is a window displaying an advertisement that is opened automatically by a website you visit. To put it mildly, these pop-ups typically do not add much value to your web-browsing experience. A rather nefarious form of pop-up window is the *pop-under*, which appears behind other browser windows. Websites use pop-unders in hopes of escaping blame for presenting you with windows you didn't ask for.

The Google Toolbar provides a solution to the annoyance of pop-up windows; the pop-up blocker is enabled by default, so you don't have to configure it. The first time it blocks a pop-up for you, it will display a dialog box informing you that the feature is active.

NOTE *Because there is little technical difference between pop-up windows (those appearing on top of your current windows) and pop-under windows (those appearing underneath your current windows), the Google Toolbar blocks both. It does not have the ability to block pop-up ads shown by AdWare like Gator, which operate outside of the browser, and therefore outside of what the Toolbar can control.*

NOTE *Most popular browsers include pop-up blocking features, Internet Explorer being a significant exception. Rumor has it that IE will include pop-up blocking in a future release; if so, it will be a welcome addition. Until then, the Google Toolbar can help keep you sane.*

Perhaps the most gratifying feature of the Toolbar is the number count of pop-ups blocked. It's found on the pop-up blocker button.

This button temporarily changes appearance when a pop-up is blocked.

The cursor changes its appearance, too.

The Toolbar tries to distinguish between those pop-ups you're likely to want and those you aren't, but it's not perfect. Sometimes when you click a link (or take some other action), the Toolbar blocks a pop-up that you'd like to see. For example, some sites use pop-up login windows or use pop-ups to show account information. You can tell the Toolbar to allow pop-ups when you click a link by holding down CTRL; the blocker is disabled while CTRL is pressed. You can also tell the blocker to always allow pop-ups from the site you're visiting; to do so, click the pop-up blocker button while on that page.

It changes to indicate that pop-up blocking is disabled for the current site.

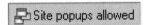

To re-enable blocking for the site, click the button again.

Disabling the blocker is helpful when it's overzealous, but there's not much to be done when it isn't aggressive enough. Undesirable pop-up windows do occasionally get through. You'll probably find, though, that browsing the Web with pop-ups blocked is very liberating.

 You can completely disable the pop-up blocker through the Google Toolbar Options dialog box, discussed in the "Other Toolbar Options" section.

AutoFill

The AutoFill feature enables you to automatically fill out web forms, the parts of web pages into which you type information. You configure AutoFill with commonly required information, such as name, address, and telephone number, and AutoFill inserts the data into the appropriate places on web pages at the press of a button. This feature saves you the hassle of having to repeatedly type the same information into forms on the Web.

If there aren't any forms on a page you're viewing, the AutoFill button is not clickable,

but the button becomes clickable on pages containing forms it can fill out.

Additionally, each field in the form for which AutoFill can store data is highlighted in yellow (see Figure 6-6) so you can tell that AutoFill is ready to operate. Notice that AutoFill recognizes most of the common fields, but doesn't recognize Favorite Color.

The first time you click the AutoFill button, the AutoFill configuration dialog box displays (shown in Figure 6-7), allowing you to enter common data. The information is stored on your computer; it is not sent to Google. If you choose to enter a credit card, it will be encrypted with a password of your choice.

Once you configure AutoFill, press the AutoFill button to insert your information into the web page (Figure 6-8). Most of the time, your information is entered into the appropriate places; however, AutoFill isn't perfect, so you should carefully check each form field before submitting the information to the website.

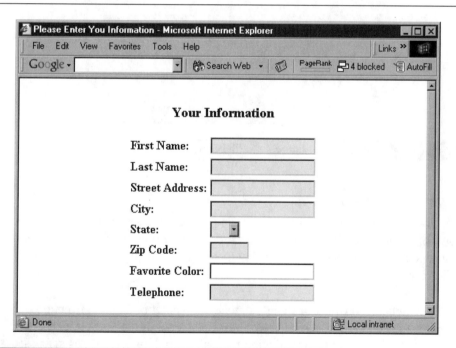

FIGURE 6-6   Fields that can be AutoFilled appear yellow.

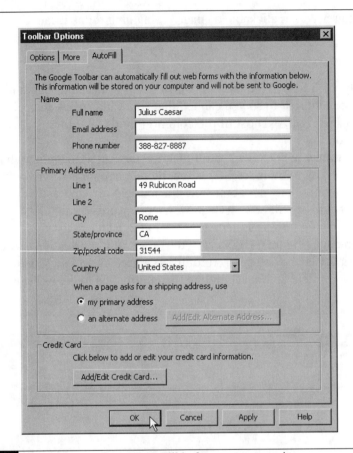

FIGURE 6-7   You must configure AutoFill before you can use it.

Page Information

The Toolbar also includes a Page Info menu, which is a convenient way to access some of Google's tools that give information about a specific page. Simply go to a page and access the Page Info drop-down menu, displayed in Figure 6-9, to get the following:

- **Cached Snapshot of Page**   Fetches the (potentially older) version of the page that Google downloaded during its crawl of the Web. It is the same as the page you get by clicking the Cached link on a result, as discussed in Chapter 4.

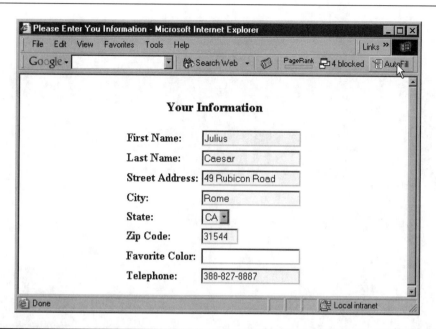

FIGURE 6-8   AutoFill inserts your information into the fields it recognizes.

- ■ **Similar Pages**   Lists pages that are apparently related to the page. This is just like the Similar Pages link on results, also described in Chapter 4, but for the current page instead of on a search result.

- ■ **Backward Links**   Lists pages which link to the current page. This is the same as the Links page-specific search in Google's Advanced Search form (see Chapter 5).

- ■ **Translate into English**   Uses Google's Language Tools machine translation function to translate the page into English. (This only appears in English language toolbars.) We discuss the Language Tools page in Chapter 5.

Other Toolbar Options

We've discussed just a few of the features offered by the Google Toolbar. All of its options are configurable through the Toolbar Options dialog box. To access this dialog box, click on the Google logo at the left of the Toolbar and select the Options menu item (see Figure 6-10).

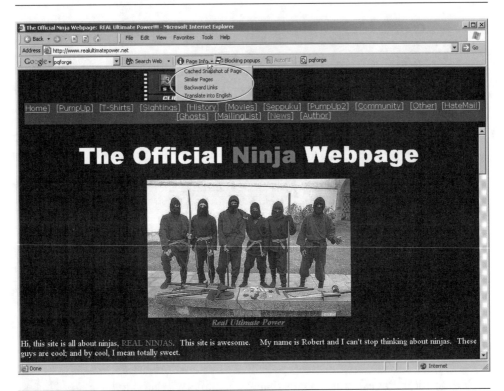

FIGURE 6-9   The Page Info menu accesses what Google knows about the current page.

To find out more information about options the Toolbar offers, select the Help item in the Google Toolbar menu (visible in Figure 6-10). The Toolbar's Help content contains discussion of each feature, as well as a Frequently Asked Questions (FAQ) list and a way to provide Google with feedback.

*A useful option for users outside the United States is the ability to configure a default search domain other than **google.com**. For example, Australian users could set the Toolbar to search **www.google.com.au**, which would allow them to locate only pages on an Australian host.*

Default Search

Even without the installing Toolbar, Internet Explorer users can get instant access to Google Search; Internet Explorer can be configured to search Google using the

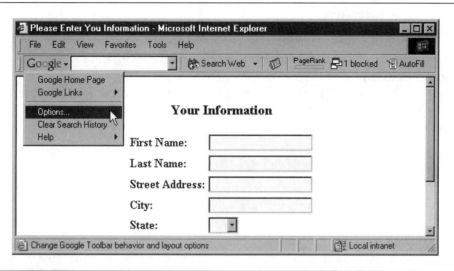

FIGURE 6-10   Configure the Google Toolbar with the Options Menu.

address bar, the place where you usually type URLs. If you enter multiple search terms into the address bar and press ENTER, the browser will perform a search for those terms. By default, this searches using MSN (the Microsoft Network), but most versions of Internet Explorer can be configured to use Google instead for these kinds of searches.

To arrange this, you will need to have Administrator privileges on your Windows computer. Download the file **http://www.google.com/google.reg** to your computer by pointing your browser at that location. Once downloaded, double-click this file and answer Yes to the dialog box. (To reverse this change, or for more guidance, see Google's page explaining this feature at **http://www.google.com/options/defaults.html#default**.)

At the time of this writing, the Google Toolbar offers to configure your default search setting during installation; you can also toggle this setting using the toolbar's Options menu.

With Google configured as your default search engine, Internet Explorer will search Google when you enter search terms, or a nonexistent URL, in the address bar. Alternately, you can type a word into the address bar, hit the DOWN arrow key, and select the line that offers to Search For that word.

Browser Buttons

Yet another way to have Google search in your browser is to add Google's Browser buttons. They work for almost all modern browsers, and are a snap to install. Installation instructions are tailored to your particular browser; to find them, search for **google browser buttons** and follow the instructions given on the first results page. In Internet Explorer, it's as simple as dragging a link to your Links toolbar.

NOTE   *Browser buttons are sometimes referred to as "bookmarklets."*

Google offers three handy browser buttons:

- **The GoogleSearch button**   This button is the most useful, and you can probably surmise what it does. You should know that there are two ways to use it. The easiest way is to select some text on a page and then click the GoogleSearch button. A search on the words selected will be performed. Sometimes, of course, the words you want to search for aren't on a page; in this case, you can just click the GoogleSearch button with nothing selected. You'll be presented with a dialog box where you can enter your query, and then the search will proceed.

- **The GoogleScout button**   GoogleScout finds pages that are similar, by some measure, to the current page. Essentially, GoogleScout does a **related:** query for the current page (discussed in Chapter 4). It's handy to have a browser button for this, since crafting GoogleScout queries by hand is kind of tedious, and the button makes it easy. This duplicates the Similar Pages item on the Google Toolbar's Page Info menu, which is described in the Page Information section of this chapter.

- **The Google.com button**   This button simply takes you to Google's home page. (In fact, you can turn any link into a simple bookmark like this button simply by following the same procedure you use to install this one.)

NOTE   *If you've installed the Google Toolbar, you don't need these browser buttons. The Toolbar does anything the bookmarklets can do, and considerably more.*

Mozilla and Netscape 6

The Mozilla browser belongs to a family of browsers based on the same technology, which includes Mozilla itself, Mozilla Firebird, Netscape 6 and 7, and a host of others. These browsers are available for almost any conceivable platform, and tend to include features that make it easy to search using Google.

Mozilla Firebird includes a search box that appears by default to the right of the address bar (see Figure 6-11). This box can be used to search Google by clicking the icon on the left side of the search box and selecting Google. Now type search terms and hit ENTER to perform a Google search. This search box can also be used to find search terms within a page; with the Magnifying Glass icon showing, hit ENTER to search for and highlight the word or phrase in the search box.

6

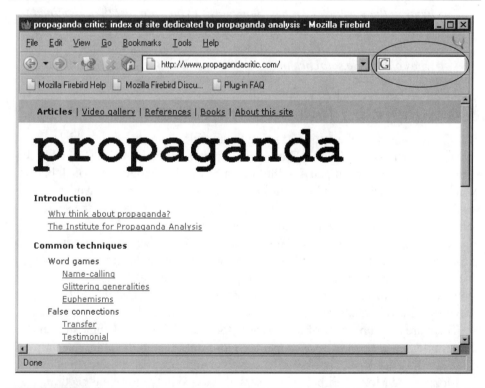

FIGURE 6-11   The Mozilla Firebird browser has a built-in Google Search box.

Although Google doesn't provide a version of the Google Toolbar that works with the Mozilla browser, volunteers in the Mozilla developer community have implemented a similar toolbar called the Googlebar that emulates all of the basic functionality of the Google Toolbar, and even includes a few extra features that the Google Toolbar lacks.

To get the Googlebar, you must be using Mozilla. Navigate to **googlebar .mozdev.org** and click the Installation link. Choose the Install link under the highest version number listed (but not the experimental version!). You'll have to restart your browser to complete the installation. Now you'll see a new toolbar with an onslaught of artful buttons, which perform searches or serve other functions (see Figure 6-12).

NOTE   *To simplify the interface, you'll probably want to remove some of the Googlebar's buttons. To do so, right-click the Googlebar and uncheck items in the various Searches submenus. If you keep just the Combined menu in the Special Searches submenu, you'll be able to perform regular Google searches by hitting* ENTER, *while still maintaining access to other types of Google searches in the Combined Searches drop-down button.*

Search Google on Macintosh Systems

Mac OS X users have the option of using the nimble Safari browser, which conveniently includes a Google Search box directly on the browser, stashed in the upper-right corner. Accompanying the search box is the Google SnapBack button, which makes it easier to explore multiple search results. After you investigate one result for a search, you can hit the SnapBack button to jump back to the search page so that you can follow other interesting result links.

The Google Toolbar isn't available for the Safari browser or for Internet Explorer for Macintosh. But, the Safari browser also integrates pop-up stopping, one of the most useful features of the Google Toolbar, and also supports the browser buttons discussed earlier in this chapter. So with all that in addition to the Google Search integration in Safari, you'll hardly miss the Google Toolbar.

There are also a number of other search tools available for Macintosh users. The simple SearchGoogle Service and the more fully featured NetService are two OS X services that make it possible to search Google from anywhere. In addition, the Mozilla and Mozilla Firebird browsers, discussed in the previous section, are

googlebar

FIGURE 6-12   The GoogleBar plugs into the Mozilla browser.

both available for Macintosh systems. Finally, GGSearch is an application that brings Google's power to your desktop. To get your hands on of any one of these tools, or to learn more about them, just search for them by name on your favorite search engine!

Chapter 7 Configure Google

How to...

- Display Google tips, messages, tabs, and buttons in another language

- Search pages written in specific languages

- Change the default number of results displayed on a page

- Filter out sexually explicit content or turn off filtering

- Configure Google to open a results page in a new browser window

Setting Preferences

You can customize the way you search by configuring your Google global preferences—options that apply across most Google services, including Google Web Search, Google Image Search, Google Groups, the Google Directory, Google News, Froogle, and Catalogs. To set these options, click the Preferences link, which is to the right of the search box on Google's home page (shown in Figure 7-1), and above the search box on Google's results page (shown in Figure 7-2).

FIGURE 7-1   The Preferences link allows you to configure Google's services.

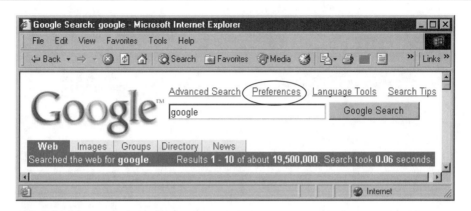

FIGURE 7-2   The Preferences link is available on some results pages.

From the Preferences page (see Figure 7-3), you can specify:

- **Interface Language**   The language in which Google displays tips, messages, and buttons.

- **Search Language**   The language of the pages Google searches.

- **SafeSearch**   Automatic omission of web pages with explicit sexual content from search results.

- **Number of results**   How many search results display per page.

- **Results window**   When enabled, clicking the link (typically the page title) for a result will open the corresponding page in a new window.

After specifying your preferences, you must save your settings by clicking one of the Save Preferences buttons (found near the top and near the bottom of the page).

Save your preferences when finished and **return to search**.   Save Preferences

Clicking this button takes you back to the page you were on when you clicked the Preferences link.

Your preferences settings apply when you use the computer on which you set them up. However, each Google domain (e.g., **www.google.fr** and **www.google.de**) is configured separately; preferences set for one domain (e.g., **google.com**) do not apply to another (e.g., **google.dk**).

FIGURE 7-3 Google's Preferences page.

Resetting Preferences

You can return to the Preferences page at any time to change your settings. However, there might be occasions when you want to reset your preferences without going to the Preferences page, e.g., you've changed the interface language to Arabic and can't read the Preferences page.

Google maintains your preferences in a cookie. A *cookie* is a small piece of information a website uses to keep track of a user's data. Deleting your cookies will "erase" Google's memory of your choices. So you can manually reset your preferences by deleting your browser's cookies.

In Internet Explorer, select the Internet Options item from the Tools menu. You'll see a dialog box similar to Figure 7-4. Click the Delete Cookies button

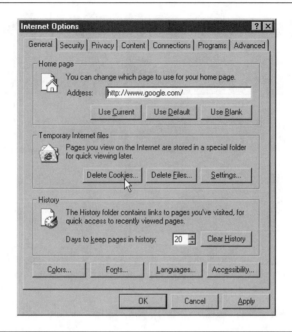

FIGURE 7-4   Erase your cookies to manually reset Google preferences.

and confirm your choice when asked. Then click the OK button to resume your browsing. If you're currently visiting a page in Google, you'll need to reload the page for your preferences to be reset.

NOTE   *Be aware that when you delete your cookies, you may also be resetting preferences for websites besides Google.*

Language Settings

Google's language settings enable many users around the world to use Google in their native languages. If you don't configure language settings, Google defaults to a language based on your browser and the Google domain you're accessing.

Interface Language

Google's *interface language* is the language in which tips, messages, links within its services, and the text on buttons are displayed. For example, if you set your interface language to Greek, messages and text on links, tabs, and buttons will be displayed in Greek, as shown in Figure 7-5.

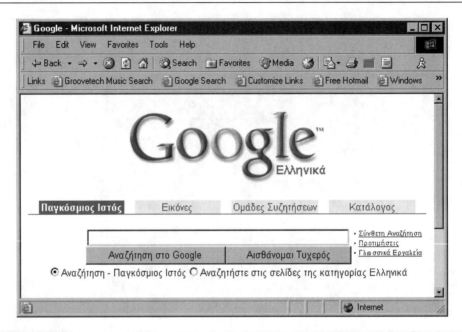

FIGURE 7-5   The interface language controls how you interact with Google.

You can configure the interface language on the Preferences page.

Interface Language   Display Google tips and messages in: English ▾
If you do not find your native language in the pulldown above, you can help Google create it through our Google in Your Language program.

The pulldown menu allows you to choose from over 80 languages. Included are all the major languages of the world, as well as many less widely spoken languages. Google even offers languages such as Pig Latin (see Figure 7-6), Elmer Fudd, Hacker, and "Bork Bork Bork!" (the dialect of the Swedish Chef from The Muppet Show).

> **NOTE**   *If you don't find your preferred language in the list, you can volunteer to translate Google's interface into that language via the "Google In Your Language" program:* ***http://services.google.com/tc/Welcome.html.***

FIGURE 7-6   Onfigurecay Ooglegay inay Igpay Atinlay

If you select an interface language other than English, when using Google Web Search you will be given the option of searching the entire Web or just pages written in your interface language. For example, with German as the interface language, the search box looks like the following:

The option on the left is to search the whole Web. The option on the right restricts the search to pages in German. If you wish to search only German pages, you need to click the German-only option on the right before clicking the search button. If you always restrict your search to a particular language, then you should probably set your Search Language preference using the Preferences page (as discussed in the Search Language section later in this chapter).

Browser Language

Each time your browser requests a web page, it sends information to the server indicating which language or languages you prefer. This is your *browser language* and it is what Google uses if you haven't set an interface language. You can configure your browser language through the Internet Options item of the Tools menu in Internet Explorer. Click the Languages button and you'll see a dialog box like the one shown in Figure 7-7.

The dialog box lists the languages your browser will request from websites, in order of preference. You can add or remove languages by using the buttons provided, as well as modify the priority of each language by highlighting (clicking) it and moving it up or down.

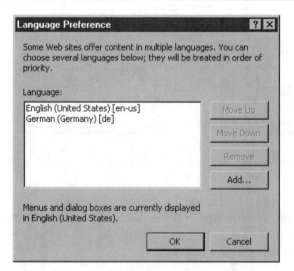

FIGURE 7-7   Languages are listed in order of preference.

Remember, Google uses your browser language only if you haven't set an interface language preference. As explained in the following section, Google also ignores your browser language if you visit a Google site in a domain other than **google.com**.

Google Domains and Interface Language

A *domain name* is the server name portion of a URL (web page address). For example, in the URL **http://www.google.com/news**, the domain name is **www.google.com**. The final part of the name indicates what kind of site it might be. The .com indicates a commercial site, but domains exist for educational institutions (.edu) and organizations (.org), as well as other entities. Most domains with three or more letters are administered by U.S. companies.

Every country has a "top level domain," a suffix of domain names allocated by that country. Country domains are two letters long; for example, fr for France and dk for Denmark. Google operates more than 70 domains in different countries, so you can go to google.fr for Google France as well as google.dk for Google Denmark. For a complete list of international Google domains, go to **http://www.google.com/ language_tools**. The bottom portion of this page contains a list of domains, as shown in Figure 7-8.

As previously mentioned, when using a non-.com Google domain, any preferences set on **www.google.com** do not apply. Each domain is configured separately. Your browser language is ignored on non-Google.com pages as well.

The default interface language of each Google domain is an official language in that country. If a country has several languages, Google usually provides you with a choice of interface languages in case the default isn't what you want. For example, Google Switzerland (**www.google.ch**) defaults to German but provides links to view the site in English, French, or Italian.

Google.ch angeboten in: <u>Englisch</u> <u>Französisch</u> <u>Italienisch</u>

Click one of these links to set your interface language preference accordingly.

If Google knows the location of your Internet connection is outside of the United States and Google has a domain for your country, you will be automatically redirected to Google's domain for your country.

FIGURE 7-8   International Google domains

Returning to the English Interface

Google provides users with an English-language "escape hatch" whenever the interface language isn't English. You can find it in the lower part of the page, as shown in the following image for the Polish-language interface:

Follow this link to set your interface language to English.

Search Language

By default, Google Web Search includes all pages on the Web. You can choose to restrict your searches to those pages written in the languages of your choice by setting the *search language*. Search language is configured through the Preferences page, as shown in Figure 7-9.

To set your search language, select the "Search only for pages written in these language(s)" option and utilize the check boxes to indicate the languages of interest. If you select the option but don't check any of the language boxes, the configuration is ignored.

If you want to restrict results to a single language for a few queries, it's probably easier to use the Google Advanced Search page than to set your configuration, search, and then reset the configuration. The Advanced Search page is discussed in Chapter 5 and can be found at **http://www.google.com/advanced_search**, or by clicking the Advanced Search link on the Google homepage. The Language option, as seen in the following image, is used to set the search language for that query:

7

Language	Return pages written in	Icelandic ▾

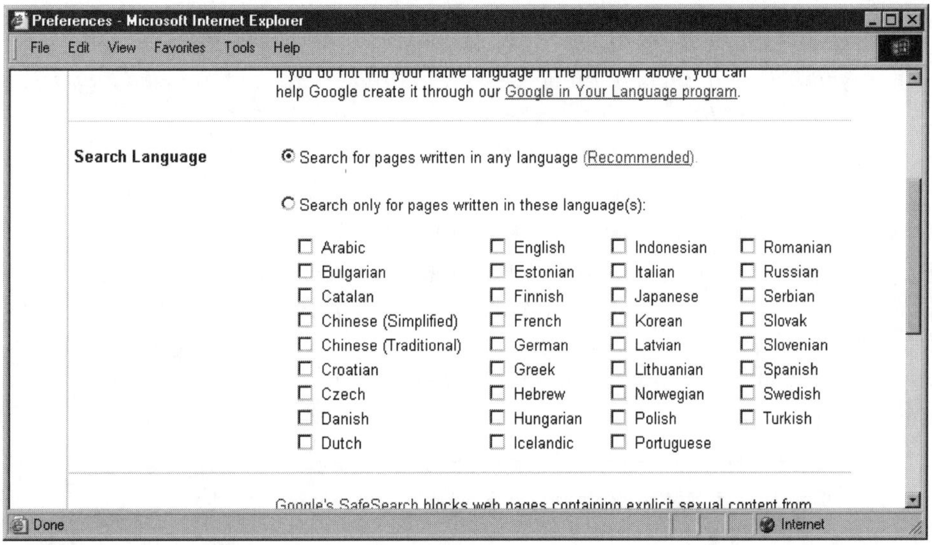

FIGURE 7-9   The Preferences page allows you to restrict results to specific languages.

Because you search fewer pages when you restrict results to particular languages, you might not find what you're seeking. Fortunately, the search box at the top of a Results page provides the option to search the whole Web or only those pages in your languages.

NOTE *Your results may include a Translate This Page link when Google finds a page in a language different from your language of choice (as specified by your Google preferences). This feature is currently available for pages published in English, French, German, Italian, Portuguese, and Spanish. We discuss this tool in Chapter 5. You can find this service at* **http://www.google.com/language_tools**.

Google Domains and Search Language

By default, searching on an international Google domain searches the entire Web. Every search box also provides you with the option of searching only pages in the language of that country. It also lets you search only the pages located within that country's domains. The search box of Google Costa Rica is shown in the following image:

We discuss using country-specific restrictions in Chapter 5.

SafeSearch Filtering	Google's SafeSearch blocks web pages containing explicit sexual content from appearing in search results.
	O Use strict filtering (Filter both explicit text and explicit images)
	⊙ Use moderate filtering (Filter explicit images only - default behavior)
	O Do not filter my search results.

FIGURE 7-10   SafeSearch excludes adult content from search results.

Safe Search

Google's SafeSearch screens sites with pornography and explicit sexual content. Moderate filtering, the default, is set to exclude most explicit images from Google Image Search results but does not affect Google Web Search or other Google search services.

Set SafeSearch filtering on the Preferences page, as shown in Figure 7-10. There are three levels: strict, moderate, and no filtering. The amount of filtering for each these settings is shown in Table 7-1.

If you would rather not have adult sites included in your results, set SafeSearch to Strict. Google's SafeSearch isn't perfect, but with strict filtering enabled, you will encounter dramatically fewer sexually explicit results.

You can set SafeSearch for a single query using the Advanced Search page (discussed in Chapter 5).

Setting	Image Search Filtering	Web Search Filtering
strict	strict	strict
moderate (default)	moderate	none
none	none	none

TABLE 7-1   SafeSearch settings and their effects

Inside Google: Matt Cutts Talks About SafeSearch

We asked Matt Cutts, the Google employee who developed SafeSearch, some questions about the development of the feature.

Authors: What inspired you to create SafeSearch?

Matt Cutts: In general, part of Google's philosophy is to filter as little as possible, so it took a client that really insisted on having a porn filter before we decided to write it.

Authors: What were some of the tradeoffs you considered?

Matt Cutts: We considered some of the manual approaches that other filters use, but that goes against another basic philosophy at Google, which is to make things as automatic and scalable as we can. So we quickly decided on an approach that leans much more toward algorithmic (computer-based) approaches than hand-picked lists of "good" and "bad" sites.

We also made the decision to build it ourselves. We evaluated outside products, but didn't find things that exactly met our needs. Another pivotal moment was doing a search for something like "sex" on another search engine and only getting something like 20–30 results. We decided that it was important to try to return as much useful content as we could rather than returning a few "approved" results. This goes back to our filter-no-more-than-necessary mindset.

Finally, we also considered categories besides pornography (things like hate speech, anarchy, bomb-making, etc). The problem is that these categories are not only on a more slippery slope, but also they are much harder to detect automatically. Trying to filter hate speech would undoubtedly filter out a few sites that *discuss* hate speech, for example those that track hate groups online. So the consensus that we reached was to concentrate only on explicit pornography. I'm happy to say that we really haven't received many complaints about SafeSearch at all, or requests that we block other behaviors. At the time, that was an unclear call, but I think we made the right decision.

Authors: Please share some stories about the history of SafeSearch.

Matt Cutts: When we first started deploying SafeSearch, we wanted to test and see if we missed any pornographic sites. It gets surprisingly mundane trying to find porn after a few hours, so I decided to enlist the help of fellow Googlers. I asked my wife to bake a big batch of cookies. I brought the cookies into work, and prepared about 250 really pornographic queries and put them in a database. Then I mailed out to Google and asked for volunteers to find porn in SafeSearch. Anyone who found porn would get a cookie as a reward. It became a tradition for a little while: about once a month, my wife would bake cookies and quite a few Googlers would go looking for porn.

Another funny thing is that misspellings are a good indicator of whether a site is porn or not. If someone writes "amature," they're probably not talking about amateur radio. Looking at our data, it seems that pornographers spell "ugh" over 480 different ways, from uuggghhhh, uuggghhhhhhhh, and uuhhhhhoohhhhyyyeeaaahhh all the way down to uuuuuuugggghhhhllllllmmmmmm.

Number of Results

The Number of Results is configurable through the Preferences page, as shown in the following image:

Number of Results   Google's default (10 results) provides the fastest results.
Display [10 ▾] results per page.

You can increase the number of results displayed per page to 20, 30, 50, or 100. The more results displayed per page, the more likely you are to find what you want on the first page of results. The downside is that the more results per page, the more slowly the page loads. How much more time it takes depends on your connection to the Internet.

If you're the kind of searcher who looks through long lists of result pages, you should consider setting your preferences to show many results. If, on the other hand, you're the type of searcher who refines your query when you don't see a desirable result in the first few, keeping the number of results per page at ten probably makes sense.

Google's Approach to Filtering

Google's filter considers many different factors in order to determine whether a page should be filtered. It checks for keywords in a page, particular phrases typical of pornographic sites, the name of the website, Open Directory categories, and other sources of information. This approach—arriving at a decision about a page based on the combination of many sources of information—is the same approach Google uses to *score* web pages. That is, to determine how "good" a page is as a result for a particular query. See the Appendix (How Google Works) for more details.

 *You should consider using both strategies when you search. Doing so makes you more likely to find what you're looking for.*

This option applies to Google Web Search, Google Groups, Google News, and Google Directory. It does not apply to Google Images or Froogle.

New Results Window

After you set the Results window option on the Preferences page: when you click on the main link (typically the page title) for a result, Google will open the corresponding page in a new window, as shown in the following image:

Results Window   ☐   Open search results in a new browser window.

This option works in all Google services.

If you use Internet Explorer, you can open results in a new window by holding down SHIFT while you click a link. In many other browsers, CTRL has the same effect.

Part II

Google Features

Chapter 8

Search News Sources with Google News

How to...

- Access online news stories from thousands of sites using Google News
- Find news articles of interest
- Get multiple perspectives on current events

Google News presents aggregated news information culled from thousands of news sources worldwide. Related articles from different sources are grouped together and updated continuously throughout the day. Google News is a great service for meeting your daily online news needs and, because it is searchable, is also useful for researching current events.

Like Froogle (see Chapter 13), Google News is a beta service. This means Google hasn't yet finalized its features or interface.

Google News

There are several ways to get to Google News. Figure 8-1 shows the Google News tab (see Chapter 1), the fifth (rightmost) tab on **google.com**'s main interface. Instead of clicking the tab, you can go directly to the service by pointing your browser at **news.google.com**.

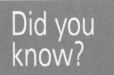

The Birth of Google News

After the tragedies of September 11, 2001, Krishna Bharat, a Google research scientist, wanted to keep track of breaking news stories from major sources on the Web. To meet this need, he built a tool to crawl the Web and organize news into ranked clusters. This demo was popular within Google and, with significant contributions by a number of Google engineers, expanded to become Google News.

FIGURE 8-1   An easy way to access Google News is via the News tab.

Another way to get to Google News is by clicking on links to it shown with your Google Web Search results. Figure 8-2 shows News links, which appear above the search results. The first two links are direct links to stories found by searching Google News for the query. The other two links are to Google News itself, enabling you to search for more articles or to jump to the News home page.

The main Google News interface (shown in Figure 8-3) is packed with information. Google tries to provide as much content as possible, so there are few images and lots of text. We discuss the interface in more detail in the Browse Google News section.

Google News presents snippets from and links to news articles all over the Web. But unlike most news sites, Google News is computer-generated. There are no editors working behind the scenes deciding which stories to display. Google's computers continually examine over 4,500 news sites and decide which stories are most relevant based on how often they appear as well as how prominently they are displayed. The content of each story on every site is also processed to determine what category the story falls into as well as other stories that might be related. The automated aggregation of content from diverse sources typically gives a well-rounded and interesting mix of information about current events. However, the process is imperfect, so stories are occasionally misclassified or improperly grouped.

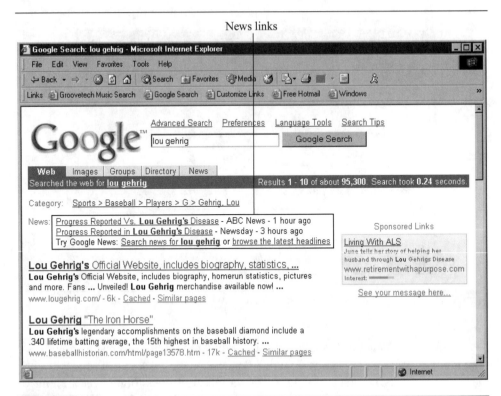

FIGURE 8-2   News links come from Google News.

The stories on Google News are updated frequently, typically about every 15 to 30 minutes. The News interface indicates how long it's been since the last update, as shown in Figure 8-4. You can hit the Refresh or Reload button on your browser to download the most recently generated page, but, conveniently, the Google News home page automatically refreshes itself every 15 minutes. This means that you don't have to refresh it manually in order to keep your eye on current stories.

NOTE   *Google appreciates feedback on how it can improve Google News. You can submit feedback by sending e-mail to **news-feedback@google.com**.*

FIGURE 8-3   The primary Google News interface is home to a lot of content.

Press Reaction to Google News

When Google News was first released, it worried many members of the press, particularly editors. The service was seen as competition, and some editors believed it posed a threat to their craft, that Google News marked the first step towards increased automation of the editorial process. In other words, that selection of stories to appear in publications would be given over to computers, making the human editor obsolete. However, the press soon realized that the primary reason Google News shows relevant content is *because* of editors who publish on the Web. Google draws upon the editorial choices of thousands of news sources to determine the most relevant stories. Today, many are big fans of the service, using it daily for research and to help decide what stories to include in their print publications.

FIGURE 8-4   Google News is refreshed approximately once every 15 minutes.

Browse Google News

The primary Google News interface (shown in Figure 8-5) is divided into several panes. You can search for news articles specifically, or the entire Web, using the search box at the top of the page. The left pane contains links to categories of stories specific to a given subject, for example Entertainment. The center pane is labeled *Top Stories* and contains featured breaking news. The right pane is split into two sections. A sample of stories from different categories is found in the top half, and clicking one of these links takes you directly to that article. A list of people, places, or things making headlines is found in the bottom portion. Click one of these links to search Google News for that term.

Further down the page are top news stories from each of Google News' categories. Only the top three are shown for each. More stories are found on the respective category pages.

Navigate to news categories   Search Google News   Random headlines

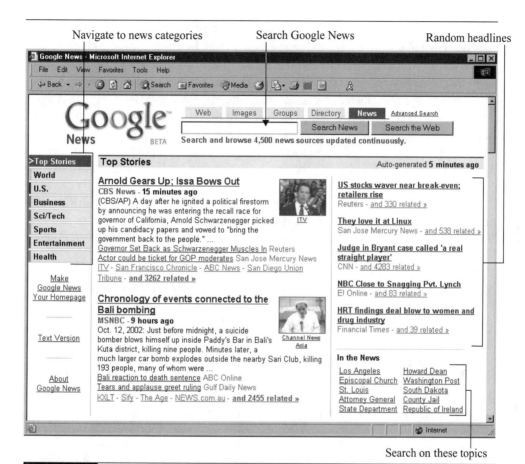

Search on these topics

FIGURE 8-5   The top of the Google News home page

The Text Version link on the left side of the page is useful if you have a slow Internet connection, and you wish to see Google News without any images.

News Stories

Google News typically knows about hundreds of articles on different sites covering each story. All the information about a story is clustered together, providing a more compact interface than if shown separately. The presentation of each story is designed to offer access to as many sources of information as possible.

Figure 8-6 shows a Google News story. An article representative of the story is chosen as the headline, and the article's title links to full text on the original site. Below the headline is the source of the article, how long ago it was published, and a snippet of its text. Next to it is usually an image, but this image isn't necessarily from the article from which the headline and snippet were taken. By taking the image from a separate source and linking the image to that source, Google provides easy access to another article. The source of the image is found directly under it. In Figure 8-6, for example, clicking the headline link takes you to a San Francisco Chronicle article, while clicking the image shows you a related article at CNN Europe.

As you can see in Figure 8-6, the titles of several related articles on different sites are found under the snippet. Below these is a list of other news sources carrying the story. Click on any of these links to take you to a related article on the site shown.

NOTE   *Google's computers choose articles to display as headlines and links. Which articles are chosen depends on how prominently articles appear on news sites, the sites on which they appear, when articles were published, and how many different sites are covering the story.*

There usually isn't enough space for Google to show all the articles covering a particular story. Instead, a link is provided to a list of all such articles. In Figure 8-6, the link reads *and 508 related,* indicating that there are 508 articles on this story. Click the link to perform a search for all related articles.

Kidnapped European tourists freed from Sahara Desert captivity; return to Germany

San Francisco Chronicle - 1 hour ago
Fourteen European tourists made their way out of the Sahara Desert by road on Tuesday, ending a six-month kidnapping ordeal at the hands of Islamic extremists linked to al-Qaida.

CNN Europe

Germany 'paid ransom' to free hostages The Scotsman
14 kidnapped tourists head home Brisbane Courier Mail
New Zealand Herald - New York Times - MSNBC - Neue Zürcher Zeitung -
and 508 related »

Other sources covering the story

FIGURE 8-6   Links to many different sources covering the story

Figure 8-7 shows the result of the search for related articles for the story in Figure 8-6. Notice the number of results found is 509, not 508. Small discrepancies are common, and are a result of the fact that, as with Google Web Search, the number of results are estimated rather than computed exactly in order to save time. Sometimes, however, the number of actual results is significantly less than the estimate. The reason for the discrepancy is that the list of related stories is filtered for duplicates. Many sites publish verbatim articles released by news services such as the Associated Press (AP) and Reuters. Duplicate copies of these articles are omitted from the results, and account for the "missing" articles.

News Categories

Google News has eight categories: World, U.S. (or another country, if you're viewing an international Google News site), Business, Sci/Tech, Sports, Entertainment, Health, and Top Stories. You start in Top Stories when you visit Google News. It contains the two top stories of the moment (shown previously in Figure 8-5) as well as top stories from each category.

8

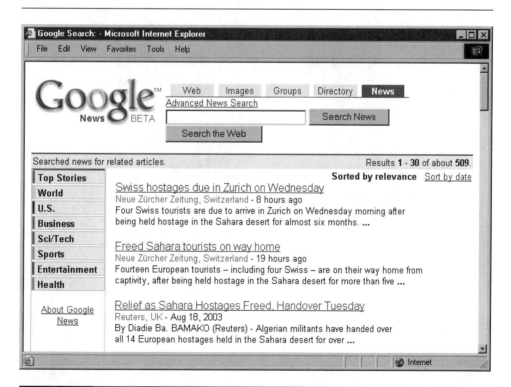

FIGURE 8-7   The list of related stories is filtered for duplicates.

Clicking the heading of a story category, for example, the Business heading as shown in the following image,

Wall St cautious trade
The Australian - **4 hours ago**
WALL Street waffled its way to a modest gain today as mixed economic news and a car bombing in Iraq revived investors' caution following yesterday's big rally.

takes you to that category. The category you're in is indicated in the menu on the left side of the page (shown in Figure 8-8), which you can also use to navigate.

Twenty of the most relevant stories are shown in each category list. Relevancy is determined in the same way as for Top Stories: by examining how prominently articles are displayed, how many sites carry the story, how recently the story broke, and similar characteristics. A heavy bias is given to recent news stories. Most stories listed in a category are less than 24 hours old.

Currently in Top Stories

Currently in Business

FIGURE 8-8   You can navigate to different categories by clicking them on the menu.

Search Google News

Search the stories in Google News with the search box found at the top of the page.

Google News Search has the same basic behavior as Google Web Search (implicit AND, case insensitivity, common word exclusion) and supports most of the basic operators (+, -, OR, quotes). It does not support the synonym operator (~) at the time of this writing. See Chapter 2 for more information about these operators.

A sample search results page is shown in Figure 8-9. A list of articles matching the query is displayed, sorted by relevance. Like other Google services, the query

FIGURE 8-9   By default, Google News Search results are sorted by relevance.

terms are presented in boldface text in the results (article headlines and text snippet). Very closely related news stories are sometimes grouped together, as you can see in the first result in Figure 8-9.

If you prefer to see results in reverse chronological order (most recently published stories first), use the Sort by date link at the top right of the Results column.

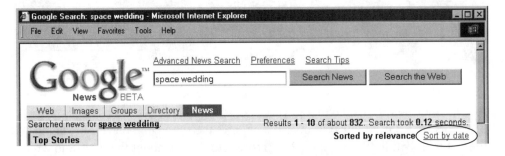

Google News does not provide the capability to sort articles in oldest-first order, but does provide a feature to search articles published between specific dates (see the "Advanced News Search" section later in this chapter).

Like Google Web Search, Google News looks for dictionary definitions for your search terms. If it finds any, it shows the terms as underlined links in the status bar portion of the Results page (below the search box).

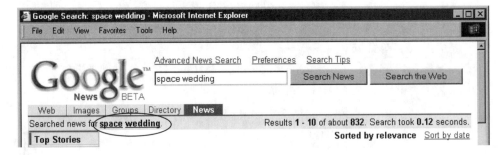

These are links to the definitions of the terms on **dictionary.com**.

Search Techniques for Google News

Google News looks for query terms in the body of articles and in their headlines. Craft your query accordingly. For example, if you were searching for stories about

Did you know?

How to Keep Tabs on Current Events

Google News Alerts (**http://www.google.com/newsalerts**) allows you sign up to receive an e-mail when new articles are published that match search terms you specify. This service can be useful for staying abreast of topics that interest you. For example, you might use Google News Alerts to keep an eye on the competition, a sports team, or a favorite celebrity.

the Tour de France bicycle race, search for words likely to appear in an article, for example **tour de france** or **lance armstrong** (who won each race from 1999 to the time of this writing). Queries such as **bike race** or **french race** are not likely to be effective, because they're not guaranteed to be found in a Tour de France article.

Because Google News searches article text and titles, you must craft general queries with care. If you were looking for news about environmental issues, **environmental news** would probably give very poor results. It would find stories containing the words "environmental" and "news." Since there will be many stories that don't include the word "news" in their title or text, the query is unnecessarily narrow. Searching for **environment** might be a bit better, but not by much because *any* story containing the word "environment" will be returned. Instead, try searching for something more specific, for example, **climate change**, **marine pollution**, or **glacier national park**.

Like Google Web Search, if you have more than one term in your query, Google News favors articles containing the terms close together over articles in which the terms are separated by lots of text. This is beneficial for many queries. It means, for example, that a query for **united nations** is more likely to turn up articles about the United Nations than random articles that happen to contain those words. It can also be a hindrance if you're not looking for news about the United Nations. You might have to specifically exclude results containing the phrase you don't want, for example, **united nations -"united nations"**, which finds articles in which the terms are not adjacent.

Since searches are performed on article titles and text, you typically cannot search for an author's name in order to see the articles he or she has published. Occasionally, an author's name is included as part of the article body.

8

Advanced News Search

The Advanced News Search interface is accessed through the Advanced Search link in the upper-right corner of Google News.

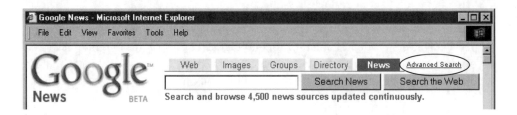

Don't let the name scare you. The Advanced News Search interface of Google News (shown in Figure 8-10) is easy to use, and provides powerful tools for restricting searches by news source, location, and date of publication.

The top portion of the Advanced News Search form is an easy way of writing queries without having to use the basic search operators (+, −, OR, and quotes), as described in Chapter 2. These operators correspond to the four boxes in the Find Results portion of the following image:

Find results	with **all** of the words		Sort by relevance ▾
	with the **exact phrase**		Google Search
	with **at least one** of the words		
	without the words		

Table 8-1 describes the meaning of these boxes, along with the operators to which they correspond.

The lower half of the interface (shown in Figure 8-11) is unique to Google News, and lets you specify more precisely what you seek by restricting your results to a subset of those that would otherwise be returned. Enter terms into the top portion of the interface and then restrict the query using the lower half. Google News will perform a query made up of all the terms you entered in the top according to the restrictions configured in the bottom.

When you navigate to the Advanced News Search interface from a Search Results page, the settings for that search are reflected in the interface. That is, if you were on the Results page for a location-restricted search and clicked the

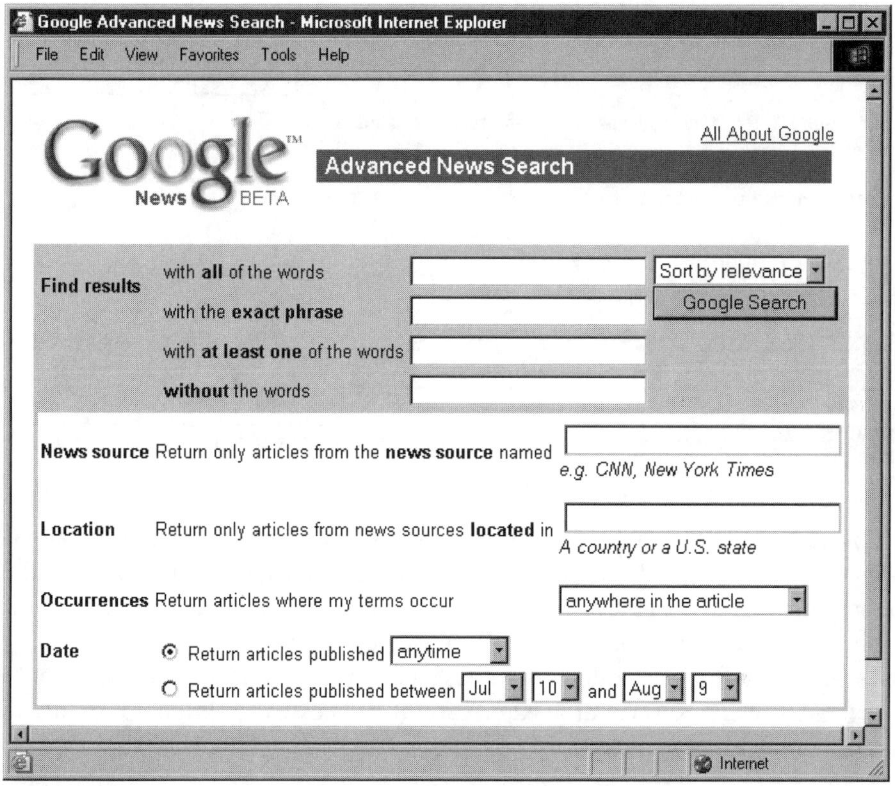

FIGURE 8-10   The Advanced News Search interface is the easiest way to restrict Google News queries.

Advanced Search feature	Matches pages...	Operator
with all of the words	with all the terms	**term1 term2 ...** (no special operator because of implicit AND)
with the exact phrase	with all the terms in the given order	**"term1 term2 ..."** (quotes)
with at least one of the words	with any of the terms	**term1 OR term2 OR ...** (OR)
without the words	without the terms	**-term1 -term2 ...** (exclusion)

TABLE 8-1   The upper half of the Advanced News Search options enable you to easily use the basic operators.

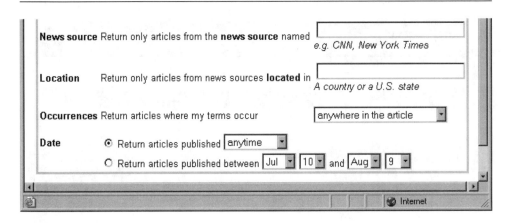

FIGURE 8-11   Use the Advanced News Search features to restrict your searches.

Advanced News Search link, the Advanced News Search interface would be already configured with the location restriction. So no need to enter the same advanced options over and over again while you refine your query. This feature is important to remember because if you forget about it, searches might be restricted from a past search without your notice. If you're having trouble finding what you want from the Advanced News Search page, carefully check each option it provides to ensure that it's set as you expect.

Google News Search Operators

Google News, like other Google services, provides specialized *operators* (query terms that have special meaning) for restricting or refining a query. For example, **source:** is used to search only articles published on one particular news site. You might use **source:reuters** along with other query terms to search articles published by the Reuters news service.

Google News operators are listed in Table 8-2. You can use them directly in the Google News Search box, but the Advanced News Search interface (shown in Figure 8-10) enables you to use them without having to remember their exact syntax. Google News crafts the query for you that includes the appropriate operators based on the values entered in the interface.

Many users prefer to use the Advanced News Search interface instead of using specialized operators directly in their terms. For example, to use the **location:** operator to search sources in a U.S. state, you must follow it with the state's abbreviation, which not everyone knows, particularly internationally. Also, while

Operator	Use	Special Rules
source:	Search only this news source.	None
location:	Search only articles published in this country or state.	None
allintitle:	Search only in article headlines.	Must be first search term. Only one "allin" operator per query.
allintext:	Search only in article bodies.	Must be first search term. Only one "allin" operator per query.
allinurl:	Search only in article URLs.	Must be first search term. Only one "allin" operator per query.

TABLE 8-2   Google News advanced operators are best used through the Advanced News Search interface.

there is an interface feature for restricting searches by article publication date, there is no operator for this feature.

Use of these operators and the Advanced News Search interface is discussed in the following sections.

Target or Exclude Specific News Sources

Be careful when searching for news from a specific source. Searching only for **new york times** will turn up articles containing the words "new," "york," and "times," rather than articles published on the New York Times' website. However, if you enter a news source as well as additional query terms, Google News will search for the additional query terms in all articles published by the given source. For example, searching for **new york times united nations** (or **united nations new york times**) will find all articles containing the words "united" and "nations" on the New York Times website. The search terms describing the source (**new york times** in this example) are detected by Google and used to restrict what source to search. Because of this, these terms are not searched for. Google searches for the non-source related terms in the query (**united nations** in this example).

Figure 8-12 shows a Search Results page for **new york times united nations**. Google News provides a link to rerun your query in case you meant to search for articles containing all the search terms, instead of just "united" and "nations" restricted to the New York Times website.

In order to prevent query terms from matching the name of a news source, use the + (inclusion) operator on part of the name. For example, +new york times united nations.

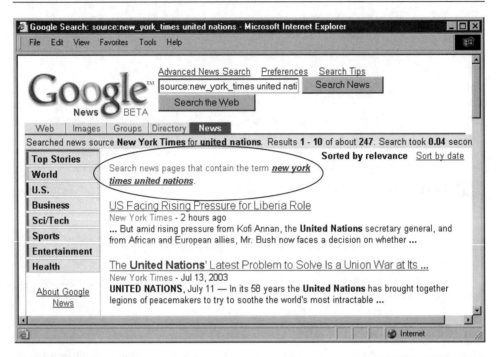

FIGURE 8-12   If some query terms happen to match a news source, a link to rerun the search is provided.

If you look carefully at the search box in Figure 8-12, you'll notice that Google News replaced the "new york times" part of the query with "source:new_york_times." Google News guessed that by "new york times" you meant the New York Times website, and replaced it with the appropriate **source:** value. Notice the value for the operator is "new_york_times," something that might be hard to guess or remember.

An easy way to search a particular source is to enter the name it is commonly known by in the News Source area of the Advanced News Search interface.

News source Return only articles from the **news source** named
e.g. CNN, New York Times

When you perform a search with a news source in this box, the appropriate **source:** term will be added to the query.

Google News searches over article URLs in addition to text and title, so if you know the domain name of a source you can use this as an alternative technique to find articles on that site. For example, the New York Times website is **nytimes.com**, so to find articles containing "united" and "nations" on that site you could search for **nytimes.com united nations**. In conjunction with the – (exclusion) operator, this provides a handy way to exclude sites from your search. For example, to search for articles about George Bush on any site but CNN, you might use **george bush –cnn**.

Search Sources in a State or Country

The **location:** operator restricts a search to only those sources in the given country or U.S. state. For example, **location:australia football** would find articles published in Australia containing the term "football" (presumably about Australian football). However, the operator requires that you enter the name of the location as it's known to Google News. In the previous example, it's clear that Australia is known as **australia**. However, other locations have names that are less easy to guess, for example U.S. states are known by the two-letter abbreviation and underscores (_) are used instead of spaces to separate multiple words in a name (e.g., New Zealand is written as new_zealand).

8

Because the value you need to enter for **location:** is probably hard to remember, it's better to use the Location field in the Advanced News Search interface.

Location   Return only articles from news sources **located** in ⌷
A country or a U.S. state

You can enter the name of a country or state here (e.g., **Saudi Arabia** or **Alabama**) and Google News will automatically include the appropriate **location:** value (e.g., "**saudi_arabia**" or "**al**") in your search.

Search for Terms only in the Text, Title, or URL

The operators **allintext:**, **allintitle:**, and **allinurl:** restrict Google News searches to the body of an article, its headline, and its URL, respectively. The easiest way to use these operators is with the Occurences portion of the Advanced News Search menu.

Occurrences Return articles where my terms occur | anywhere in the article ▼ |

If you use any of these operators directly in a query (instead of using the interface), there are two things to be aware of. First, you can only use these operators one at a time. However, this is not a problem since it doesn't make much sense to search for terms *only* in the URL and *only* in the headline at the same time. Second, these operators must come first in your list of search terms. Google News does not support ORing them together. For example, searching for **announces allintitle:Microsoft** wouldn't work. You must instead search for **allintitle:Microsoft announces**.

Search by Time of Publication

To restrict your search to articles published within a time span, use the Date portion of the Advanced News Search interface.

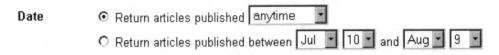

The top pull-down menu lets you search articles published in the last hour, day, week, or month. The bottom menu permits specification of any date range within the previous 30 days.

There are no operators to specify date restrictions directly in your queries. Instead, once you've searched using a date restriction from the Advanced News Search interface, pull-down menus for date selection will be found under the search box, as shown in Figure 8-13. These menus are present as long as you continue to

Date restriction pull-down menus

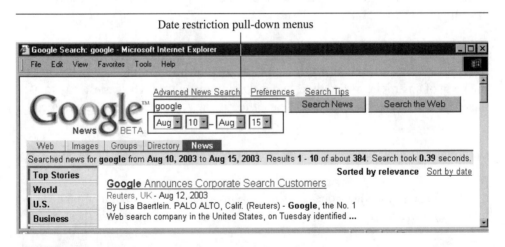

FIGURE 8-13   Subsequent searches use date restriction.

search, permitting you to refine date-sensitive queries without having to return to the Advanced News Search interface.

The easiest way to stop searching by date (e.g., get rid of the date pull-down menus below the search box) is to click on a Category link. You could also go the Advanced News Search page, select "Return articles published anytime" from the Date area, and perform a search.

Summary of Search Techniques

A summary of search techniques for Google News is found in Table 8-3. In addition to these techniques, we'd like to reiterate the most important things to keep in mind when searching for news:

- Google News supports most of the basic Google searching operators (+, –, OR, quotes) and has similar behavior (implicit AND, case insensitivity).

- Search for terms likely to appear in the headlines or text of articles you wish to find.

- Be specific: use more query terms to narrow your results. Try to make search terms as specific as possible, as searches on Google News for broad concepts or general ideas tend to return poor results.

In order to	Do this...
only search articles from a particular source	Use the "News Source portion of the Advanced News Search interface or include the name of the source in addition to other query terms. You could also include the site (e.g., cnn.com) as a query term.
exclude results from a particular site	Use the exclusion operator (–) applied to the site (e.g., –cnn.com).
only search articles in a particular country or U.S. state	Use the Location portion of the Advanced News Search interface.
search for terms only in article headlines	Use the Occurences portion of the Advanced News Search interface or include the **allintitle:** operator as the first query term.
search for terms only in article bodies	Use the Occurences portion of the Advanced News Search interface or include the **allintext:** operator as the first query term.
search for terms only in article URLs	Use the Occurences portion of the Advanced News Search interface or include the **allinurl:** operator as the first query term.
search only over articles published within a date range	Use the Date portion of the Advanced News Search interface.

TABLE 8-3   Summary of specialized Google News search techniques

Possible Uses

The most obvious way to use Google News is as a daily news resource. Many users find the lack of prominent images and other adornments appealing because it permits more information to be shown on each page. At the time of this writing, Google News also has the advantage of being advertisement-free. Google News' lack of ads and its text-focused approach are in stark contrast with many other major news sites.

Other uses for Google News include the following:

- **Digging deeper into a story** A single news source typically has only a few articles about a particular story. Google News provides access to articles on thousands of news sites, so chances are good that you can find lots of information on a current event of interest.

- **Comparative current events** Google News provides the opportunity to read articles about the same events from multiple perspectives. For example, you could read an election article on CNN and then read an account of the same story from related sources provided by Google. You could use a location restriction to see how sites in other countries reported the story. This can be an enlightening activity!

- **News around the world** If you restrict your search to a location but don't enter any search terms, you get the major stories published in that area. For example, to see stories published in Illinois, you could enter **Illinois** in the Location field of the Advanced News Search page, or search for **location:il**.

- **Education about the media** By looking at what stories are published by whom and when, you can learn a lot about how news is reported. For example, you can observe how a story tends to break in one place and is then reproduced in various forms on other news sites. You can get a feeling for the political leanings of various news sources, as well as judge how accurately you think their reports are compared to those of other sites. Following the evolution of news stories over time using date restrictions is also interesting, as is observing what stories make headlines in one place, but seem to go unnoticed in another.

- **Press releases** Google News includes a very large number of press releases from around the world (a search for **press release** typically gives tens of thousands of results). If you work in manufacturing, for example, you could search for **manufacturing press release** to see what other companies in your industry are up to.

Limitations of Google News

Google News provides access to articles published within the previous 30 days. Google doesn't link to older articles because many news sources move old articles into subscription areas and charge users for accessing them.

Another limitation is that breaking stories tend to dominate the Google News home page. Top stories can be quickly crowded out (replaced) by bigger or more recent news. It's easy to miss important events unless you visit Google News daily (or more often) and read news categories, as opposed to just the front page. News articles in categories are rarely more than a day old.

Catching up on current events with Google News after having been away can be a bit frustrating because top stories usually assume the reader has some knowledge of the recent past events. Searching with date restrictions is helpful for this task, but the inability to sort in chronological order is often a hindrance. It's probably not any easier to get caught up-to-date on other sites, but it's more noticeable on Google News because the stories are always so fresh.

The final limitation with Google News we'd like to mention is both a boon and an annoyance. Articles on sites requiring free registration (signup) are often linked to directly by Google News (with permission, of course). You can view these articles without a subscription when you follow the link from News. However, if you wish to view other content on the site (for example, by clicking a link in the article), you are often required to sign up for an account. For the most part, these accounts are free if you are willing to provide your e-mail address.

NOTE *Many people create a "throw away" e-mail address specifically for the purpose of signing up for these accounts. Search the Web for **free e-mail account** to find free, web-based e-mail services. Sign up and use the new e-mail address to activate an account on a news site. Once your news account is created, you typically don't ever have to use the e-mail address again.*

International Google News Domains

In addition to the original U.S.-centered news service, Google has expanded its international news offerings to seven versions (at the time of this writing). More will follow.

International news sites are offered by country. You can see a current list of available countries at the very bottom of the main Google News page.

Not all international Google domains have a News tab. If one does, it is typically linked to the news site for that country. But sometimes a News tab is provided even if that country doesn't have its own Google News site. In such cases, the tab links to a News site likely to be useful for residents of that country. For example, the News tab on Google Switzerland (**www.google.ch**) links to the Google News Germany (**news.google.de**).

If you've set your browser or interface language (see Chapter 7), Google uses these settings to determine which site to show you. For example, if you visit **news.google.com** with German configured as your browser language, Google News Germany displays. If you're shown a version of the site that is different from what you want, you should select the desired site from the links to international versions found at the bottom of every page.

NOTE *The search language setting (see Chapter 7) has no effect on Google News.*

Chapter 9

Search Discussion Forums with Google Groups

How to...

■ Understand where the Google Groups information comes from

■ Browse online discussion forums

■ Search discussion forums for interesting information

■ Post articles to discussion forums

The Internet is home to many different kinds of discussion forums. There are chat rooms, bulletin boards, e-mail lists, and newsgroups of all kinds. A *newsgroup* is, generally, a public forum to which people from around the Internet can post messages. Posted messages are made available within hours to other users of the group, and people converse on all manner of subjects by reading and replying to the messages left by other participants. A newsgroup is like a huge chat room in which messages take hours or days (instead of seconds) to appear. The advantages of a newsgroup over a chat room are that the discussion is more structured and the participants don't all have to be online at once.

The most enormous newsgroup system on the Internet is Usenet (*yooz-net*). It's home to thousands of individual newsgroups in which millions of people discuss as many different topics as there are in conversations in the offline world.

Google Groups provides a convenient web-based interface for browsing, searching, and posting to Usenet newsgroups. It's a great tool to find the unedited advice, opinions, and recommendations of a truly mind-boggling number of people. While a complete explanation of Usenet is outside the scope of this book, we will give a basic introduction to accessing Usenet through Google Groups. If you're interested in learning more, simply do a Google Web Search for **usenet**.

Usenet

Usenet predates the Web by a large margin. In 1979, Duke graduate students Jim Ellis and Tom Truscott implemented a primitive bulletin board system intended to let users of UNIX computers distribute information to each other. Steve Bellovin and Steve Daniel linked the system at Duke to systems at the University of North Carolina, and within a couple of years the seeds of Usenet found fertile ground at academic, research, and technology centers all over the country.

The Usenet system is interesting because it operates entirely in a distributed and decentralized fashion. By *distributed* we mean that it's composed of thousands of machines in many different parts of the world that work together to make sure everyone gets everyone else's posts (messages). By *decentralized* we mean that no one is in control of Usenet. We mean it. Each computer network that permits users to read and post to Usenet is owned and operated by a different entity. For example, the systems at Columbia University that provide Usenet access to students are entirely independent from those run by your Internet Service Provider (ISP), and neither are affiliated with Google. All these diverse systems cooperate in order to ensure that each has an up-to-date copy of the most recent newsgroup postings available for its readers. No one owns Usenet. There's no governing body, standards board, or police force. It's a geeky democratic cooperative of computers permitting people worldwide to see each others' messages. In fact, Usenet got its name for this very reason. Usenet stands for User's Network.

NOTE   *You can find Google's introduction to Usenet at **http://groups.google.com/ googlegroups/basics.html**. A more in-depth discussion of what Usenet is and is not can be found in the Usenet FAQ (Frequently Asked Questions) at **http://www.faqs.org/faqs/Usenet/what-is/part1/**.*

9

Usenet newsgroups are an excellent source of information of the kind likely to come up in conversation or via e-mail. You can find all kinds of discussions on newsgroups, for example, recommendations on digital cameras, suggestions for where to go on vacation with toddlers, setup instructions for a new digital scanner, and opinions on the new Britney Spears album. You can also find lots of *spam* (widely distributed junk messages), griping, lengthy diatribes, delusional babbling, and *flames* (insulting criticism or remarks meant to incite anger). Since Usenet is essentially a free-for-all, you have to take the good along with the bad.

The Usenet Hierarchy

Usenet is composed of several thousand newsgroups covering topics from atheism, investing, job opportunities, music, sports, and feminism to David Letterman, Madonna, and Jimmy Buffett. Because there are so many different newsgroups, they're named in a hierarchical fashion for easier access and understanding.

The name of a newsgroup is made up of several parts, the first of which gives its general subject matter and the successive parts describe with increasing specifics what kind of discussion belongs there. For example, the newsgroup rec.food.recipes is a *rec*reation newsgroup where talk about *food* and, in particular, *recipes* is appropriate.

Said another way, newsgroups are grouped into several large areas, each of which is broken into subareas. The different parts of a newsgroup's name are separated by a period (.), and indicate an area and subarea it contains a discussion of. The first part of a name is called its "top-level area" or hierarchy. Consider, for instance, the name rec.sports.tennis. The newsgroup is in the recreation area of the newgroup hierarchy, in the sports subarea, and is intended for discussion of tennis. The major top-level areas available through Google Groups, along with the description of each, are shown in Table 9-1. You don't have to memorize them; we list them to help you understand how newsgroups are organized. The Google Groups home page lists them as well.

Top-level area	Subject matter
alt.	Alternative discussions (any conceivable topic)
biz.	Business products, services, reviews, etc.
comp.	Relating to computers
humanities.	Fine art, literature, philosophy, etc.
misc.	Miscellaneous topics, e.g., employment, health, etc.
news.	Relating to Usenet itself
rec.	Relating to recreation, e.g., games, hobbies, sports
sci.	Relating to the sciences
soc.	Relating to social issues, culture
talk.	Long arguments, current issues and debates, frequently political

TABLE 9-1   A Newsgroup's Top-level Area Gives You a General Idea of Its Subject Matter

In order to give you a flavor of the kinds of newsgroups that exist, here's a short sample:

alt.aldus.pagemaker

alt.atheism.moderated

alt.fan.letterman

alt.personals.ads

biz.books.technical

misc.invest.real-estate

misc.jobs.offered

rec.aviation.soaring

rec.food.recipes

rec.music.classical.guitar

soc.feminism

> NOTE   *Newsgroups have at least two parts to their names, but aren't limited to three. For example, there is a newsgroup alt.barney.dinosaur.die.die.die for those who dislike the children's TV character.*

Newsgroup Posts

Within each newsgroup are found messages (also referred to as *articles*, *postings*, or *posts*) that look like e-mail between one user and another. But instead of just being sent between two people, these messages are made available to anyone who wishes to read Usenet (and therefore anyone who uses Google Groups). The distinction between newsgroups and e-mail is important. E-mail is sent from one person to a specific set of recipients, and is placed in your personal inbox when received. Usenet postings are sent from one person to the world, and are placed in a public newsgroup for browsing by anyone with the time and inclination to read them.

 Sometimes, when someone posts a message to a newsgroup, they also send you e-mail at the same time. They typically do this when replying to one of your posts, to make sure you know the discussion on the group is continuing.

When you start reading newsgroups, you might find that participants make use of specialized jargon, often refer to events in a newsgroup's past, and are fond of cracking oblique in-jokes that go over the heads of most newcomers. Google provides a glossary of some common Usenet terms (**http://groups.google.com/ googlegroups/glossary.html**), but this list isn't exhaustive. The more you read, the more of these bits of Usenet culture you'll pick up on.

Moderated Groups

Discussion groups can be unmoderated or moderated. Anyone can post whatever he/she wants at any time to an unmoderated group. Postings to a moderated group are automatically sent to a *moderator*, someone (or several people) democratically selected by newsgroup participants to make ensure the conversation stays on topic. Moderators have the option of allowing a post to be published, editing it before publication, or simply refusing to permit it to be posted.

As you can imagine, unmoderated newsgroups can often contain significant amounts of "noise," chatter only loosely related (if at all) to the topics at hand. Moderated newsgroups often contain fewer but higher-quality posts. Most moderated newsgroups have a ".moderated" suffix, for example rec.martial-arts.moderated.

Google Groups

Google Groups provides a nearly complete archive of Usenet newsgroup postings from 1981 to the present. Newly published articles are continuously added to the service, so you can find ongoing current discussions in addition to those from the past. In all, Google Groups contains more than 800 million messages (and growing).

The information you can find with Google Groups differs significantly from that which you can find with Google Web Search. While some people put up

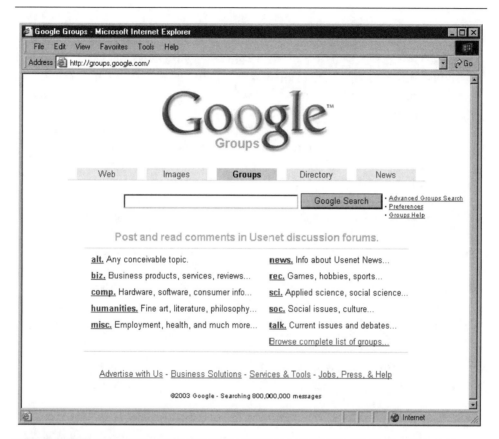

9

FIGURE 9-1   Google Groups enables you to read, search, and post to thousands of discussion forums.

personal web pages and blogs (web logs) to express their opinions, these mediums aren't very interactive. On the other hand, Usenet is very interactive. Use Google Groups with this in mind. If you want to find personal opinions, gossip, or any other sort of conversational information, consider searching Google Groups.

The main Google Groups interface is shown in Figure 9-1. To get there, click the Groups tab on the Google home page or go directly to **groups.google.com**.

Piecing Together the Groups Archive

Because Usenet is decentralized, it isn't anyone's duty to collect and store old postings. Messages are usually stored only as long as someone might conceivably want to read them, say a few months or years, and then they are deleted to make room for new posts. This presented a major problem for Google when it decided to make Usenet postings searchable: there was really no place to find a complete list of newsgroup postings from more than a few years prior.

Deja.com collected a large archive of Usenet discussions from 1995 on, and made them available on the Web along with an interface for posting. In February of 2001, Google acquired Deja.com's Usenet-related services and data. This provided a great base for Google Groups, but was far from complete.

Google engineer Michael Schmitt spent months carrying out detective work in an effort to piece together the lost history of Usenet posts from before 1995. When he began searching, he found that rumors of old backups were more easily obtained than the backups themselves. Apparently, every Usenet old-timer knew someone who had a friend who used to work at a place where some engineer's father's lab partner had kept an archive. Most of these improbable leads turned out to be dead ends. But luckily for Google, some did not:

- Data from 1981 to about 1991 were archived onto magnetic tape by Henry Spencer, then a member of the Zoology department at the University of Toronto. These 141 tapes eventually made their way to David Wiseman at the University of Western Ontario. Over the course of the next ten years, with the help of graduate students such as Bruce Jones from UC San Diego, Wiseman extracted the information from tape onto more modern media. These two million posts are not the largest part of Google's archive, but they're the oldest.

- Articles from 1992 and 1993 were recovered from CD-ROMs produced by Kent Landfield for users whose Internet connections were too slow to otherwise read Usenet.

- Much of the data from 1989 to 1996 was contributed by Jurgen Christoffel at GMD (the German National Research Center for Information Technology).

In December 2001, Google released its Usenet archive dating back to 1981. Estimates place the number of posts missing from the Google Groups archive to be several million, mostly from the late '70s and early '80s. This might seem like a lot, but compared to the nearly one billion posts available in Groups, it's not bad for a year's worth of detective work!

Browse Google Groups

If you know the name of the newsgroup you want to browse, enter it into the Google Groups search box and press ENTER or the Google Search button. For example, search for **rec.food.recipes**. You'll be shown the newsgroup reading interface that we discuss in the Read Newsgroup Messages section.

> **NOTE** *We only discuss using the major Usenet hierarchies—those listed on the Google Groups front page. There are hundreds if not thousands of additional miscellaneous, regional, and specialized groups that fall outside of the "normal" hierarchy. To find them, click the Browse Complete List of Groups link on the Google Groups home page. You can use them just like you'd use the "normal" hierarchy.*

Find Newsgroups

If you don't know the name of a newsgroup you might be interested in, there are two good ways of finding one. The first is to browse lists of newsgroups. Click one of the top-level areas found in the bottom portion of the Google Groups home page (Figure 9-1) to show you a list of the subareas it contains. For example, Figure 9-2 shows the result of clicking the rec. link, the newsgroups having to do with recreation. You can navigate through subareas by clicking any of these links. If there are too many subareas to show on one page, Google provides a pull-down menu and a link enabling you to see more. They're found just above the colored status line in Figure 9-2.

Next to each newsgroup is a column labeled Activity containing a shaded bar. This bar indicates the amount of posting that goes on in the group. The more shading, the more frequently messages are posted. In Figure 9-2, you can see that rec.motorcycle has very little activity, whereas rec.motorcycles has a lot. The activity meter is there to help you choose which groups to visit. Most people feel that the more activity the better, though to be fair, some low-activity newsgroups have very good discussions.

> **NOTE** *Sometimes there's no real reason for one newsgroup (e.g., rec.motorcycle) to be "dead" while a similar one (rec.motorcycles) has lots of active participants. People tend to gravitate to popular groups, sometimes for no other reason than they're popular.*

See more
subareas

FIGURE 9-2 Browsing through the Usenet hierarchy enables you to find newsgroups of interest.

Some links in Figure 9-2 have a suffix of .* and are followed by a number (e.g., 36 Groups). This means that the topic in question is further broken up into more specific newsgroups. In Figure 9-2, you can see that there are 21 newsgroups to be found under rec.crafts.

The second way to find a newsgroup of interest is to search Google Groups for a topic. Figure 9-3 shows the search results for **travel**. Above the actual search results, in the section labeled Related Groups, Google shows a set of links to newsgroups it believes to have something to do with your query.

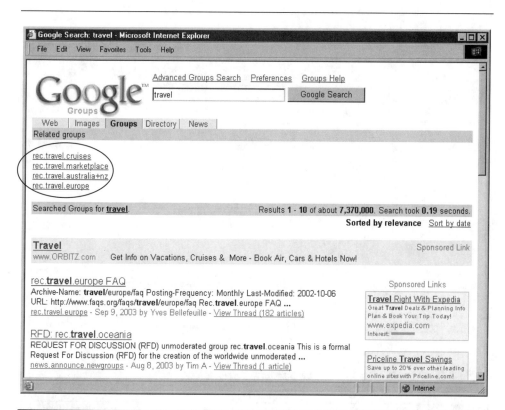

FIGURE 9-3   Google Groups shows some related newsgroups when you search for
a topic.

You can click one of these suggested newsgroups to start reading it, but there's
no guarantee Google has shown you *all* or *the best* related newsgroups. In fact, the
list in Figure 9-3 looks pretty incomplete. What about Africa and Asia? A very
useful trick is to combine the suggestions Google provides with a little knowledge
of how the Usenet hierarchy works. In Figure 9-3, you can see that all the suggested
groups begin with rec.travel. Based on this fact, you can guess that if you look
under rec.travel, you'll find a more comprehensive list. Figure 9-4 shows a search
for **rec.travel**. Sure enough, at the top of this page of results is a much better list
of potentially interesting newsgroups.

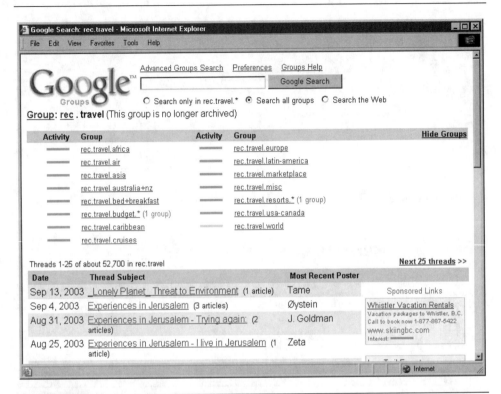

FIGURE 9-4   Searching for a general area of Usenet (in this case rec.travel) is often an effective way of finding newsgroups of interest.

Read Newsgroup Messages

Figure 9-5 shows the newsgroup reading interface, in this case for the group rec.travel.europe. If there were further subgroups under rec.travel.europe, they'd be shown above the posts like in Figure 9-4. But since there aren't, Google just shows you the messages in the current newsgroup.

The most recent posts are listed first, and for each message it shows the date it was published, the subject, and the name of the most recent person to contribute to the discussion. On the right side of the page are a series of shaded boxes. These are paid advertisements that Google believes are relevant to the topics in the newsgroup, and these are how Google makes money from this service.

Because there are often many discussions on different topics happening simultaneously, showing *all* the messages in a newsgroup in chronological order

FIGURE 9-5   The most recent threads of conversation in a discussion group are shown first.

would result in a chaotic jumble of posts. It would be hard to follow a series of replies because all the intervening messages people leave on other subjects would get in the way. For example, consider how hard it would be to follow a conversation in a chat room in which a hundred people were simultaneously discussing ten different subjects.

Instead, Google shows posts grouped together by thread. A *thread* is a post along with any follow-up articles published in reply. By keeping all the articles posted with the same subject together in one place, Google makes it easy to follow a conversation of interest.

The number of messages in each thread is listed just after the thread's subject. For example, in Figure 9-5 you can see that there are five posts in the most recent thread (with the subject Looking For A Travel Agency In Paris For Train Bookings). Only the 25 most recently active threads are shown on the first page. To see more, click the Next 25 Threads link at the upper- or lower-right of the page (in Figure 9-5, only the upper link is visible). Because some groups have such a high volume of posts, you might have to browse through a few pages worth of threads to see what's been posted in the last few days.

 If you've set the Number of Results preference as discussed in Chapter 7, Google will show that many threads per page only if it is more than 25.

View Posts

Clicking a thread's subject takes you to the thread view, the interface used to read the content of individual posts. As you can see in Figure 9-6, Google Groups provides two views of the thread. On the left is a narrow window showing the order in which the articles in it were posted. Each row corresponds to an article and includes the date it was posted and the name of the author, which is linked to the article itself. A red triangle points to the article displayed in the right window (aka the content pane). By default, the right pane shows the most recent article in the thread, but you can scroll the pane up or down to view preceding posts. Click links in the left pane to scroll the window automatically to the article selected.

NOTE *You can drag the divider between the two panes to give each pane more or less space.*

Historic Posts

As you might imagine, Google Groups makes for some interesting modern archeology. You can observe new ideas and phrases emerging by when they appear in posts, and read about historical events as discussed by those on Usenet at the time.

Google created a timeline of many interesting posts for its launch of the full Usenet archive dating back to 1981. Included are such posts as the first mention of MTV, AIDS, the Y2K problem (guess when!), and spam. You can find the timeline at **http://www.google.com/googlegroups/archive_announce_20.html** or simply by doing a Google Web Search for **google groups timeline**.

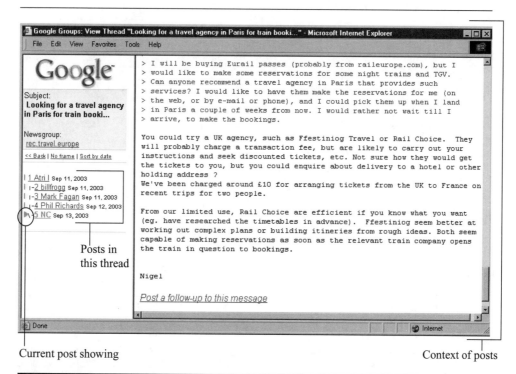

FIGURE 9-6   Google Groups framed thread view

Sometimes there are dozens or even hundreds of articles in a single thread. Figure 9-7 shows such a thread. Because there are too many articles to show at once in the right pane, only some are shown. The left pane indicates which articles are shown with a colored dashed line. The other lines connecting posters indicate who replied to whom. In other words, a line connects each article to the post it replies to. The indentation indicates this as well. For example, you can see that the currently displayed article by Jim Gillogly was replied to by Cristiano, which was replied to by Tom St. Denis, and so forth. You can also see by the dashed lines leading down vertically from various posts that other participants replied as well. (Their posts can be found by scrolling the left pane down).

Because the two-paned interface is a bit complicated from the browser's point of view, its Back button doesn't always work as you might expect on Google Groups. Consider using the navigation links in the left pane, as shown in Figure 9-7.

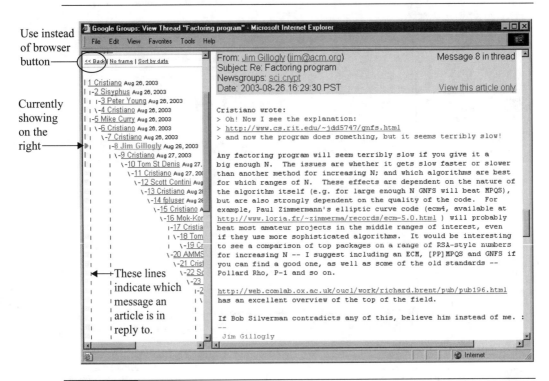

Use instead of browser button

Currently showing on the right

These lines indicate which message an article is in reply to.

FIGURE 9-7 The left pane helps you understand who replied to whom in very long threads.

Avoiding Spam on Usenet

It's common to see e-mail addresses in Usenet posts with large, seemingly out-of-place words in them, for example **someone@somewhereNOSPAM.com**. People who use e-mail addresses like that are trying to avoid spam by modifying their real e-mail address to something that looks normal to a computer, but that a human immediately notices as odd. The idea is that spammer's e-mail-harvesting software will collect and use the fake address (**someone@somewhereNOSPAM .com**), while a real person interested in e-mailing them will be able to guess the correct one (**someone@somewhere.com**).

Eliminate the Thread View Pane

If you don't like the split interface shown in Figures 9-6 and 9-7, you can use the link in the left pane, next to the Back link, that says No Frame (each pane is called a frame). Click this link to get rid of the left frame, which leaves you with the articles that make up the thread, as shown in Figure 9-8. If the thread contains many articles, you might have to use the navigation links provided (Figure 9-8) to move forward or backward through the articles.

Other Features

We've discussed the major features you use to browse newsgroups, but we haven't covered them all. For example, when viewing a post, click the author's name to get a list of all the articles posted by the author. The best way to learn about the features Google Groups has to offer is to learn by experience. Pay attention to the links provided in the interface, and experiment with what they do. You won't break anything!

9

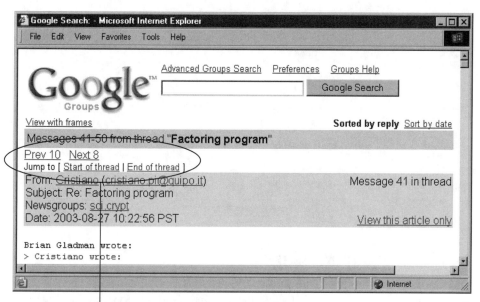

Use these links to navigate to posts in thread

FIGURE 9-8   The No Frame option does away with the left pane.

Usenet Posts Per Year

Usenet Usage Exploded As More People Came Online in the '90s.

Year	Number of Posts
1981	4,000
1982	27,000
1983	62,000
1984	110,000
1985	160,000
1986	100,000
1987	120,000
1988	185,000
1989	480,000
1990	1,200,000
1991	2,000,000
1992	10,000,000
1993	8,000,000
1994	15,000,000
1995	21,000,000
1996	53,000,000
1997	80,000,000
1998	107,000,000
1999	130,000,000
2000	132,000,000
2001	150,000,000

Post Newsgroup Messages

You're not confined to just reading discussions with Google Groups; you can participate in them as well. To learn more, visit Google's posting FAQ at **http://groups.google.com/googlegroups/posting_faq.html**, or just do a Google Web Search for **google groups posting** and visit the first link. Signing up for an account only takes a few minutes, and a valid e-mail address is the sole requirement.

Before you go ahead and post, you should take a minute to familiarize yourself with the Usenet culture. Doing so will help your posts be better received, and result in more responses. The most annoying thing in the world to Usenet regulars is a newcomer who doesn't bother to respect the protocol of the group.

The easiest way to learn what's acceptable on Usenet is by observing how others use it. Once you've read a few dozen threads and witnessed a few flame wars erupt, you should get a feel for what's appropriate and what's not. To help you get there a bit faster (and to make sure you don't unintentionally set off a flame war of your own), it's a good idea to keep in mind some basic tips that will help you fit into the Usenet community more easily. You can find some excellent tips at **http://groups.google.com/googlegroups/posting_style.html**, or do a Google Web Search for **google groups posting style** and click the first result.

NOTE *If you post to Usenet via Google Groups, your e-mail address will be distributed widely and you may receive spam as a result. Consider getting a second email address from Yahoo, Hotmail, or some other free service to use for your public postings.*

9

Search Google Groups

Use the Google Groups Search box like you'd use the Google Web Search box. Instead of showing you results that are web pages, Google Groups shows you Usenet postings that match the query.

Google Groups searches have the same behavior as web searches: they use implicit AND, are case-insensitive, and ignore punctuation and common words. The basic operators +, −, and OR work as you would expect, but they don't recognize the synonym operator (~) and their handling of quoted phrases is a bit weird. Common words in quoted phrases will match *any* word, as if they were replaced with a * (recall from Chapter 2 that a * in a quoted phrase matches any word). So a search for **"the best printer"** is equivalent to **"* best printer"**. To get around this, use the inclusion operator on common words within quotes, for example **"+the best printer."**

Figure 9-9 shows search results for **tips on traveling with toddlers**. As discussed in the Read Newsgroup Messages section, Google Groups shows you newsgroups related to your query in addition to posts that match. In Figure 9-9, you can see that the group rec.arts.disney.parks is recommended. Below the group recommendation are the posts that match. For each matching article, Google Groups shows the title of the thread in which the post was found, a snippet of its text, and its posting information (the newsgroup, date, and author). Posts are listed in order of relevance by default, but you can click the Sort By Date link in the upper-right portion of the page to see the most recent messages first.

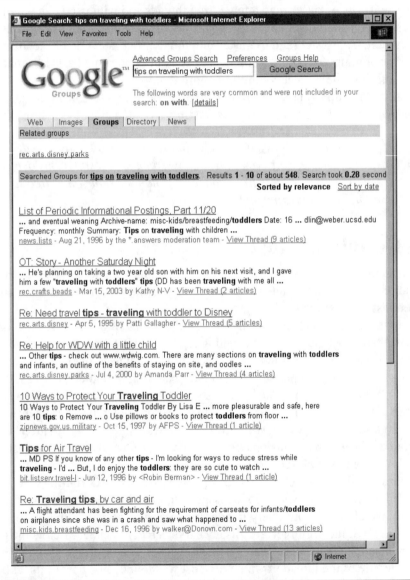

FIGURE 9-9   Results on Groups are related newsgroups and posts.

Click the View Thread link included with each result to see the article in the context of its thread. It uses the same interface discussed in the View Posts section.

Click the title of a result to see just that post. Figure 9-10 shows an article viewed this way. Under the status bar and above the actual post, Google shows advertisements; in this case, three lines in a lightly shaded box labeled Sponsored Links on the right. Within the post, Google Groups highlights your search terms to make them easier to find ("tips," "toddlers," and "traveling" are highlighted in Figure 9-10). If you want to see the article in the context of its thread, click the View: Complete Thread link.

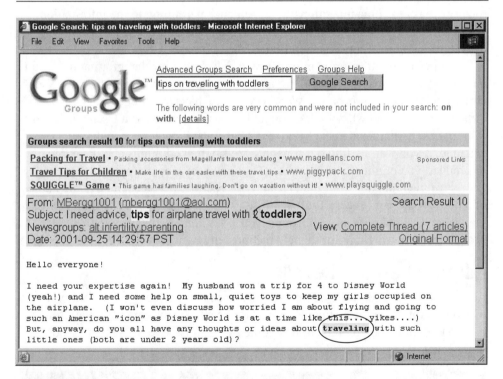

FIGURE 9-10   When you view a Google Groups search result, your terms are highlighted wherever they appear in the text.

Select Search Terms

When you search with Google Groups, it looks for your query terms in a number of different places:

- Name of the person who posted
- Subject of the post
- Body (text) of the post
- Newsgroup name

Search for words you would expect to find in these places, particularly in the subject and body. Searching for phrases can be particularly effective because it's relatively easy to come up with part of a sentence pertaining to the information you're after. For example, you might search for **"bed and breakfast in paris"** to find discussions of travel accommodations in France.

If you want to find specific information, think about how the information would be phrased or discussed in a newsgroup posting. Information isn't always as nicely labeled on Usenet as it is on the Web, so you may have to try phrasing a query in different ways to find what you're looking for. Also, be aware that Usenet is largely informal, so participants make heavy use of slang and conversational tone. For example, if you want to find out if people are saying bad things about a company or product, you might search for what they would say, for example **"dsl sucks."**

As we mentioned in the Find Newsgroups section, if you search for the name of a newsgroup (e.g., **rec.animals.wildlife**), you'll be taken directly there. Once you've got the hang of Google Groups, you'll find that you have a few favorite groups and that searching for them is the most efficient way to begin reading them.

Advanced Groups Search

Like other Google services, Groups offers a special advanced search form you can use to fashion very precise queries. Links to the advanced search form are found next to the search box on the Groups home page, and above the search box on other pages.

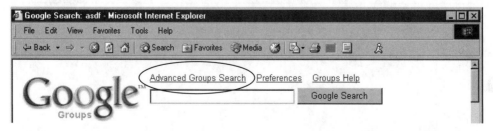

The Advanced Groups Search form is shown in Figure 9-11. Like the advanced search pages for other services, the top portion of the form (the shaded region) enables you to create queries using the basic operators without having to include them manually (see Table 9-2). It also lets you control the number of results shown per page as well as how they're sorted. The bottom portion lets you use Groups-specific search options, some of which correspond to special operators.

Newsgroup

The Newsgroup field (see Figure 9-11) specifies that you're only interested in finding posts within the specified groups. You can use the exact name of a newsgroup, for example **misc.jobs.offered**, or enter multiple groups separated by a space. The * operator in conjunction with a partial newsgroup name is used to indicate interest in groups with any words in place of the *. For example, **rec.music*** would search all groups whose names begin with "rec.music" (such as rec.music.beatles). Using ***music*** would restrict the search to groups whose name contain the word "music," for example rec.music.beatles, alt.music.dance, and alt.music.makers.dj.

If you enter the name of a newsgroup as a search term (instead of in the Newsgroup field of the advanced search form), you can get similar behavior. Google Groups will find articles in the group you specified because it searches the name of the group to which an article was published. But it will also find posts in other groups that happen to include its name. Most of the time you can get away with this technique, and it's certainly easier to type **sci.agriculture.beekeeping hive** directly into the search box than to bring up the advanced search form and enter "hive" in the With All of the Words field and "sci.agriculture.beekeeping" in the Newsgroup field.

Subject

The Subject field is straightforward: it specifies that you're only interested in posts with subjects matching the given terms.

Author

The "Author" can be a name or e-mail address. You can also use part of a name or e-mail address, for example **jim** or **aol.com**.

You should be aware that many people post to Usenet under *handles* (made up pseudonyms), and don't necessarily include valid e-mail addresses in their posts. They do this not only to protect their identity, but also to prevent spammers from getting their real information.

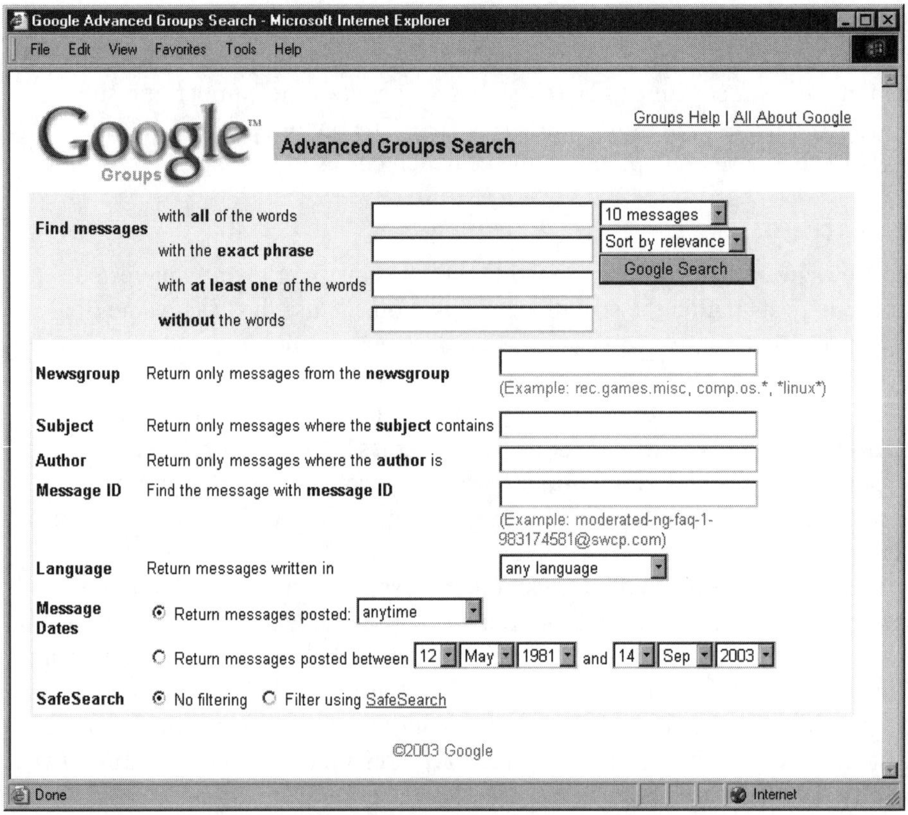

FIGURE 9-11   The Advanced Groups Search form enables you to specify all kinds of information about the articles you want to find.

Advanced Search feature	Operator
with all the words	**term1 term2** … (no special operator because of implicit AND)
with the exact phrase	**"term1 term2 …"** (quotes)
with at least one of the words	**term1 OR term2 OR** … (OR)
without the words	**-term1 -term2** … (exclusion)

TABLE 9-2   The Top Portion of the Advanced Search Options Facilitates Easy Usage of the Basic Operators

Message ID

Chances are you won't have much use for this field. The Message ID field is for Usenet experts seeking a specific message. Since each Usenet post has a unique identifier, experts can use this field to find a specific message they know to be in the Groups archive. For example, people occasionally search for famous/legendary posts by Message ID.

Language

Usenet has many participants from all over the world, so it's not uncommon to find posts in languages other than English. Using this option overrides any Google-wide Search Language preference you may have set (see Chapter 7), allowing you to change your language of choice for the search you perform with this form.

Message Dates

If you're seeking time-sensitive information, restrict the messages you find according to their post dates. The most common use of Message Dates is to find only recent articles by restricting the date to be within the last month or so. But, you can also use date restrictions to do historical research, for example, to see what people were saying about Microsoft in the mid-'80s.

Because there is no operator that enables you to specify a date restriction directly in your queries, pull-down menus for date selection are included under the search box on results pages when you've performed a date-restricted search:

These menus are present as long as you continue to search, permitting you to refine date-sensitive queries without having to return to the advanced search form.

To get rid of these date-related pull-down menus (e.g., to stop searching by date), the easiest thing to do is to click on the Google Groups logo at the upper-left of the page. You could also go to the advanced search form, select Return Messages Posted Anytime from the Date area, and perform a search.

SafeSearch

This option on the advanced search form (see Figure 9-11) enables you to override your Google-wide SafeSearch settings (see Chapter 7) for a search performed with this page.

Using SafeSearch with Google Groups cuts down on the number of posts you see containing explicitly sexual language. It does *not* filter out hate speech, discussion of criminal activity, descriptions of graphic violence, and other potentially objectionable material. One might wonder about our society's choice of priorities in the matter, but luckily this is a book about Google, not morality.

Advanced Search Operators

The Advanced Groups Search options and the operators to which they correspond are shown in Table 9-3. If an operator for an option you use exists, it is automatically inserted into the query. For example, a search for "madonna" in the Subject field runs the query **insubject: madonna** for you. You can, of course, specify the operators listed in Table 9-3 directly in your queries.

Avoid an Advanced Search Pitfall

The Advanced Groups Search form works the same way as the Advanced News Search form in the sense that when you go to it from a search results page, the settings for that search are reflected in its interface. For example, if you were on the results page for a date-restricted search and clicked the Advanced Groups Search link, the form would already be configured with the date restriction. This lets you refine a query without having to reset every single option, but also risks frustrating your attempts to find something if you forget that options are set. Be sure to carefully check each option before searching, or better yet, go to the Google Groups home page and start over.

Option	Operator
Newsgroup	**group:**
Subject	**insubject:**
Author	**author:**
Message ID	none
Language	none
Message Dates	none
SafeSearch	none (see Chapter 7)

TABLE 9-3   Advanced Groups Search Options and the Operators to Which They Correspond

Possible Uses

There are three common ways people use Google Groups: to read or participate in Usenet discussions, as a repository of information to be searched for answers, and as a forum in which they can ask questions.

Participate in Discussions

Usenet was created to facilitate discussions among Internet users, and for most people, Google Groups is the easiest way to participate. Usenet users follow different groups for different reasons. Some people read about hobbies or entertainment. Others read those related to an academic interest or their profession. The frequency of participation varies as well. Some read religiously, following every thread, while others check in occasionally to see what's up. Whatever the case, many people find that it's a good way to stay abreast of new developments, find bits of interesting information, and gauge public opinion.

Mining Usenet

The following kinds of information are often more easily found with Google Groups than with Web Search:

- Unpolished product reviews in the form of personal opinions

- Advice on what kind of (fill in the blank) to buy

- Travel tips

- Problem-solving advice

- Solutions to technical problems (how to set up a digital scanner, etc.)

- Up-to-the-minute gossip about celebrities and current events

What these boil down to is information in the form of personal experiences. Since Google Groups is a record of millions of conversations, it should come as no surprise that the majority of the information you can find with it comes in the form of personal opinions, anecdotes, and experiences.

If you're looking for information that might be expressed like this, it's almost always a good idea to try your query with Google Web Search first. If the information you find is satisfactory, great. If not, consult Google Groups. A good rule of thumb is to use Google Groups if you're looking for discussion, conversational information, or opinions on specialized topics.

If you're looking for specific information on Google Groups, many times you don't even have to ask for it. Chances are, someone has already asked, so you can take advantage of any responses you can find by searching for them. Treating Google Groups as a giant question-and-answer database is one of the most effective ways to use it.

Try searching for words or phrases that would be part of a question someone (like you) might ask. Considering the titles and snippets of the results returned is usually sufficient to determine whether a post contains your question. If it does, go ahead andview its thread and look for the answer. If not, try rephrasing the query. If you still can't find the answer, you might consider asking for it, but not before checking the Frequently Asked Questions.

Frequently Asked Questions

New participants in a newsgroup tend to ask the same questions. Old-timers become tired of repeatedly answering, so they often put together a Frequently Asked Questions (FAQ) list for the group. FAQs contain exactly what you would expect: a list of questions that are frequently asked, along with their answers. When they exist, FAQs are regularly posted to the newsgroup, so if you can identify a newsgroup related to the information you're seeking, you can search it for **faq** (e.g., **rec.travel.europe faq** or **faq group: rec.travel.europe**) and see if it is useful. FAQs are often posted on the Web as well, so you can find them by visiting **www.faqs.org** or doing a Google Web Search, for example with **rec.travel.europe faq**.

Post a Question

If you can't find some information you're after by searching Groups and other Google services, consider posting your question to Usenet via Google Groups. Posting a question requires signing up for an account and finding an appropriate newsgroup, but these tasks typically only take a few minutes.

Before you post, be sure the answer to your question isn't in the FAQ. In crafting your post, take advantage of the fact that many people on Usenet like to show off their knowledge, and often like to get downright pedantic. Phrase your question in a way someone on a factoid ego trip would be dying to answer. For example, use a respectful tone and implore the wise experts in the newsgroup to educate you on the very interesting topic you propose. Or take a guess at the answer in hopes that someone will correct you. Once you do post, be aware that it takes several hours for articles to propagate to the majority of Usenet, so don't get frustrated if no one answers your query right away.

If no one responds satisfactorily to your query on Usenet, considering asking Google Answers (see Chapter 12).

9

Chapter 10

Find Pictures with Google Images

How to...

■ Find images on the Web using Google Images

■ Restrict the images you find to a particular format, size, or coloration

L ike Google News and Google Groups, Google Images is a specialized search service that Google provides to help you find a specific kind of content, in this case, images.

You could find images by performing a Google Web Search and looking at the images on results pages, but doing so isn't a very efficient way to find what you want. You search Google Images in the same way as Google Web Search, but instead of showing you web pages that match your query, Google Images shows you graphics, pictures, and icons that match.

NOTE   *If you're adverse to adult content, you should configure your SafeSearch settings (Chapter 7) before experimenting with Google Images.*

Search Google Images

To get to Google Images, click the Images tab on the Google home page (see Chapter 1) or go directly to **images.google.com**. Figure 10-1 shows the primary Google Images interface.

Like Google Web Search, Google Images is a search service. To find what you're after, enter a query and search for it. Unlike Google News and Google Groups, there is no way to browse Google Images. This really isn't a problem though, because, like Google Web Search, querying for something of interest is usually the most efficient way to find what you want.

Searching Google Images is a lot like searching the Web with Google, except that it finds images instead of web pages. Google Images has a database of more than 425 million different images, yet these images do not belong to Google. Instead, they are images found in web pages all over the Internet. Google images analyzes how each image appears in a web page in order to determine what the image portrays. About two dozen different pieces of information are used to make this determination, including the image's caption, its filename, and the text surrounding the image on the page.

FIGURE 10-1   Google Images lets you find pictures online.

NOTE   *While it might sound like a good idea for computers to analyze each image in order to recognize the object(s) it contains, doing so reliably is extremely hard. Even the most modern technology fails to properly recognize objects in images with high accuracy. Because of this limitation, Google chose to determine an image's subject matter based on the context of the page.*

Google Images Results

To search for an image, enter search terms in the search box shown in Figure 10-1 and press ENTER or the Google Search button. Figure 10-2 shows the results page for the query **bear**. The top portion of the page looks like the results page for Google Web Search, but the results are rows of images. Rows are shaded in

alternate colors to make them easy to see, and the images display in a roughly uniform size. These smaller versions of images are called *thumbnails*.

Figure 10-3 shows a Google Images result. Click the thumbnail to link to the image viewer and see the image at full size in its original context. Below the thumbnail is the filename of the image as well as its dimensions (in pixels) and size (in bytes). Below the dimensions is the URL where the image was found.

Image Viewer Interface

Clicking a result thumbnail takes you to a rather awkward image-viewer interface, shown in Figure 10-4. For copyright reasons (as discussed in the Copyrights section later in this chapter), Google can't immediately show you the full-size image. It shows a scaled-down version in the top pane and the web page where the image was found in the bottom pane.

Thumbnail link to image viewer

Filename ⟶ **bear**.gif

Image dimensions ⟶ 400 x 355 pixels - 61k ⟵ File size

www.windowschicago.com/

Page where image was found

FIGURE 10-3   Anatomy of a Google Images Search result

10

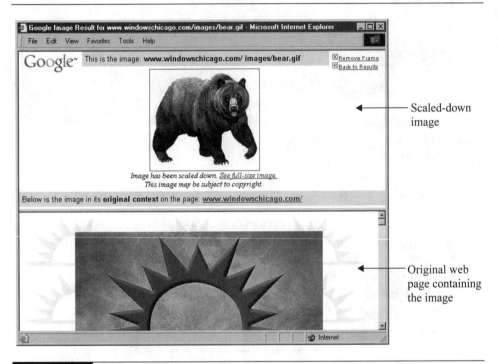

FIGURE 10-4   The Image Viewer interface is split-screened.

Click the image in the top pane to load the full-sized image (finally!). To save it to your hard disk, right-click the full-sized image and select Save Picture As…, shown in Figure 10-5. Alternately, select the Save As… option from the browser's File menu; however, this technique is less useful because it doesn't always correctly guess the image's filename. On many operating systems you can also drag the image with your mouse onto your desktop or into a folder.

 *You can also save the image from the image-viewer interface. Right-click the scaled down version in the top pane and select Save Target As….*

Although the page on which the image appears is visible in the bottom pane, the viewing area is typically too small to be of much use. To load the page in the

FIGURE 10-5   To save an image, right-click it.

full browser window, click the original page's URL at the bottom of the upper pane, or the Remove Frame link at the top-right corner (see Figure 10-6).

Craft Image Search Queries

Google Images Search is based on the text of the page in which the image is found, so select search terms as you might for Google Web Search (see Chapter 2). Because there is often only a small amount of information on the page that applies to an image, Google Images Search isn't quite as precise as Google Web Search. For

FIGURE 10-6   Load the original page in the full browser window.

example, Figure 10-7 shows the results for **larry page sergey brin**, Google's cofounders. The last result on the first row is a picture of Eric Schmidt, Google's CEO. Google Images returned his picture because it appears in web pages very close to those of Page and Brin; therefore, Google Images believes it to be relevant even though you didn't ask for it.

The basic search operators (+, –, OR, quotes) work as they do for Google Web Search, but the synonym operator ~ doesn't work very well at the time of this writing. The search behavior for Google Images is the same as Google Web Search (implicit AND, common word exclusion, punctuation exclusion, case-insensitivity), and it supports the full range of web search advanced operators (see Chapter 5). Google Images Search also supports a variety of advanced image-specific operators.

FIGURE 10-7   Google Images Search can be less precise than Google Web Search.

Did you know?

Most Popular People Searches

The most popular searches for people on Google Images Search are almost always stars of music, film, or sports. For women, Britney Spears, Pamela Anderson, Jennifer Lopez, Anna Kournikova, Angelina Jolie, and Christina Aguilera are consistently on the list. The top searches for men vary considerably from month to month, but usually include Eminem, Brad Pitt, David Beckham, Justin Timberlake, 50 Cent, and Johnny Depp.

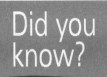

Possible Uses of Google Images

Some things you might use Google Images for are the following:

- To find pictures of celebrities
- To view famous works of art
- To check if anyone you know has their picture on the Web
- To find clip art to add to a presentation or document
- To find icons or user-interface components for use in a web page
- To find background wallpaper for your computer desktop
- To find pictures for children

Advanced Image Search

The Advanced Image Search form is accessible by the link at the right-hand side of the main Google Images interface (Figure 10-8, top) and a link at the top of Google Images Results pages (Figure 10-8, bottom). This form provides a way to specify more precisely the type of image you're seeking.

The top portion of the Advanced Image Search form (Figure 10-9) is an easy way to write queries without having to use the basic search operators (+, −, OR, and quotes), as described in Chapter 2. Table 10-1 describes the meaning of these boxes, along with the operators to which they correspond.

Advanced Search feature	Matches images...	Operator
related to all of the words	related to all the terms	**term1 term2 ...** (no special operator because of implicit AND)
related to the exact phrase	related to all the terms in the given order	**"term1 term2 ..."** (quotes)
related to any of the words	related to any of the terms	**term1 OR term2 OR ...** (OR)
not related to the words	not related to the terms	**-term1 -term2 ...** (exclusion)

TABLE 10-1 The Upper Half of the Advanced Image Search Options Enables You to Easily Use the Basic Operators

FIGURE 10-8   Access the Advanced Image Search interface from the main Google Images interface (top), or the Google Images Results pages (bottom).

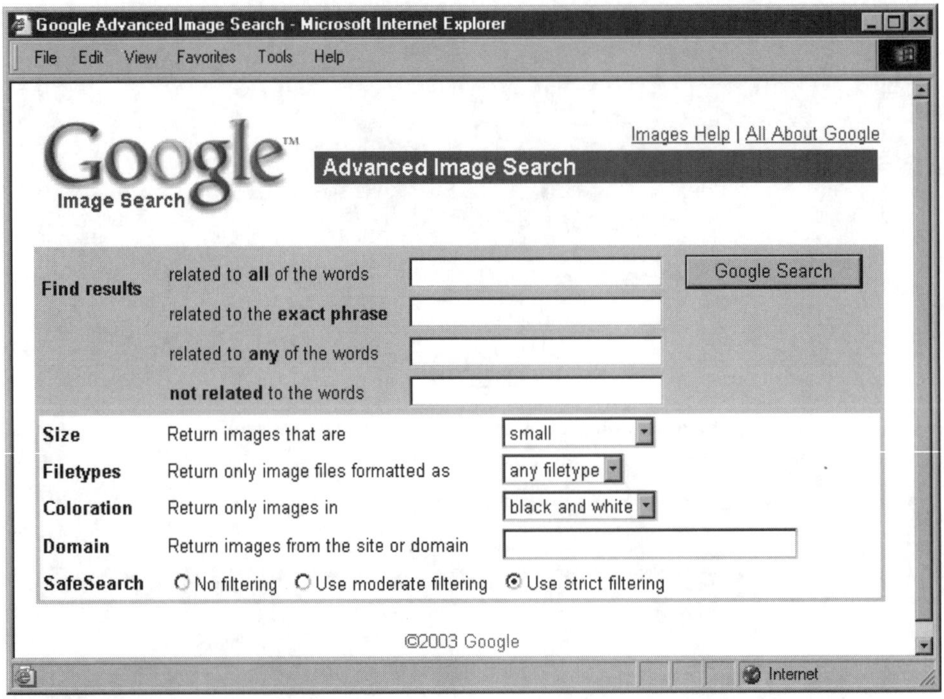

FIGURE 10-9 The Advanced Image Search form enables you to specify details about the images you seek.

The lower half of the Advanced Image Search form (Figure 10-9) is unique to Google Images, and lets you restrict your results to a subset of images that would otherwise be returned. Enter terms into the top portion of the interface and then refine the images it will find using the lower half. Google Images will perform a query made up of the terms you entered in the top portion according to the restrictions configured in the bottom.

When you navigate to the Advanced Image Search interface from a Search Results page, the settings for the previous search are reflected in the interface. That is, if you were on the Results page for a search restricted for image size and then clicked the Advanced Search link, the form would be already configured with the size restriction. So there's no need to repeatedly enter the same advanced options while you refine your query.

Option	Values	Meaning	Operator
Size	any size, icon-size, small, medium, large, very large, wallpaper-sized	images of these relative dimensions will be found	none
Filetypes	any filetype, JPG, GIF, PNG	only images in this format will be found	filetype:
Coloration	any colors, black and white, grayscale, full color	images with this color depth will be found	none
Domain	a domain name, for example **umich.edu**	find images from this domain	site:
SafeSearch	no filtering, moderate filtering, strict filtering	controls adult content filter	none (but configurable through Google's preferences, see Chapter 7)

TABLE 10-2   Advanced Image Search Options

The Advanced Image Search options for Google Images Search are shown in Table 10-2.

Image Size

The "Size" restriction doesn't refer to the size (in bytes) of the file, but rather to its height and width (in pixels). Table 10-3 lists the approximate dimensions of the values listed for Size.

Size value	Approximate dimensions
icon-size	50x50 or less
small	100x100
medium	200x200
large	300x300
very large	500x500
wallpaper-sized	800x600 or more

TABLE 10-3   Use the Size Option to Find Images of a Particular Dimension

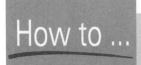 **Set Wallpaper for Your Computer Desktop**

You can use the Size option of the Advanced Image Search form to find wallpaper-sized images. Such images are typically large enough to use as backgrounds for your computer desktop, as its "wallpaper." Follow these steps to set your wallpaper on Windows 2000 and XP:

1. Find an image using Google Images and save it to an easy-to-find location on your hard drive.

2. Right-click the desktop, the blank area on top of which windows and menus appear.

3. Select the Properties item from the menu that appears. You should see a Display Properties window that looks something like the following:

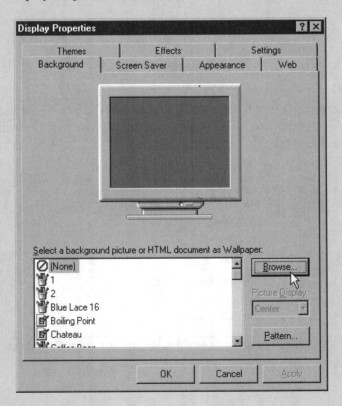

4. Press the Browse button to show a dialog box that permits you to select a wallpaper image.

5. Use the pull-down menu labeled Files of Type to select All Picture Files, as shown here:

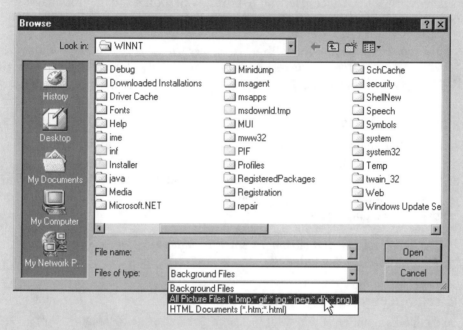

6. Find your image using the file interface provided (or type the path to the file into the File Name box).

7. Double-click the image.

8. The miniature screen in the Display window shows you what the wallpaper will look like. You can use the Position option to change how the image displays; for example, you can tile it so that copies of the image are placed side-by-side to cover the whole background.

9. Press the OK button on the Display window.

Image Type

File type is used to find images in a specific format. The JPG (pronounced "jay-peg") format is typically used for photographs and is in widespread use on the Web. It employs compression to reduce file size at the expense of image quality. The GIF ("giff" as in "gift") format is used for drawings and line art, for example, icons, diagrams, and clip art. The PNG format is a relatively new replacement for GIFs, but is not yet in widespread use.

Restricting by file type is useful if you want to restrict your search to photographs (use JPG) or art that you wish to include in a presentation or document (use GIF). Otherwise, you're probably best off searching for images of any format.

 *Some JPG images on the Web are named with a .jpeg instead of a .jpg file extension. Although there's no option for it on the Advanced Image Search form, you can search for these images using the operator **filetype:jpeg**.*

Image Coloration

The Coloration option is useful if you're looking for an image to include in a document or presentation. For example, you might not want a full-color image if you wish to include it in a letter printed on a black-and-white printer. Conversely, you might wish to find only full-color images if you wish to include them on your web page or in a photo gallery.

 *To find images of a particular color, include the color in your search terms, for example **blue cat**.*

Search Specific Sites

Use the Domain option if you want to search a specific site for images. For example, if you enter **cnn.com** in the Domain field and then search for **tiger woods,** you can find all of CNN's pictures of the golfer.

 *When the domain restriction option is used, only hosts ending with the given domain name are searched. So when you use **www.somesite.com**, it won't search images found on somesite.com. When you use **somesite.com**, it will find images on **www.somesite.com** because the domain ends with .somesite.com. It is, therefore, best to use the fewest number of domain components (items between the dots) as possible to ensure the most inclusive search. You could even specify .com to search all sites ending in .com or .nz to search all sites in New Zealand.*

SafeSearch

Recall that SafeSearch—Google's adult content filter—is set to Moderate Filtering by default. Configuring SafeSearch as a Google option, as discussed in Chapter 7, applies your choice of settings to all of Google's services, including Google Images Search. If you're adverse to adult content, you should definitely configure your Google-wide SafeSearch preference to Strict Filtering. It's not perfect, but it significantly reduces the chances you'll find adult content with Google Images.

The SafeSearch option in the Advanced Image Search form controls the setting of the adult filter on a per-search basis. That is, it lets you adjust the filter settings for the search you do with the Advanced Image Search form, regardless of what your Google-wide SafeSearch preference is.

Manual Use of Advanced Operators

The Advanced Image Search form inserts the **filetype:** and **site:** operators into your query when you use these fields. You can also use them manually just like the Advanced Web Search operators discussed in Chapter 5. Just enter them directly into the search box. For example, to find JPG images of Tiger Woods on CNN's website, you might use **tiger woods filetype:jpg site:cnn.com**.

Copyrights

Copyright laws govern how you may use any images you find online. In the United States, you can use an image for educational, news reporting, criticism, research, or other not-for-profit purpose without violating copyright laws. However, if you want to use an image for commercial purposes, you need the explicit permission of the creator of the image. Typically, this is the owner of the website, but even if this isn't the case, the owner is a good starting point for getting permission.

> NOTE *Copyright laws apply regardless of whether the image or web page contains a copyright notice. A copyright notice serves as an indication that the content owner is serious about protecting their copyrighted material, but the absence of a notice doesn't nullify their rights under U.S. law.*

The reality of the Web is that people use the images of others all the time, typically without explicit permission. Doing so is usually tolerated so long as the images borrowed aren't of significant value to a company in terms of money, reputation, or time. Icons and simple line art used to adorn web pages are examples of images that are widely reused. But unauthorized publication of copyrighted pictures people pay to see, for example pornographic material, is likely to result in serious legal consequences.

10

Did you know?

The Digital Millennium Copyright Act

The Digital Millennium Copyright Act (DMCA) was passed in the United States in 1998. It updates copyright law to include new protections specific to digital media. Many technologists take issue with certain provisions of this act, particularly those that make it unlawful to circumvent any attempt at copyright protection. This part of the DMCA makes it unlawful for scientists doing research in computer security to attempt to analyze the security of products without the explicit permission of the manufacturer. For example, academic researchers are prevented from analyzing DVD and CD copy-protection software, as well as electronic book formats claiming to protect electronic text. Companies rarely give researchers permission to analyze their products for fear the scientists will discover a weakness. Critics argue that this actually decreases the security of such products because the "good guys" cannot test product security, thereby making it unlikely a weakness will be discovered by anyone but a hacker.

Provisions of the DMCA affect Google Search as well. The DMCA makes it unlawful to distribute "tools or technology" that can be used for copyright circumvention. Links on the Web are considered such "technology," so it is unlawful to even link to a site containing banned or unauthorized copyrighted information. This means that when Google receives a DMCA complaint from a copyright holder, by law a link to the website in question cannot be included in search results. Note that it doesn't take a court order to require a link from Google's Search results be removed; it takes only a notice from the copyright owner contending that the link is a breach of the DMCA.

When Google receives a DMCA complaint, it replaces the link that would normally be found in the search results with a link to the complaint received. It is interesting to note that the DMCA complaint explicitly states the URL of the pages that must be removed!

 *You can find more information about U.S. copyright laws at the Library of Congress' website on copyright issues at **http://www.loc.gov/copyright/**.*

If you're outside the United States, you should be aware that although copyright laws vary from country to country, because of extensive international treaties, U.S. copyright protection extends to works produced in other countries. International copyright laws grant roughly the same protection as those in the United States, so if you're in doubt, it's best to investigate the laws in your country.

 *You can find lots of information about international copyright laws at **http://www.ifrro.org/**, the International Federation of Reproduction Rights Organizations.*

10

Chapter 11

Browse Topics by Category with the Google Directory

How to...

- Locate information by browsing Categories
- Search the Google Directory
- Improve your searches using the Google Directory
- Understand how Google Web Search draws upon the Google Directory

The Google Directory is organized into categories, classifications of pages by subjects. Unlike Google's Web search engine, whose index is built by computers that examine the Web, entries in the Google Directory are selected by people. Each entry is evaluated, classified, and annotated by volunteer subject-matter experts. The entries are then ranked according to Google's PageRank technology.

NOTE   *For more information about PageRank, see the Appendix.*

Consider using the Directory instead of Google's Web Search whenever you want to:

- Familiarize yourself with a topic.
- Get suggestions for ways to narrow your search.
- Find ideas for query terms.
- View only pages that have been evaluated by a human editor.

Search only pages within a category.The Google Directory is more useful for some things than others. Its strengths are in tasks that utilize its hierarchical classification of web pages. For example, it's good for finding information about a general topic because that topic is typically a Directory category. Similarly, it's good for browsing information about subjects with which you're not familiar. The Google Directory is not so good for finding very specific information. Since a much smaller set of pages are available through the Directory than through Web Search, you might have trouble locating something found on few or highly specialized sites. The important thing to remember is that the Google Directory augments—but does not replace—Google Web Search.

The Open Directory

A *directory* is a human-maintained library of websites organized by topic. In comparison, Google Web Search uses an *index*, a computer-created library of websites that provides no structured interface to users. Since directories are built and edited by hand, they typically contain fewer websites than a machine-maintained index.

NOTE   *For more information about how indexes work, see the Appendix.*

The Google Directory draws much of its information from the Open Directory Project (**www.dmoz.org**). The Open Directory is a free, volunteer-run directory hosted by Netscape Communications Corporation. In addition to Google and Netscape, the Open Directory collaborates with AOL, DirectHit, HotBot, and Lycos.

The Open Directory is a *decentralized* directory, meaning that the editors who maintain it aren't part of a large company or corporation. Instead, they are more than 50,000 volunteers from around the world who organize pages into categories in their free time. Their goal is to bring understanding to the Web by presenting it in an organized fashion. Each category has editors responsible for adding new pages and deleting pages that are no longer on the Web. The web pages selected by these editors are organized into a number of broad categories which have many subcategories.

Anyone may submit a page to be considered for inclusion in the Open Directory by providing the URL, a description, and the single best category for the entry. There are instructions on how to add a site on the Web at **http://dmoz.org/ add.html**.

Before adding a new page, an editor verifies that the subject of the page matches the category, and ensures the description of the site is accurate. Manually editing these directory listings is time-consuming. Consequently, the Open Directory contains far fewer documents than Google's Web index, but those that are included are usually of high quality.

NOTE   *You can learn more about the Open Directory (and becoming an editor) at* ***http://www.dmoz.org/about.html****.*

The Google Directory

The Google Directory draws its 1.5 million URLs from the Open Directory, which contains almost 4 million. Google doesn't use the entire Open Directory because it pulls information from it at a rate much slower than the Open Directory adds new content. Google augments the Open Directory's content with its PageRank data, Google's measure of how popular a site is (see the Appendix). Aside from the difference in size and the presence of PageRank data, the content of the directories is essentially the same.

Use the Google Directory when you want to explore by browsing topics. Its hierarchical categories of topics are useful for finding general information about subjects you are not familiar with. They're not so useful for finding specific information. For example, you're likely to find good information in the Directory if you want to get general information about photography or digital cameras, but you're unlikely to find detailed technical data about a Canon Powershot s45 camera.

To explore by topics, click the Directory tab or visit **directory.google.com** to go to the Google Directory home page, shown in Figure 11-1.

FIGURE 11-1   The Google Directory contains links to websites sorted by category.

United States Department of **Homeland Security**

Description: A federal agency whose primary mission is to help prevent, protect against, and respond to acts of...
Category: <u>Society</u> > <u>Law</u> > <u>Law Enforcement</u> > <u>Government Agencies</u>
<u>www.whitehouse.gov/homeland/</u> - <u>Similar pages</u>

FIGURE 11-2   Category and Description are from the Google Directory.

You get the benefit of Google Directory from Google's regular web search. As explained in Chapter 5, when a result is included in the Google Directory, a description of the site and the category in which it appears is listed below the snippet in your search result (see Figure 11-2).

Google Web Search also provides a link to each category your query matches. These links appear at the top of the Web Search Results page, as shown in Figure 11-3.

When you want more resources on a topic, click on a category link to be taken to the Google Directory. It will show you a page that may contain subcategories, related categories, and links to relevant web pages on that topic.

Categories

The Google Directory contains links to websites sorted by category. Each category is subdivided into more specific subcategories. For example, as you can see in Figure 11-4, Arts is subdivided into over 40 categories including Literature, Movies, Music, and these topics are further subdivided.

FIGURE 11-3   Link into the Google Directory from Google Web Search.

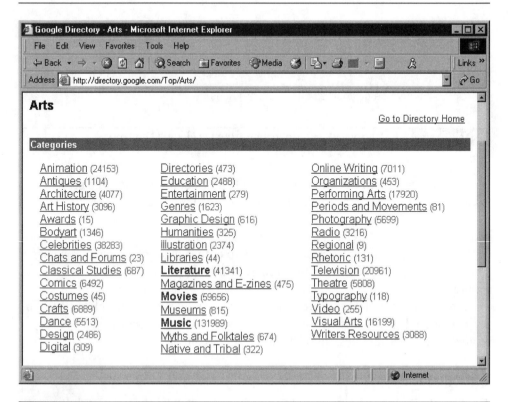

FIGURE 11-4   Categories can contain more specific subcategories.

Some categories contain only links to pages, while others contain only subcategories or a mixture of the two. For example, the Arts category contains only subcategories (see Figure 11-4), but the Arts > Awards category shown in Figure 11-5 contains both subcategories and web pages. The "deeper" you explore into subcategories, the more specific the topic. For example, Arts > Literature contains sites about literature in general (e.g., online libraries), whereas Arts > Literature > Children's contains sites specific to children's books (e.g., the Junior Great Books Website).

Next, we'll describe how to browse and search the Google Directory, which is the best way to become familiar with its contents.

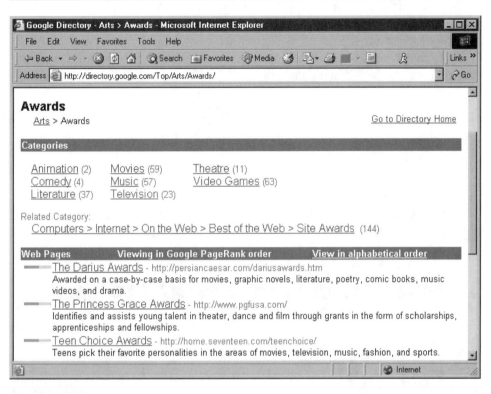

FIGURE 11-5   Categories can contain both subcategories and web pages.

Browsing the Google Directory

When you click on a category, the Google Directory displays a navigational row below the search box showing your current category. As shown in the following image, the > signs in Arts > Movies > Genres > Documentary indicate subcategories; that is, Documentary is a subcategory of Genres, which is a subcategory of Movies, which is a subcategory of the top-level Arts category.

Documentary
Arts > Movies > Genres > Documentary   Go to Directory Home

You can click on a link to jump to a category. As in the case of other Google services, you can jump to the Google Directory home page by clicking the Google Directory logo at any time.

If the category contains subcategories, you will see them listed in the navigation row, as shown in the following image:

In parentheses next to the category are the numbers of subcategories, related categories, and web pages in that category. The names of very large categories, those containing thousands of sites, will appear in bold face type (see Figure 11-6).

FIGURE 11-6   The names of large categories appear in bold.

Sometimes there are too many subcategories to show them all. For example, the Arts > Movies > Titles category has 50,000 subcategories, each of which correspond to a movie. Instead of showing all 50,000 subcategories, the Google Directory displays an alphabet in which each letter is linked to subcategories beginning with that letter, as shown in the following image:

Categories

Titles Categorized by Letter:
0 1 2 3 4 5 6 7 8 9 A B C D E F G H I J K L M N O P Q R S T U V W X Y Z

Depending on the category, popular subcategories might be shown in conjunction with the alphabet, as shown in Figure 11-7.

Any closely related categories are displayed below any subcategories. The related categories for Art > Movies > Genres > Documentary are the following:

Related Categories:
  Arts > Television > Programs > Documentaries (75)
  Arts > Movies > Filmmaking > Documentary (38)

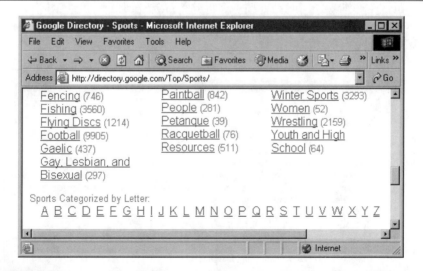

FIGURE 11-7   In the Sports category, popular subcategories are listed before the index.

11

Links to related categories enable you to jump easily to a similar or related topic. For example, to go from Arts > Movies > Genres > Documentaries to pages about documentary filmmaking, click on the related category link Arts > Movies > Filmmaking > Documentary.

Links to web pages contained in a category are listed on the bottom section of the page. Figure 11-8 shows part of the list of pages for Arts > Movies > Genres > Documentaries. The horizontal rating bar on the left indicates the importance of the web page as determined by Google's PageRank technology.

BBC Documentaries - http://www.bbc.co.uk/bbcfour/documentaries/
Features on films in the documentary strand and interviews with independent filmmakers.

These PageRank bars tell you at a glance whether other people on the Web consider a page to be of high quality. More important sites, ones with more fully shaded PageRank bars, are listed first. PageRank is discussed in further detail in Appendix A. If you want to see the links to the sites in alphabetical order, just click on the View in Alphabetical Order link that is on the right side in the list heading, as shown in Figure 11-8.

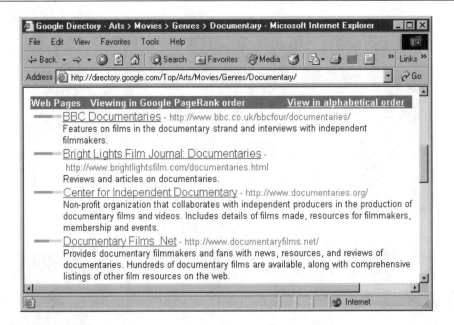

FIGURE 11-8   Pages for Arts > Movies > Genres > Documentaries sorted by PageRank

Searching the Google Directory

Searching the Google Directory supports all the basic operators (+,–, ~, OR, quotes) and has the same behavior (implicit AND, case-insensitivity, ignores punctuation) as Google Web Search. However, when you search the Google Directory, it only finds pages within the directory's hand-edited lists (rather than the Google Web Search index).

A results page for the Google Directory, see Figure 11-9, is similar to the results page of Google Web Search, except related categories are shown more prominently. Ads may be shown in shaded text boxes on this page.

If you're viewing a category, by default you search within that category. You're also given the option to search the entire Web. You can see these options in Figure 11-10, which shows the search box for the History category. Neither of these options permits you to search the entire directory. To do so, you must go to the Google Directory home page and search from there.

11

FIGURE 11-9   Results page of Google Directory search

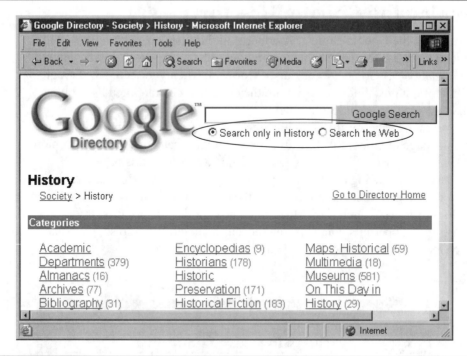

FIGURE 11-10   Options for searching after you browse a category

Directory Search Quality

Google Web Search has more than 2,000 times as many searchable pages as the Google Directory. The pages in the Directory are hand picked, so they tend to be of high quality. But because there are fewer of them, there isn't as much information available through the Directory as through Google Web Search. For example, searching the directory for **job search tips** returns around 6,000 results. The same query on Google Web Search provides more than 2 million results.

Another potential drawback of the Directory is that each category is maintained independently of the others so there is no guarantee that any particular category will be up-to-date. Some editors don't do a good job of keeping their sections current, and this can be frustrating if you're interested in a topic that changes rapidly.

Possible Uses

You get the benefit of the Directory's descriptions and links to its categories from Google's regular web search. So, you should use the Google Directory when you want to do any of the following:

Familiarize yourself with a topic   Browse the Directory for an unfamiliar subject to learn more about the topic. For example, the Art category gives a good overview of many different aspects of art. A web search for **art** is not nearly as helpful for grasping the big picture.

Get suggestions for ways to narrow your search   When you obtain too many results, consider exploring categories, subcategories, and related categories to find what you're seeking.

Come up with ideas for query terms   Consider using the names of categories to refine your search and specify more precisely what you want. For example, if you're interested in nutrition, the Health > Nutrition category provides a cornucopia of ideas for searches.

Grasp the scope of a given category   Since a category is a comprehensive resource on a given subject, you can use the Directory to get an idea of its extent. For example, navigating through the category Regional > Countries provides a list of many countries.

Find categories associated with a particular topic   When you're not sure in which category you can find the information you're seeking, search for that specific information. For example, search for **ebay tips** to learn that you can find insights on how to use the auction site in the category Home > Consumer Information > Auctions.

Find lists of items   There are lists of staggering size in the Google Directory. For example, Art > Literature > Authors contains thousands of authors categorized by the first letter of their last name, and Arts > Literature > World Literature contains categories for authors of more than 50 countries.

11

Google Directory Tips

Here are a few tips for working with the Google Directory:

- Most categories specific to a geographical area (for example, government, education, and travel) are found under Regional.

- Try searching only pages within a category. This is a good way to narrow your searches if they're returning too much information.

- Don't overlook alphabetized lists of subcategories. Some of the best information in the Directory can be found there. For example, the alphabetized index of subcategories in Arts > Music > Bands and Artists is easy to overlook:

Bands and Artists Categorized by Letter:
0 1 2 3 4 5 6 7 8 9 A B C D E F G H
I J K L M N O P Q R S T U V W X Y Z

Yet there are about 50,000 sites about thousands of individual groups accessible through this index!

Google Directory in Non-English Languages

At the bottom of the English-version Google Directory home page, you'll find a World category, as shown in the following image:

World
Deutsch, Español, Français, Italiano, Japanese, Korean, Nederlands, Polska, Svenska, ...

The World category contains all of the non-English content in the Directory. There are more than 60 language categories containing anywhere from less than 100 pages (for languages such as Bangla, Farsi, and Punjabi) to more than 100,000 pages (for French, German, and Spanish).

Each language category contains general subcategories much like those found at the top level of the Google Directory. Subcategories of the Icelandic language (World > Íslenska) are shown in Figure 11-11.

If you set your interface language to a non-English language (see Chapter 7), messages and tips are sometimes in your interface language and other times in

FIGURE 11-11   Pages in Icelandic are found within World > Íslenska.

English. For example, after setting your language interface to German, messages and tips display in English when you access the Google Directory (by pointing your browser to directory.google.com). However, click on the Google Directory tab and the messages and tips display in German, and instead of the Directory home page, you will see the content of the subcategory World > Deutsch.

> NOTE   *Different languages are maintained by different editors. Consequently, you may notice variations in style and page layout.*

Chapter 12

Ask Researchers Questions with Google Answers

How to...

- ■ Browse questions and their answers
- ■ Ask a researcher a question
- ■ Form effective questions
- ■ Price your question appropriately

Having trouble creating a query to find the information you seek? Don't have time to research the topic yourself? Consider asking Google Answers, where you can get assistance from researchers with expertise in online searching.

How It Works

Google Answers (**answers.google.com**) allows you to ask researchers questions for a price between US$2 and US$200. One great thing about this service is that you get to name your own price. Whatever the answer to your question is worth to you, that's what you pay. Asking a question requires a Google account, but you don't need an account if you only wish to browse Google Answers.

Here's how to ask a question. We'll explain each step in more detail in subsequent sections.

1. Pose your question. In general, the more details you provide, the better results you'll receive.

2. Specify the price (between US$2 and US$200) you are willing to pay for an answer based on your question's difficulty, urgency, and the value of the answer to you. A nonrefundable US$0.50 listing fee will be added.

3. Receive an answer. A Google Answers researcher will answer your question using information from the Web. The result will be posted to Google Answers and e-mailed to you, if you requested the latter option during the signup process.

Google Answers has safeguards ensuring your satisfaction. If you're not happy with the answer provided, you pay only the listing fee, currently US$0.50. Researchers are not required to answer every question, but pricing your query fairly usually ensures that a researcher will respond.

Origin of Google Answers

During the early days of Google, both Larry Page and Sergey Brin (Google's cofounders) responded directly to e-mail from users asking for help finding information on the Web. When Google grew to be larger, Larry and Sergey decided they wanted an online "Question Economy" where users could submit questions and receive answers. Googlers Susan Wojcicki and Andrew Fikes investigated the possibilities.

To get an idea of the kinds of questions people might ask, they ran an ad campaign on Google asking users to submit questions. It was apparent that the ad began running at a time when most of the western hemisphere was asleep, because they received questions like, "Who are the sellers of wheat straw in Mumbai?" Some people didn't take the ads seriously and submitted questions such as, "Who put the bop in the bop-shoo-bop-shee-bop?"

Once the initial exploratory phase was complete, Lexi Baugher and Nina Kim joined the Answers team and work began in earnest on building the product. It took about four months of development, and officially launched in April 2002.

Researchers are paid individually, so it's up to individual researchers which questions they will answer. A question that is hard to answer but low-priced isn't likely to receive a response.

Are you reluctant to use Google Answers? Do you think you can find the information you want if you search a bit longer? If you feel that way, you're not alone. Nevertheless, many people who have asked a question of Google Answers are now fans of the service. Not only does it save them time, but the answers they receive are packed with useful information and links. It's a wonderful service that's well worth checking out, whether you're a novice or experienced searcher.

 NOTE   *Google Answers is offered only in English at the time of this writing. Questions about or involving other languages are answered, but Google does not provide an interface in other languages.*

Who Are the Researchers?

The relationship between Google and the researchers is fairly loose. Researchers are hired as contractors, and are paid on a per-question basis. The application process involves submitting background information, answering interview questions, and researching a number of test questions as if they were posed by a user. Some researchers are pulled from the ranks of users who consistently make helpful comments on questions. However Google is not, at the time of this writing, accepting applications for new researchers. Researchers have a wide variety of backgrounds. Some have advanced degrees or work in library science, but neither is a requirement. The ability to find information quickly on the Web is the primary requirement for becoming a researcher, and their ability to consistently do so is monitored by Google. The rating system for answers is one way they do this. Results are also spot-checked by administrators for quality.

Because some researchers consistently provide good quality results, they develop a following. Any question you see with a subject like ONLY FOR PINKFREUD-GA is intended for a specific researcher, in this case "pinkfreud-ga."

NOTE   *You can see the ratings for all the answers a researcher has posted by clicking on the researcher's name.*

Because Google Answers researchers aren't full-time Google employees, they don't work from a central location. They work online, at their convenience. This is beneficial from your perspective as a user: it means questions can be answered at any time. You won't have to wait for business hours or the end of a holiday weekend to receive a response.

Inside Google: Questions About Answers

The authors asked Google Answers Researcher "pinkfreud" to answer a few questions of our own:

Authors: Can you describe how you started with Answers, and how you feel about it?

Pinkfreud: I am a 55-year-old former civil servant. Since I am disabled by a chronic illness, and unable to work outside my home, Google Answers has been a godsend to me. I first discovered the site in June 2002, after seeing a link that had been posted in the Off Topic forum at AnandTech. At the time, no new applications were being considered, so I did not expect ever to become a Google Answers Researcher. I was so in love with the site that I spent several hours a day offering free assistance in the "Comments" section. To my eternal delight, my labors were noticed by Researchers, several of whom petitioned the Powers That Be to add me to the team. I am now approaching my 600th answer, and I'm still loving Google Answers. For most of my life, I've had a head filled with useless information. Now I finally have a use for some of it!

Authors: What's the funniest question you've answered?

Pinkfreud: It's a bit difficult to describe the funniest question I've ever answered. There have been some dandies. If I have to choose, I'll say that the question with which I had the most fun was, "What Color is Penguin Poop?" (http://answers.google.com/answers/threadview?id=240878). Somehow it just seemed that the "penguin poop" question was destined for me. After all, my nickname is "Pink."

Authors: The most difficult question?

Pinkfreud: The most difficult project I've tackled was also one of the most rewarding (both financially and emotionally). A customer asked for my assistance with a program that she was developing for cable television. While I have long been a fan of classic television shows, this question really gave my mind a workout. To complicate things, I became very ill while working on my answer. Had it not been for the assistance of some wonderful GAR (Google Answers Researchers) friends, I might not have been able to complete this: "History of Marriage on TV" (http://answers.google.com/answers/threadview?id=192280). (It is a question about the evolution of how marriage was portrayed on TV shows, asked by someone putting together a segment of a show on this topic.)

It was quite entertaining to view the cable TV program which featured some of the info I had gathered. And, much to my delight, when the final credits rolled, "pinkfreud-ga" was included under the heading "Research by..." (Google Answers and three of my colleagues were also mentioned in the credits. Hooray for us!)

Tour of Google Answers

A link to Google Answers is shown when a web search returns few results:

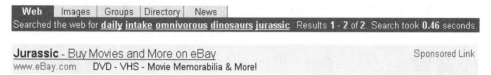

If a query returns no results, a more prominent link is shown. Figure 12-1 shows a search with zero results.

Because Google strives for a minimal user interface, Google Answers is not otherwise prominently linked from **google.com**. The fastest way to get there without performing a search is to point your browser to **answers.google.com**.

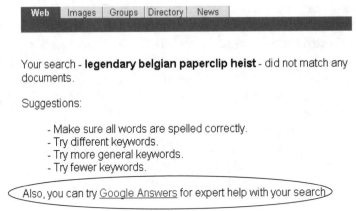

Your search - **legendary belgian paperclip heist** - did not match any
documents.

Suggestions:

- Make sure all words are spelled correctly.
- Try different keywords.
- Try more general keywords.
- Try fewer keywords.

Also, you can try Google Answers for expert help with your search

FIGURE 12-1   Google Answers is suggested if you can't find the information you need.

The primary way to use Google Answers is to ask a question. But others might
have asked the same or similar questions, so spending time browsing questions and
their answers can save you money. Browsing questions can also be fun, as well as
educational.

Figure 12-2 shows the main user interface for Google Answers. Two aspects of
the interface are useful if you want to ask a question. The first is the Log In link, which
can be used to ask a question or to check the status of a question you've asked. The
second is a text entry box in which you can ask a question directly. Entering a question
in this area and clicking the Ask Question button will take you through a series of
steps that includes account creation if you don't have an account, or login if you do.

All questions asked and all answers provided by researchers are available for
browsing and searching. You can search for words that appear in a question or answer,
(see Figure 12-2). You can also browse questions by topic. Google Answers groups
questions by category to make it easier to find questions that might be of interest.
You can see topic categories in the lower portion of Figure 12-2.

NOTE   *The categories in Google Answers are different from those of the Google
Directory (Chapter 11).*

Browse by topic

FIGURE 12-2   The main Google Answers user interface

Search Google Answers

For convenience, the search box appears in many pages throughout Google
Answers, for example, at the top of the page if you click on the Arts and
Entertainment category, as shown in Figure 12-3.

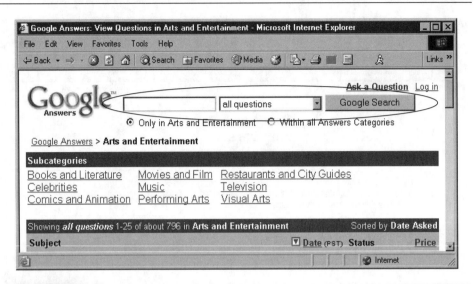

FIGURE 12-3   Google Answers search box appears throughout the site.

This search box supports the major operators described in Chapter 3, namely +, −, OR, and quoting terms. Like Google Web Search, it uses implicit AND, ignores punctuation, and is not case-sensitive. Unlike Google Web Search, results are presented in reverse chronological order (most recently asked question first), by default. Click the Date and Price links, shown in Figure 12-4, to sort results according to those fields.

If you sort by date or price, you will see a triangular indicator, as shown in the following image:

This icon indicates whether the field is sorted in increasing (triangle pointed upwards) or decreasing (triangle pointing downwards) order. To switch from increasing to decreasing order, click the triangular indicator.

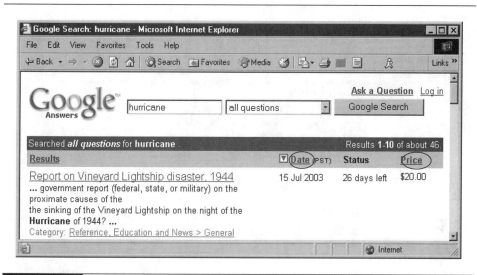

FIGURE 12-4 Sort Google Answers search results

Browse Google Answers

When you pose a question, you select the topic category that best applies to your question. You can browse all the questions in a particular category by clicking one listed on the main Google Answers page. Figure 12-5 shows these categories.

Click a category to see a list of all the questions ever asked that pertain to that topic. For example, click the Arts and Entertainment category to see the list of questions about arts and entertainment. An example of what you will see is shown in Figure 12-6.

Near the top of Figure 12-6 is a list of subcategories that can be selected by clicking on the link to further refine the topic. In the lower half of the figure is the subject list of all questions in the current category. Clicking on a subject takes you to the full text of the question. Subjects give a one-line summary of the question, as shown in the following image:

Showing *all questions* 1-25 of about 796 in **Arts and Entertainment**		Sorted by **Date Asked**	
Subject	▼ **Date** (PST)	**Status**	**Price**
Where to find good seats for concerts Asked by: xxmissmandyxx-ga	18 Jul 2003	29 days left 1 comment	$5.00
Web site featuring ugly scandinavian guy named "Henrik" Asked by: bigsticks-ga , Answered by: pinkfreud-ga	18 Jul 2003	Answered 2 comments	$2.00

12

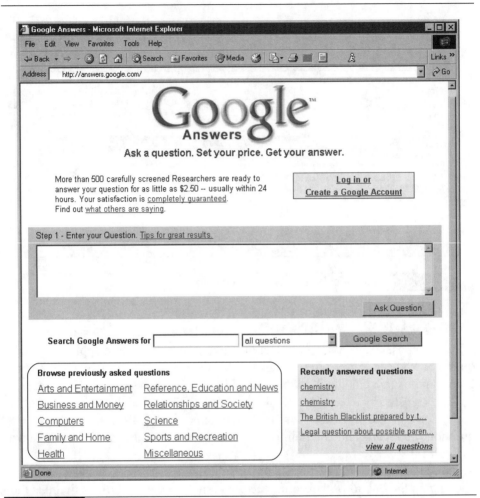

FIGURE 12-5   Categories of questions available for browsing

Text under the subject indicates who posed the question, and, if it has been answered, the researcher who did so. For example:

Showing *all questions* 1-25 of about 796 in **Arts and Entertainment**		Sorted by **Date Asked**	
Subject	▼ **Date** (PST)	**Status**	**Price**
Where to find good seats for concerts Asked by: xxmissmandyxx-ga	18 Jul 2003	29 days left 1 comment	$5.00
Web site featuring ugly scandinavian guy named "Henrik" Asked by: bigsticks-ga , Answered by: pinkfreud-ga	18 Jul 2003	Answered 2 comments	$2.00

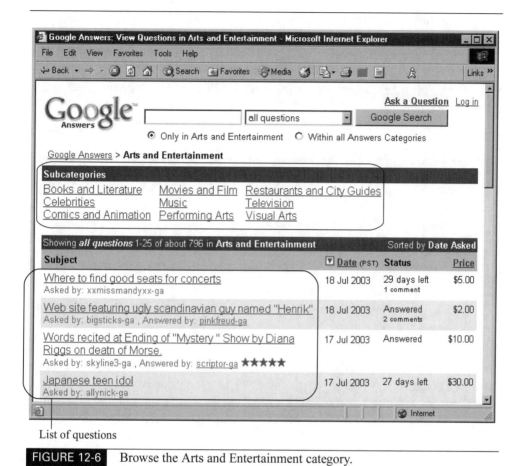

List of questions

FIGURE 12-6 Browse the Arts and Entertainment category.

You might also see a series of stars, as shown in the following image:

Showing *all questions* 1-25 of about 796 in **Arts and Entertainment**		Sorted by **Date Asked**	
Subject	▼ **Date** (PST)	**Status**	**Price**
Where to find good seats for concerts Asked by: xxmissmandyxx-ga	18 Jul 2003	29 days left 1 comment	$5.00
Web site featuring ugly scandinavian guy named "Henrik" Asked by: bigsticks-ga , Answered by: pinkfreud-ga	18 Jul 2003	Answered 2 comments	$2.00
Words recited at Ending of "Mystery " Show by Diana Riggs on deatn of Morse. Asked by: skyline3-ga , Answered by: scriptor-ga	17 Jul 2003	Answered	$10.00
Japanese teen idol Asked by: allynick-ga	17 Jul 2003	27 days left	$30.00

The stars indicate the asker's rating of the researcher's answer. Five stars is the best, one star is the worst.

The most recent questions in the list are shown first. You can see the oldest questions first by clicking the Date link at the top of the date column. Similarly, you can sort by increasing or decreasing price by clicking the Price link at the top of the price column.

The Status column gives more information about the question.

Showing *all questions* 1-25 of about 796 in **Arts and Entertainment**		Sorted by **Date Asked**	
Subject	▼ Date (PST)	Status	Price
Where to find good seats for concerts Asked by: xxmissmandyxx-ga	18 Jul 2003	29 days left 1 comment	$5.00
Web site featuring ugly scandinavian guy named "Henrik" Asked by: bigsticks-ga , Answered by: pinkfreud-ga	18 Jul 2003	Answered 2 comments	$2.00
Words recited at Ending of "Mystery " Show by Diana Riggs on deatn of Morse. Asked by: skyline3-ga , Answered by: scriptor-ga ★★★★★	17 Jul 2003	Answered	$10.00
Japanese teen idol Asked by: allynick-ga	17 Jul 2003	27 days left	$30.00

This column indicates whether the question has been answered and whether anyone has added comments. An answered question will have the value Answered. A question in the process of being answered is "locked," which we explain in more detail in the "Ask a Question" section. A padlock in the status column indicates a locked question.

Showing *all questions* 1-25 of about 7918 in **Miscellaneous**		Sorted by **Date Asked**	
Subject	▼ Date (PST)	Status	Price
Criminal Defense Attorneys Asked by: along-ga	18 Aug 2003	29 days left	$100.00
IBM's "Big Blue" nickname Asked by: zpatch-ga	18 Aug 2003	29 days left 🔒	$10.00

The time remaining before an unanswered question expires is also listed under the Status column. There is a maximum time limit of 30 days for each question to be answered; otherwise, the question's status is changed to Expired. This could happen if the question is difficult, poorly worded, or if the amount the asker is willing to pay is insufficient for the amount of work required to find the answer.

The Status field also indicates whether anyone has commented upon the question. A comment is different from an answer. Only researchers may post answers; comments may be posted by users and researchers alike. Comments are displayed when viewing a question, and we discuss more about the question viewing process in the following section.

Anatomy of the Question View

The interface for viewing a question is shown in Figure 12-7. Questions and answers are often several paragraphs long, so you might have to scroll down the page to see all the content.

There are two major areas of interest visible in the Question view. The first is the series of shaded boxes at the top of the screen labeled Sponsored Links (see Figure 12-7). These boxes contain advertisements that Google has selected as being relevant to the question you're viewing. The second is the question itself, which is located under the ads, as shown in the following image:

Question

Subject: **military spending**	Posted: 03 Jul 2003 11:40 PDT
Category: Reference, Education and News	Expires: 02 Aug 2003 11:40 PDT
Asked by: **soprisave-ga**	Question ID: 224812
List Price: $2.00	

```
We are trying to determine the cost of a military jet doing a flyover
of our town on july 4th,
```

Sometimes a user asks a question without giving enough detail for a researcher to provide an answer. This is the case with this question, because different types of military aircraft have different operating costs. If a researcher needs a clarification, he or she will post a request for clarification below the original question.

Request for Question Clarification by tutuzdad-ga on 03 Jul 2003 12:34 PDT

```
What kind of jet is it? What branch of service is the jet assigned to?
What town are you referring to?
```

12

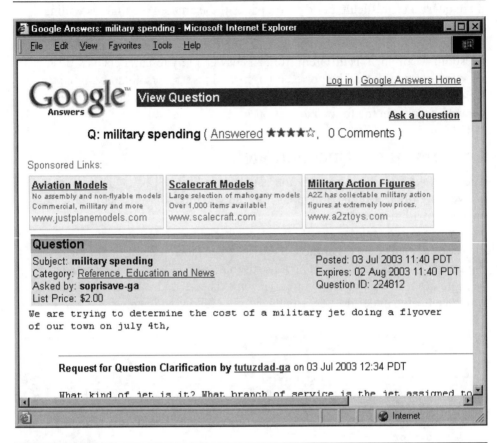

FIGURE 12-7   The Question view

If the asker responds with a clarification, it will be found below the researcher's query. This process often goes through several iterations until the researcher has enough information to provide a clear answer to the question.

Scroll down the page to find the Answer section.

Answer

Subject: **Re: military spending**
Answered By: <u>tutuzdad-ga</u> on 03 Jul 2003 19:19 PDT
Rated: ★★★★☆

```
Dear soprisave-ga;

Thank you for allowing me an opportunity to answer your interesting
question.
```

In addition to the researcher's answer, this section might contain further clarification, for example, if the researcher later turned up new information he or she wished to add.

Scroll further down the page to reveal the remaining two sections, as shown in the following image:

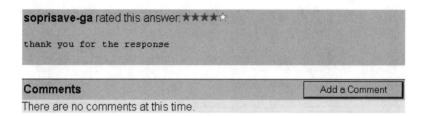

In the shaded region is the asker's rating of the answer as well as any comments he or she might have. Below the asker's feedback is the Comments section. As previously mentioned, both users and researchers can add comments to a page. Often comments consist of extra information found by users or an interesting discussion of the answer.

Ask a Question

Browsing other people's questions can be interesting and educational, but you get the most out of Google Answers by asking a question of your own. Later in this chapter, we suggest different types of questions for which Google Answers is very useful.

Sign Up for an Account

You need a Google account to ask a question. If you already have a Google Groups account (see Chapter 9), you already have a Google Answers account. You use the same e-mail address and password you use to log in to Google Groups.

To create an account, click the Log In link found in the upper-right corner of almost all pages on Google Answers, then click the Sign Up Now link on the resulting page (shown in Figure 12-8). There is also a Create a Google Account link on the main Google Answers page (**answers.google.com**). Yet another way you can create an account is to just start asking a question. You'll be given an opportunity to create an account along the way.

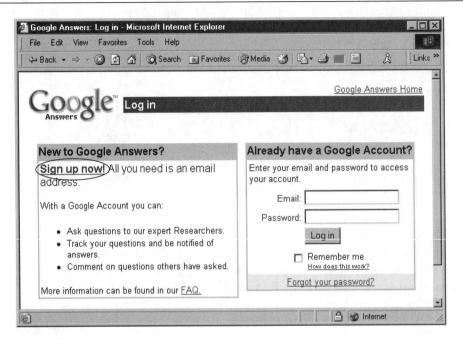

FIGURE 12-8   Sign up for a new account or log in if you have an existing account.

 *If you're concerned about entering personal information, you can read Google's privacy policy at* **http://google.com/privacy.html**.

Account creation is straightforward. It requires an e-mail address so Google can send you an alert when your question has been answered. When you sign up, you will receive a confirmation e-mail that contains a URL you must click to activate your account. Once your e-mail address is confirmed, you will get to choose a nickname and how (if at all) you'd like to receive updates about your questions via e-mail.

Account Information

Once you have an account, log in to Google Answers by using the Log In link found on **answers.google.com** or on the upper-right corner of most Google Answers pages. Once logged in, you'll see a page resembling that shown in Figure 12-9. This is the

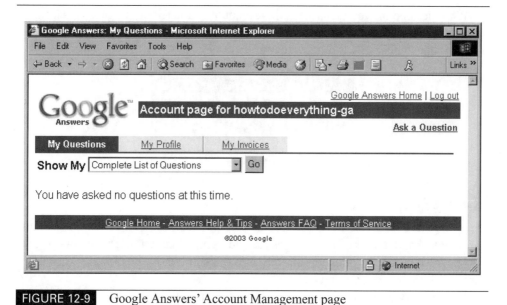

FIGURE 12-9   Google Answers' Account Management page

Account Management page, which lets you change your e-mail address and password, list the questions you've asked, and perform other tasks.

NOTE   *When you log in, Google Answers often sends you directly to the question you were last browsing.*

There are currently three tabs on this page, as shown in the following image:

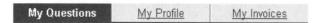

The first tab (My Questions) is active by default, and shows any questions you have asked. Click on any of the questions listed to view that question. You can change your view of the questions by using the pull-down menu at the top of the list.

The second tab (My Profile) lets you add or modify billing information, and the third tab (My Invoices) shows any charges placed on your credit card.

12

While logged in, you can access this Account Management page by clicking the My Account link wherever it appears. For example, in the upper-right corner of most pages you will see the following:

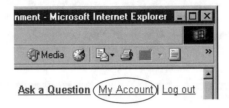

Pose a Question

Once logged in, you can ask a question by clicking the Ask a Question link in the upper right-hand corner of most pages (including the Account Management page). You can also type your question directly into the text box in the Google Answers home page (**answers.google.com**).

The primary question-asking interface is shown in Figure 12-10. In the Subject field, enter a short phrase that describes the nature of your question. In the Question field, state your question. In the Price field, list the price you are prepared to pay for the answer to your question. Choose the Category and Subcategory that best fits your question.

The most important information you must provide is the question you ask and the price you set. The quality of the answer you receive depends heavily on what you enter for both.

Write Effective Questions

How should you phrase a question so you get a good answer? For starters, good questions are not open-ended.

Question: The more details you provide, the better the results you'll receive. How to ask a

How can I make $2.5 million?

This isn't necessarily a poor question because of *what* it asks. It's a poor question because of *how* it asks it. It's not clear what kind of answer is desired. Does the asker want a business plan? Career advice? Blueprints for a machine capable of

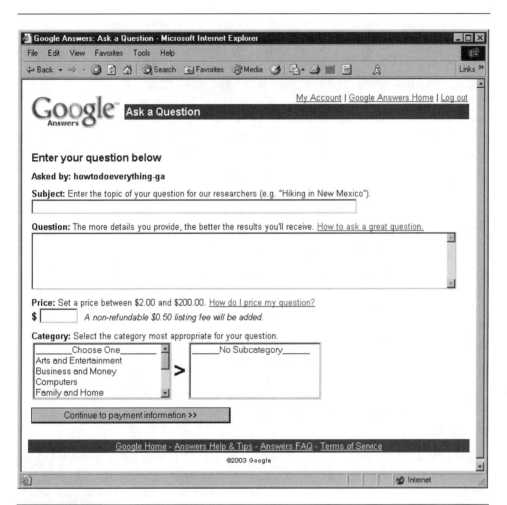

FIGURE 12-10   Ask Google Answers a question.

printing 2,500,000 dollar bills? Good questions are phrased so that any reader would clearly understand what kind of answer is required. A more effective question might be the following:

Question: The more details you provide, the better the results you'll receive. How to ask a

```
How can I locate a trustworthy member of the Nigerian
National Petroleum Corporation to whom I can wire
$10,000 in exchange for $2.5 million at such time as
he or she can withdraw money from a dedicated account
at the Central Bank of Nigeria? Provide name and phone number.
```

Strive to phrase your question so there is only one possible answer: the answer you want in the form most useful to you. Some principles for achieving this result are described in the following five sections.

Explain Exactly What You Are Looking For   Precisely define not just the information you'd like to receive, but also the ideal form in which you'd like your answer. Questions can be answered in many ways, for example, with a number, a definition, a list of references to books or web pages, a set of instructions, a list of query terms, or an explanation. Be ridiculously clear about what you want.

Explain Exactly What You Are *Not* Looking for   All a researcher has to work with is the text of your question. Be sure the researcher has enough information to avoid providing you with a useless answer. Give a summary of what you already know, a list of answers that are unsatisfactory, and provide any closely related questions that you're explicitly not interested in the answers to.

Give Context   Google Answers provides an easy way for a researcher to ask for clarification of a question. When a researcher asks for clarification, it's almost always because there wasn't enough background information needed to answer the question. The answers to many questions depend upon details about you. For example, a legal question is likely to depend on the country and state of residence, and exercise advice is likely to differ based on age and any medical conditions the asker might have. Often, *why* you're looking for something is just as important as *what* you're looking for. The answer to a history question could be very different depending on whether the asker is merely curious or gathering information for a Ph.D. thesis.

Provide Detail   Leave as little to chance as possible. If there is any potential for confusion, provide enough detail so the researcher will know exactly what you're talking about. At times, it might be helpful to provide a reference to material related to your question.

Ask Politely   The way a question is asked is also important. For best results, pose your question in a neutral tone and be polite. If you're asking a question about religion or politics, be sensitive to the fact that researchers might not agree with your opinions. And while your grammar and spelling don't need to be perfect, poorly written questions often result in misunderstandings.

A vague, imprecise question is hard to answer and typically requires several rounds of clarification. A clear, unambiguous question requires no clarification, so asking such questions results in getting answers more quickly.

Figure 12-11 shows a question following the suggested tips.

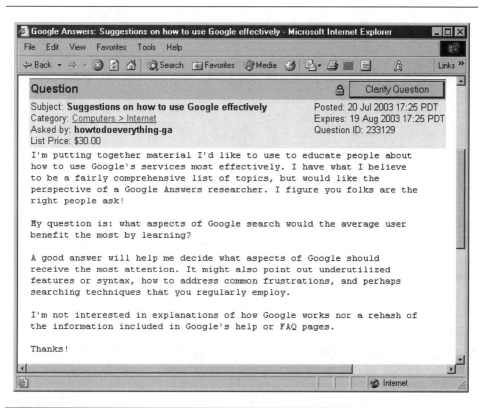

FIGURE 12-11   Using Google Answers to improve this book.

 *Google's suggestions on how to form questions can be found at* ***http://answers.google.com/answers/help.html***.

Focus Your Question

It's not a good idea to cram a bunch of unrelated questions into one Google Answers post. The question shown in Figure 12-12 exhibits this problem. Many researchers have a particular area of expertise about which they can answer questions effectively. By mixing questions from separate subjects, an expert is less likely to provide an answer because parts fall outside the researcher's area of expertise.

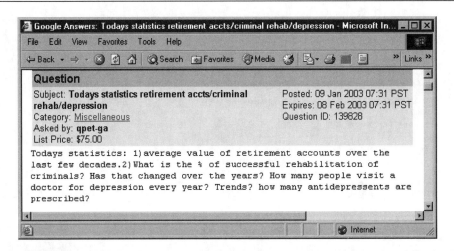

FIGURE 12-12   Unrelated questions belong in separate posts.

Inappropriate Questions

Google discourages and occasionally removes certain kinds of questions. The Google Answers Help page (**http://answers.google.com/answers/help.html**) says forbidden questions are any that do the following:

- Contain your personal contact information (e-mail, phone number, full name)

- Request private information about individuals

- Want assistance in conducting illegal activities

- Are meant to sell or advertise products

- Refer or relate to adult content

- Are homework or exam questions

- Seek specific information about Google or Google Answers

In practice, some guidelines are enforced more strictly than others. Any requests for the private information of an individual—for example their address or employer—are always turned down, as are advertisements and questions construed to be assisting illegal activity. Other rules, like the prohibition on homework or questions about Google, are typically not enforced.

How to Set a Price

Google lets you offer from US$2 to US$200 for an answer. In general, you should set your price to however much the information is worth to you. Because you can raise your price after the question is posted, you might offer a low price initially in hopes of getting a "bargain." This isn't a bad strategy because there are many researchers who answer questions inexpensively. Use common sense to judge what might be *too* low, as clearly the author of the question in Figure 12-13 did not.

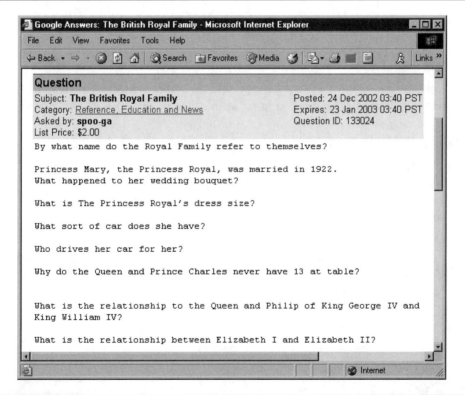

FIGURE 12-13   A Google Answers user asks eight unrelated questions for a total price of $2.

Some pricing strategies are as follows:

- Price according to the level of detail you expect. Assume you're hiring the researcher at a reasonable hourly rate, perhaps $25/hour. Use this rate to help calculate how much to offer. For example, if you ask the researcher to explain something at length or summarize a bunch of data, consider the time they will spend writing the response. For prices over $50, researchers typically respond with thorough, detailed answers, sometimes many pages long.

- Price according to how quickly you need the answer. If you need the information immediately, offering a high price usually brings a response within an hour. Low-priced questions can languish unanswered for days, and many are never answered at all.

- Browse Google Answers to get an idea of what others have offered for similar questions. Sorting questions by price is a helpful tool for seeing the extreme ends of the range.

Google Answers gives pricing suggestions at **http://answers.google.com/answers/pricing.html**, and we summarize this data in Table 12-1.

Post Your Question

After entering the subject, question, price, category, and subcategory, you will be taken to a payment page. Fill out the billing information (or verify existing information) and then carefully review the preview of your question found at the bottom of the page (shown in Figure 12-14).

Price Range	Answer	Work Required
$2–$5	Single link or piece of information	Less than 30 minutes
$10–$15	Several paragraphs and many links	About 30 minutes
$20–$50	Detailed information to hard questions	An hour or so
$100	In-depth research to very hard questions	Two to four hours
$200	Very thorough, very detailed research	More than four hours

TABLE 12-1   Google Answers' suggested price ranges

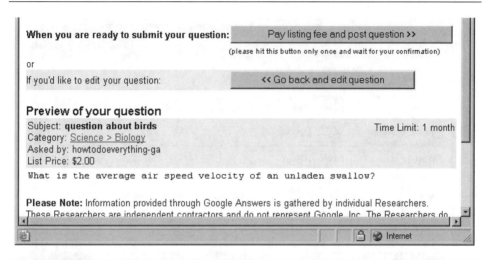

FIGURE 12-14 Check your proposed question carefully.

This is your last chance to edit your question. To do so, use the Go Back and Edit Question button visible in Figure 12-14. Once a question has been posted, it cannot be changed, whether it is open or not. However, you can post clarifications of the question after posting.

To post your question, click the Pay Listing Fee and Post Question button visible in Figure 12-14. Your credit card will be charge a nominal fee (currently $0.50) for use of Google Answers, but you won't be charged for an answer until a researcher provides one.

Researchers receive 75 percent of the price of an answered question. Google keeps the other 25 percent as well as the service fee.

After You Post a Question

A posted question awaiting an answer is listed with the status OPEN in the My Questions portion of your account view, as shown in Figure 12-15. Other possible status values are shown in Table 12-2. You can make changes to an open question by viewing it and utilizing the following three buttons:

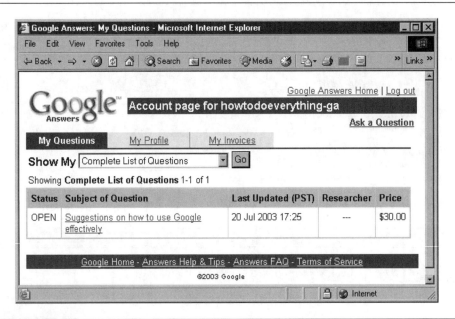

FIGURE 12-15   No researcher has yet answered the question.

The question parameters are its category and the price you're willing to pay for an answer. You can also clarify the question if you think of some way to improve your question. Closing the question indicates you are no longer interested in the answer. You forfeit the service fee, but will not be charged for an answer.

Researchers have the opportunity to answer open questions. Because the 500 or so Google Answers researchers are paid individually, Google ensures that each question is answered by at most one researcher. When a researcher decides to answer

Status Value	Meaning
OPEN	The question has been posted but has not yet been answered.
REQUIRES ATTENTION	A researcher has responded to your question with an answer or a request for clarification.
CLOSED	The question has been answered and rated, or was closed by the asker.

TABLE 12-2   Question status values

a question, he or she "locks" it and begins their response. Locking the question signals to other researchers the question has been taken. Find out whether or not your question is locked by viewing it. If the question is locked, the heading area will contain a padlock icon and text indicating that you cannot modify the question parameters at the current time.

A locked question will not necessarily be answered. The researcher might decide not to provide an answer after looking into the question. For example, the question might be significantly harder than it first appeared. A researcher lets other researchers take a crack at it by unlocking the question. A question remains locked for four hours at most, so there's no danger a researcher might permanently lock your question and block anyone else from answering it. Four hours should be sufficient time to answer, given the cap of $200 per question.

If your question is marked as needing attention, as shown in the following image,

there are several things that could be required. View the question by clicking its status or subject. You'll see the reason the question needs attention spelled out at the top of the page in large red writing. The two primary reasons your question might need attention are explained in the following two sections.

You Need to Clarify the Question   A researcher has asked you to provide more information necessary to answer the question. You can find the request for clarification below the text of the question and should reply to the researcher using the button provided. The interface for entering a reply is shown in Figure12-16.

You Need to Add a Rating   Your answer is ready! You can find it immediately below the text of your question. As part of the researcher's answer you will find the following two buttons:

If you're not satisfied with the answer, click the Request Answer Clarification button to post a note to the researcher and read the Unsatisfactory Answers section that follows. If you are happy with the answer, click the Rate Answer button. When rating the answer, a small interface is provided for you to post a comment as well as tip the researcher if you feel so inclined. Once you've rated the answer by selecting

12

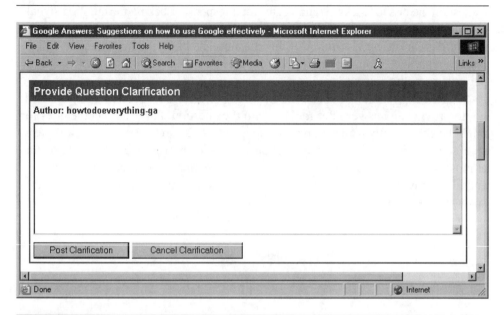

FIGURE 12-16   Question clarifications will be posted below the request for clarification.

a number of stars and possibly entering a comment and tip, the question will be displayed with status CLOSED in the My Questions section of the account view.

Unanswered Questions

If after a few days your question hasn't been answered and no one has asked for clarification, there are two possible causes. First, the price you offered was too low. While you might think researchers would tell you this, Google discourages researchers from commenting on price. If you suspect your price might be too low, change it or post a clarification asking what price might be acceptable. After 30 days without an answer, a question is closed, marked Expired in the Status field of the question browsing interface, and can no longer be answered. It might therefore be prudent to gradually raise the price of an unanswered question as it approaches expiration.

The second common reason for an unanswered question has already been mentioned: some questions are simply too hard. Since researchers are very good at finding things online, they know what kinds of information are within their reach. They shy away from questions whose answers are likely to be unobtainable.

 *If you're not sure why your question remains unanswered, the best thing to do is post a clarification asking for advice. If a researcher doesn't respond, a user will often post a comment.*

Unsatisfactory Answers

In the event you receive an unsatisfactory answer, you should work with the researcher before asking for a refund. Posting a request for answer clarification (through the View Question interface) permits you to notify the researcher that you are unsatisfied. Be sure to include the specific aspects of the answer you find lacking, and suggest ways for the answer to be improved. Give the researcher some time to reply, and be prepared to elaborate on your requirements if the researcher asks.

If attempts to resolve the problem with the researcher reach an impasse, one option is to repost your question. This allows another researcher to attempt an answer. Requesting a repost doesn't cost you anything. The service fee is waived and the charge you paid for the first answer is applied to any new answer you receive.

The interface used to request a repost is the same as that used to request a refund. The URL is **http://answers.google.com/answers/main?cmd= refundrequest**. (This URL is hard to type, so it might be easier to find a link to the page through the Answers FAQ, which is linked to at the bottom of every Google Answers page.

Requesting a repost or a refund requires the question ID and an explanation. The question ID is displayed in the Question view, as shown in Figure 12-17. Don't forget the explanation. Without it, Google will not repost or refund your money.

12

Question

Subject: **bird question**   Posted: 21 Jul 2003 19:27 PDT
Category: Science > Physics   Expires: 20 Aug 2003 19:27 PDT
Asked by: **howtodoeverything-ga**   Question ID: 233578
List Price: $2.00

What is the air speed velocity of an unladen swallow?

FIGURE 12-17   Question ID is required to request a repost or refund.

Possible Uses for Google Answers

There are many ways to use Google Answers. It can be applied to a wide variety of needs, many of which might not occur to you when you first use the service. We list some of the most popular uses here, but this list is by no means comprehensive.

Improve Your Searching Skills   Google Answers is a great way to test and improve your search skills. In addition to replying with the answer to a particular question, most researchers also list the search terms they used as well as pages they found containing the desired information. Pick an interesting question and search for the answer. Compare the information you find with the information found by the researcher. Did he or she employ any techniques you did not? Also, check each web page in which the researcher found relevant information. What kinds of queries are likely to bring up that web page? Might there be related pages with similar information you could use in the future?

Memory Aid   While searching for something, you may find you have forgotten enough specific details so as to be unable to form an effective query. For example, perhaps you're looking for the name of a song about which you recall the subject matter, release date, and genre, but not the artist or exact title. You could go "fishing"

Inside Google: Andrew Fikes, This is Your Life

We asked Andrew Fikes, one of Google Answers' primary developers, to say a few things about himself:

I joined Google in January 2001. I was attracted to the food, the logo, and the people. Before Google, I earned an M.S. in Computer Science from Stanford and a B.S. in Computer Engineering from Texas A&M University. I started at Google building tools in the QA department, and manually testing the early toolbar and enterprise releases. I'm a Texan by heart, and hopefully someday by location. I love all sorts of things, including fishing, farming, wine, cooking, and carving. I've been as far north as Kotzebue, AK, and as far south as La Paz, Bolivia. I've visited the world's largest goldpan, the world's largest thermometer, and have stood directly under the world's largest weathervane.

for the answer by repeatedly performing Google searches with variations on the information you recall, but asking Google Answers is often a more effective approach. Researchers can find what you're looking for given only the sketchy details. An example of this type of query is the following:

Question	
Subject: **Finding people who are neighbors**	Posted: 12 Jul 2003 13:45 PDT
Category: Family and Home	Expires: 11 Aug 2003 13:45 PDT
Asked by: **lilli412-ga**	Question ID: 229200
List Price: $3.00	

```
There is a website where it will list all the neighbors of an address.
I forgot what it is.  Can you help me out?
```

Save Time   Not all users post questions because they can't otherwise find the answer. Many do so because they don't have the time to find the answer themselves. They'd rather have a researcher find it while they are doing something else. Posting to Google Answers is a good way to save your valuable time.

Science Questions   Many users find the Science category of Google Answers to be very useful. Many researchers have a degree in a scientific field and provide answers to questions at all levels, from basic physics to highly specialized fields of chemistry. The diversity of researchers' backgrounds means there is almost always someone with the required background who will be able to answer your question. An example of a science question is the following:

Question	
Subject: **How to measure zeta potential**	Posted: 05 Jul 2003 19:21 PDT
Category: Science > Chemistry	Expires: 04 Aug 2003 19:21 PDT
Asked by: **tlimg-ga**	Question ID: 225532
List Price: $20.00	

```
I'm trying to find out the zeta potential of cerium oxide.
```

Computer Questions   Many Google researchers are experts when it comes to computers. Give your technically inclined child or relative a break by putting the Google Answers experts to work for you.

Market Research   Requests for market research are common. The rating of an answer to a high-priced market research request is usually four or five stars because researchers are able to provide in-depth competitive and background business data. Low-priced market research requests are most often ignored because gathering this data is a time-consuming process (which is probably why the question was asked in the first place).

Statistics   Statistics you may need might not be found neatly labeled on the Web. Consequently, you might want to turn to Google Answers to find the data. An example of a statistics request is the following:

Question	
Subject: **Animal kingdom**	Posted: 12 Jun 2003 12:37 PDT
Category: Science	Expires: 12 Jul 2003 12:37 PDT
Asked by: **zarb-ga**	Question ID: 216580
List Price: $2.00	

Which animal kills most human beings in a year?

Historical Facts   Researchers typically answer questions about history in detail and with considerable enthusiasm. Asking questions about historical people or events on Google Answers is a good way to get information not included in the average history book or encyclopedia. Be sure to request that the answer includes multiple references or points of view, so you're guaranteed a well-rounded reply. An interesting question of this variety is the following:

Question	
Subject: **Congressman qualifications**	Posted: 19 Jul 2003 15:07 PDT
Category: Reference, Education and News > General Reference	Expires: 18 Aug 2003 15:07 PDT
Asked by: **martine3-ga**	Question ID: 232857
List Price: $10.00	

Since Article I, Section 2 of the US Constitution says noone can be a House of Rep member unless he's been 7 years a citizen of the US (and 9 years for Senate), how did newly admitted states, such as Texas, fill their initial House and Senate seats since they were previously Texan citizens and just became American citizens upon admission to the US?

Geographical Information   It's not always easy to confine your search to a particular geographical area with most Google services. For example, including +**california** in a Google Web Search query restricts it to pages containing the word "california," but there's no guarantee such pages are in, or even about, California. Finding an answer to a question depending on geographical information is often easier through Answers than through the other services Google offers.

Unofficial Legal or Medical Advice   Researchers draw upon personal experience and a wide variety of professional websites to answer these kinds of questions. Browsing answers to these questions shows they are usually answered with a high degree of accuracy by researchers apparently knowledgeable in the field. On one hand, getting "professional" advice from Google Answers is appealing because it's easier and less expensive than hiring or visiting a specialist. On the other hand, it's risky because there's no guarantee of the accuracy of the information. Lawyers, doctors, accountants, and other professionals are certified for a reason: to ensure they're qualified to give advice in their field. There's no guarantee this is the case with Google Answers researchers.

Hints on Homework   Despite the fact that homework questions are officially discouraged, you can find quite a few examples of them, particularly in the Science and Computers sections. Google Answers is not intended to facilitate cheating on homework, but asking researchers for a hint is OK by most standards. Just be sure to indicate you're working on a homework problem so they don't reveal the complete answer. Not surprisingly, researchers are also quite good at providing references that make good starting points for writing papers, but researchers probably won't be interested in writing entire essays.

"Dumb" Questions   This is the perfect place for anonymously posing a question you might have been wondering about for a while, but were afraid to ask. For example:

Question	
Subject: **surface area in the colon (aka large intestine)**	Posted: 06 Jun 2003 15:06 PDT
Category: <u>Science</u>	Expires: 06 Jul 2003 15:06 PDT
Asked by: **svdh-ga**	Question ID: 214155
List Price: $25.00	

```
What is the surface area of the colon (also called the large
intestine)?  Please do not give me the surface area of the small
intestine; that information is easy to find.
```

Is Google Answers Effective?

Whether you find Google Answers to be a useful service depends on your needs. Anecdotal evidence suggests many people find the service to be a valuable, if somewhat infrequently used, part of Google's offerings. But a better way to estimate the site's usefulness is to read over a large number of questions and characterize any trends you notice. We did this and here's what we found.

Over half of all questions are answered, and the majority of answers that are rated are given four or five stars. Inspection of unanswered questions reveals the majority to be open-ended or far under priced, or both. A surprising number of unanswered questions received requests for clarifications but no response.

Some unanswered questions request information that is probably not available online. Google restricts the answers provided by researchers to information that can be found and referenced in open online sources. This means questions are not likely to receive a satisfactory answer if they require visiting a place (other than a library), talking to a person, or delving into the private data of some company or other entity.

Another way to evaluate the service is by how long it takes a researcher to answer a typical question. Here Google Answers really shines: the overwhelming majority of questions are answered within one day, with more than half answered within a few hours.

This data suggests that Google Answers is effective at quickly providing the information you need as long as the answers can be found in a library or somewhere on the Internet, and you follow the advice on posing good questions given in this chapter:

Limitations of Google Answers

When Google Answers was released in early 2002, many speculated that the service threatened the livelihood of librarians. In retrospect, this fear seems a bit unfounded. There will be a need for librarians as long as there are libraries, and Google Answers will never make such a useful institution or profession obsolete.

There are other reasons an Answers researcher will never replace librarians. First, librarians provide their service for free, while Google Answers costs money. Second, for many people, libraries are more accessible than the Google Answers website. There is a library within walking distance of many people, and using the library doesn't require a computer or Internet connection. Third, librarians can provide you with pointers to many books on the subject of interest. A Google Answers researcher can provide you with websites, but there's no guarantee that any of them will contain, in-depth content you might require.

Consider also that the quality of content in print is, in general, probably better than that found online. It's very easy to post erroneous information on the Web, but somewhat harder to get it published in a book. For important questions you probably shouldn't rely on Google Answers as an authoritative source. For example, questions critical to your health or finances are best answered by experts.

12

Chapter 13

Find Bargains with Froogle

How to…

- Find online stores selling a particular product
- Browse different types of products for sale
- Find the lowest price on an item

Froogle—a pun on *frugal* and *Google*—is Google's spin on comparative shopping services such as MySimon (**www.mysimon.com**) and BizRate (**www.bizrate.com**). Like other Google services, it provides the ability to browse and search specialized online content, in this case, products for sale.

If you're in the market to buy something online, using a service like Froogle is often the most efficient way of going about it. Froogle saves you the trouble of performing a web search for the item, visiting a bunch of results pages, and figuring out which ones offer the best deal. Instead, you can search Froogle and immediately see where the item can be purchased and at what price. Froogle is one of the most useful—and underutilized—services that Google offers.

Introducing Froogle

Froogle isn't a shopping service; it's a search service. Said another way, Froogle isn't an online store. It's a service you use to search for products available for sale in thousands of stores all over the Web.

The products Froogle knows about come from two sources. The first source is online stores that Google sees when crawling the Web (see Appendix A), that is, when examining web pages for inclusion in its search engine. When Google encounters what it believes to be an online store, it collects information about the products it offers and their prices. The second source is information submitted by online retailers. They sign up for a merchant account with Froogle and regularly provide it with an up-to-date list of items for sale.

Froogle is a *beta* Google service. This means that Google is still developing it by tweaking its user interface and improving its features. In Google's words, Beta is geek speak for a pilot program or test version of a product. It means that the Froogle you see today is likely to evolve and improve over time. You shouldn't let this stop you from using it. The only difference you're likely to notice between Froogle and other Google services is that small details of its user interface are more prone to change, usually in response to user feedback.

Because Froogle is a beta service, Google doesn't link to it prominently from the **google.com** home page or from other services, at least not at the time of this writing. There is a small link to Froogle from the Advanced Search form for Google Web Search (Chapter 5), but an easier way to get to Froogle is to point your browser at **froogle.google.com** (**froogle.com** also works). You could also do a Google Web Search for **froogle**.

Figure 13-1 shows the primary Froogle interface. You can use it to browse products for sale online, or search for something you'd like to price or purchase.

FIGURE 13-1   Froogle enables you to search for products available for sale online.

13

Browse Products

Froogle groups products into the categories shown in the bottom half of Figure 13-1. These categories are hierarchical, meaning that categories can contain subcategories that further refine the type of items Froogle knows about. Click on a category to take you either to a list of products (discussed in the following section) or to subcategories. Figure 13-2 shows the subcategories you'll see if you click on Arts & Entertainment.

You can use navigational links found under the title of the category to jump back to a more general category or simply click the Froogle logo in the upper-left corner to go to the Froogle home page.

Lists of Products

Once you've navigated to a sufficiently specific category, Froogle presents you with a list of products. Figure 13-3 shows the product list for Sports & Outdoors >

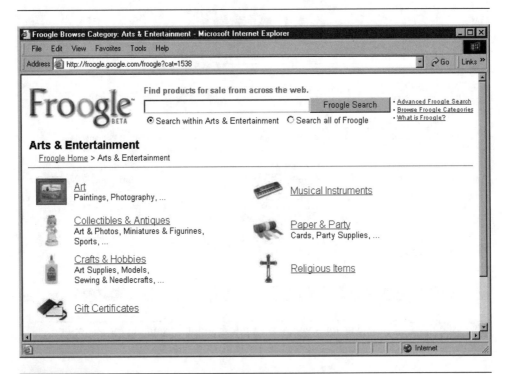

FIGURE 13-2   You can use the links under the category title (Arts & Entertainment) to navigate back to more a more general category.

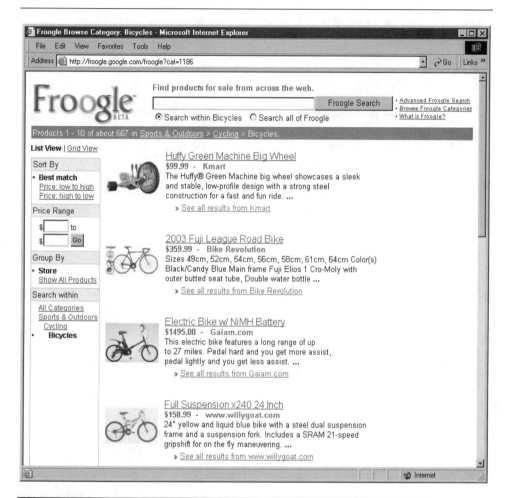

FIGURE 13-3   A list of Froogle products

Cycling > Bicycles (the > means In Subcategory). By default, products are listed
in a very rough order of relevancy to the category, but this ordering often isn't very
useful. We discuss later in this section how to order the products by price.

  The top, green status bar tells you how many products Google knows about in
this category and enables you to navigate to more general categories by clicking
the links provided.

The Grid View link on the left side shows the page with the products arranged in rows instead of a single column. This view (shown in Figure 13-4) enables you

FIGURE 13-4   The Grid View displays more products at once, but less information about each.

to see more pictures of products at once, but doesn't show as much information about each individual listing. If you don't like this format, you can switch back by clicking the List View link, located to the left of Grid View.

We've said that the list of products Froogle shows is in rough order of relevancy, by default. But since different products are likely to be relevant in different ways to different people, this ordering isn't always useful. More often, you want to see products ordered by price, or those that fall within a particular price range.

Figure 13-5 shows the navigation items found on the left side of a Froogle list. The Sort By links list the items in the category according to price. (Best Match is the somewhat dubious default ordering according to relevancy). The Price Range field restricts the products shown to only those within the price range you enter. Fill in the lowest priced item you wish to see in the first box, the highest priced in the second, and press the Go button. If you enter only a low price, Froogle shows you all the items at that price and above. If you enter only a high price, Froogle shows all the items of that price and below.

The name of the Group By links shown in Figure 13-5 is a bit misleading. By default, Froogle only shows you one product in the current category from each store. This is to prevent stores that have hundreds of similar items for sale from swamping the list of products. If you'd like to see all products in the category that each store has for sale, just click the Show All Products link. Click the Store link to switch it back.

> NOTE *The name Group By is so misleading that we wouldn't be surprised if it was changed to something more descriptive as Froogle evolves out of beta.*

The Search Within links are primarily useful after you've performed a search. While you're browsing products, they provide links to categories within which the current products reside.

Individual Products

Figure 13-6 shows a Froogle product item, which requires little in the way of explanation. The product name is a link to the item in the store that sells it. Its price and the store on which it is found are listed below. A short snippet of text from the site describing the item is included, as is a link to see more products in this category for sale from the same store. If you're viewing with Show All

FIGURE 13-5 The left side navigation of a Froogle product list

Products (all results for a store are included, instead of just one), this last link isn't necessary, and isn't shown.

Because some of Froogle's product information is extracted from web pages, you might encounter items that have incorrect or missing images. Typically, you can find the correct product image by clicking the product title link to go to the store on which it is for sale.

Full Suspension x240 24 Inch
$158.99 - www.willygoat.com
24" yellow and liquid blue bike with a steel dual suspension frame and a suspension fork. Includes a SRAM 21-speed gripshift for on the fly maneuvering. ...
» See all results from www.willygoat.com

FIGURE 13-6 Each Froogle product shown includes price and description information extracted from the store in which it is for sale.

Search Froogle

Use Froogle's Search box in the same way you'd use the search features of other Google services. It supports the basic operators +, –, quotes, and OR, but doesn't recognize the synonym operator (~). Froogle's search uses implicit AND, is case-insensitive, and ignores punctuation, but is an exception to the typical behavior because it doesn't ignore common words (aka stopwords). Since only products are being searched, the designers reasoned that all the words entered are likely to be significant (e.g., **the who cd**), so they chose to allow common words to influence the search results.

On many comparison shopping services, merchants can pay to have their products appear first in the list of results for a search. In keeping with Google's policy of not selling placement in search results (Chapter 1), Froogle doesn't employ this practice. Instead, Google shows advertisements alongside search results in a separate area. Figure 13-7 shows a search for **computer desk**. The shaded boxes in the rightmost column titled Sponsored Links are ads, and are how Google makes money by running Froogle.

Select Search Terms

Froogle searches product titles, descriptions, and store names, so select terms are likely to appear in one of these places. To find a specific product, just search for its name. You can also search for a general kind of product by searching for terms that would appear in its description, for example **cd player**.

Be aware that including the manufacturer in your query when searching for a specific product can restrict your results unnecessarily. For example, searching Froogle for **playstation 2** results in about 580,000 hits. A search for **sony playstation 2** results in only 180,000 matches because it only returns those stores selling Playstation 2s that include the word "Sony" in the title or description.

Refine Your Query

Searches for a general type of product might be complicated by the fact that there could be different *kinds* of the product you seek. For example, **cd player** returns results for portable CD players, car stereos, home stereo components, and CD players for DJs. Adding more search terms can refine the query by making it more specific, but it's easy to unintentionally make the query *too* specific. Searching for **home cd player** only finds CD players whose titles or descriptions include the

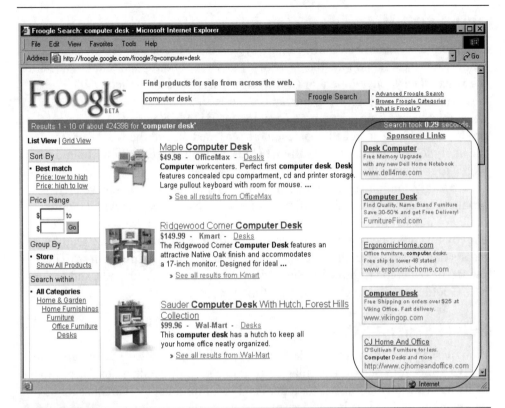

FIGURE 13-7   Advertisements are shown to the right of search results.

word "home." There are probably many home CD players of potential interest that don't include this word. Instead of adding terms that *might* be found for a product, consider using the exclusion operator to omit results you *know* you don't want. If you're in the market for a home CD player, you could search for **cd player –dj** or better yet, **cd player –dj –car –portable**.

If you're looking for a general kind of product, browsing to an appropriate category is often more effective than searching. You might visit Electronics > Audio > Portable Audio > CD Players to see portable devices or visit Electronics > Audio > Car Audio & Video > Stereos & Changers to find a CD player for your car.

When viewing a category, the search box at the top of the page defaults to searching within that category.

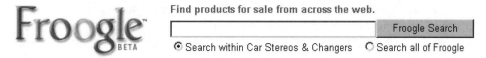

Searching within a category can give you better results than searching all of Froogle because searches are narrowly targeted to items of the kind you want.

If you don't find what you're looking for by searching within the category, you can run your search in other closely related categories using the Search Within links on the left navigation column. Figure 13-8 shows a search for **cd player** within the Car Stereos & Changers category. In the Search Within area, Stereos & Changers is indicated as the current category. The other links perform your search on a related category (such as MP3 Players), or a more general category (such as Audio).

FIGURE 13-8   The Search Within links enable you to quickly run your search in related categories.

13

Keep an eye on the Search Within links to avoid a subtle pitfall of Froogle's interface. They're often the only indication of which Froogle category the box at the top of the page searches. You might think that entering a query into the search box in Figure 13-8 would search all of Froogle. But notice that Stereos & Changers is indicated as the category to Search Within, meaning the search box will search only that category. To search all of Froogle, either click the All Categories link in the Search Within area or click the Froogle logo to go back to the home page. An awareness of this subtlety can save you frustration when searching for an unrelated product after searching within a category.

Advanced Froogle Search

You can find a link to the Advanced Froogle Search form in its customary place, to the right of the search box on any Froogle page.

The Advanced Froogle Search form (shown in Figure 13-9) allows you to specify more precisely the products you wish to find. As usual, the top part of the form (the shaded region) enables you to form queries without having to manually use the basic search operators (+, −, OR, and quotes). The basic operators (Chapter 2) are automatically applied to the terms you enter in each of these boxes according to their meanings in Table 13-1.

The lower half of the interface is for Froogle-specific search options. The Price Restriction and Category options are self-explanatory. The Occurences option instructs Froogle to find your search terms in a particular part of a product listing. You can tell it to search both product title and description (the default) or restrict your search to only one of these fields.

Advanced Search Feature	Operator
with all the words	**term1 term2** ... (no special operator because of implicit AND)
with the exact phrase	**"term1 term2 ..."** (quotes)
with at least one of the words	**term1 OR term2 OR** ... (OR)
without the words	**−term1 −term2** ... (exclusion)

TABLE 13-1   The Top Portion of the Advanced Search Options Facilitate Easy Usage of the Basic Operators.

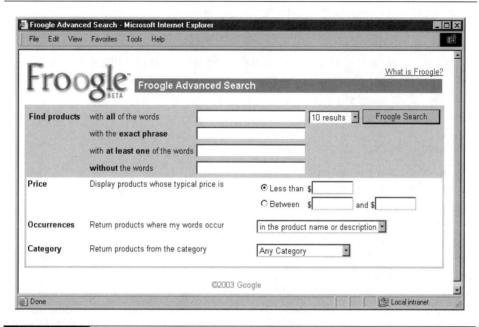

FIGURE 13-10 The Advanced Froogle Search form provides an easy way to specify more complicated queries.

Occurences options correspond to operators as shown in Table 13-2. These operators are automatically inserted in your query when you use this option. For example, using the Advanced Search form to find products "with all the words" **ant farm** and using the Only In The Product Name option causes Froogle to search for **allintitle: ant farm**. You can, of course, use these operators directly in a query without using the Advanced Search form.

13

NOTE *You can only use one of the **allintitle:** and **allintext:** operators in a query, and it must be the first search term.*

Option	Operator
in the product name or description	none (default behavior)
only in the product name	**allintitle:**
only in the product description	**allintext:**

TABLE 13-2   Occurences Options and Their Froogle-specific Operators

Since most of the features provided by the Advanced Froogle Search form are available through the normal Froogle interface, the Advanced Search form is primarily useful as a way to craft more complicated queries without having to specify the operators manually. Using the Category feature on the form can sometimes be more convenient than browsing to a category and then searching within it.

Possible Uses

Froogle is great for finding offbeat or unusual items. If you're in the market for a **robotic lawnmower** or a **pull my finger doll**, chances are Froogle can tell you where to buy one.

We also find Froogle to be an excellent resource for finding the best price on a specific item we're interested in purchasing. If you have a particular item in mind, it's almost always worthwhile to check Froogle to locate the best price when making a purchase.

On the other hand, Froogle isn't always as useful if you only have a general type of product in mind. Nonspecific queries such as **desk**, **camera**, or **computer** often give *too many* results of too many different kinds to be very useful. For example, searching for **laptop** turns up more than 500,000 products spanning the gamut from refurbished budget computers to high-end multimedia portables, Macintoshes to PCs, and with all manner of different configurations and options. Sometimes it can be better to research products with other sources and then search Froogle for pricing information on specific models, for example **12" apple powerbook** or **ibm thinkpad T30**.

One of Froogle's limitations is its inability to narrow a particular type of product by one of its characteristics. For example, there's no way to search for TVs with 30" or larger viewing area. Similarly, there's no way to specify that you'd like to find mopeds with engines smaller than 80cc's. For these reasons, consider using Froogle primarily to find something specific. It works best when you want to find the lowest price, a particular accessory, or when you want to find comparably priced competing items for something you're considering buying. If you're looking for something nonspecific, such as a computer, consider using other sources for research.

Chapter 14

Other Cool Features

How to...

- ■ See the most popular queries on Google Search
- ■ Use experimental and less well-known features such as Google Catalog
- ■ Use third-party features that draw information from Google

Peek behind the austere white curtain of Google's home page and you'll find more features of interest. With over a thousand employees, a formidable research department, and a corporate environment that encourages experimentation, it's no surprise that Google has a few tricks up its sleeve. In addition, thanks in part to the Google Application Programming Interface (API), an interface that Google makes available to software developers, third parties have built some cool features on top of Google's service.

Google Zeitgeist

Zeitgeist is a German word meaning "spirit of the times." It refers to the collective mindset of a group of people during a particular time period. The concept of Zeitgeist embodies what people are thinking about, their interests, and their likes and dislikes.

 To pronounce Zeitgeist, the first syllable rhymes with "kite" and the second rhymes with "heist."

Since millions of people perform Google Web Searches every day, the queries Google receives tell a lot about what's on peoples' minds. While it's not a perfect Zeitgeist, examining what people search for in different parts of the world gives Google a glimpse into popular culture and the people, places, or things that are hot topics. Google aggregates this information and presents interesting aspects of it on a regular basis, typically weekly, monthly, and yearly.

Google Zeitgeist can be found at **http://www.google.com/press/zeitgeist.html**, or simply by searching for **google zeitgeist** (an I'm Feeling Lucky search works great). Figure 14-1 shows the Google Zeitgeist page. The left column lists the top ten gaining queries for the week—the searches that showed the biggest increase in popularity. The right column shows the opposite—the ten queries whose popularity declined by the biggest margin.

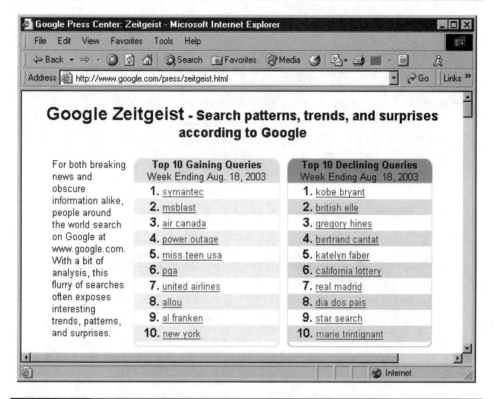

FIGURE 14-1   Google Zeitgeist gives insight into the relative popularity of common queries.

The top gaining and declining queries typically reflect the ebb and flow of the top stories in the media. For example, in the week shown in Figure 14-1, the MSBlast virus and Symantec (a company that makes antivirus software) were making national news; thus, **symantec** and **msblast** were the top gaining queries (positions one and two, respectively).

Scroll down the page to find assorted Zeitgeist statistics: the top gaining and declining queries for the prior month, a variety of statistics about the users who accessed Google's website, Top Five lists for subjects like TV Shows, and a sample of what people are searching for on Google's international domains.

14

The Ghost of Google Past

Historical snapshots of Google Zeitgeist are archived at **http://www.google.com/press/zeitgeist/archive.html** (or search for **google zeitgeist archive**). There you can find the weekly, monthly, and yearly Google Zeitgeist pages since the feature was introduced in January 2001. Figure 14-2 shows part of this list.

The yearly Zeitgeist pages are particularly interesting because they include top searches for the year in many categories (e.g., Most Popular Queries, Top Celebrities, and Top Video Games) as well as a time showing search statistics for each month. Figure 14-3 shows part of the timeline for 2002.

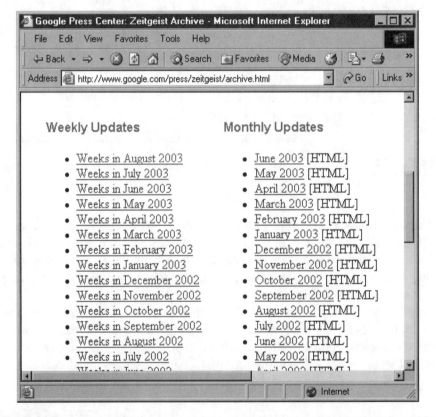

FIGURE 14-2   Google Zeitgeist information for past weeks and months is available in the archive.

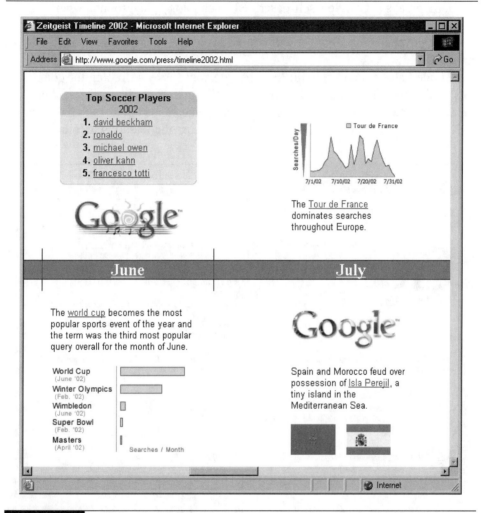

FIGURE 14-3   Yearly Google Zeitgeist pages include a timeline annotated with interesting facts.

Google Labs

Part of Google's engineering culture is to experiment with new services and applications around Google's technology. Some new projects, such as Google News, are eventually integrated into Google's main service offerings; others never reach the public eye at all. Then there are those that fall somewhere in between: interesting enough to showcase to the world, but not sufficiently practical or complete to justify releasing as part of a new service and promoting to users.

Google Labs is Google's self-described "technology playground" where experimental features are exhibited. It's a place for Google engineers to make available novel applications that will not or haven't yet made it onto Google's main site.

Google Labs is found at **http://labs.google.com** (or by searching for **google labs**) and is shown in Figure 14-4. To explore the prototypes listed there, click their links. Afterwards, if you feel so inclined, you can use the links found under each prototype to send feedback to Google or discuss the feature with others.

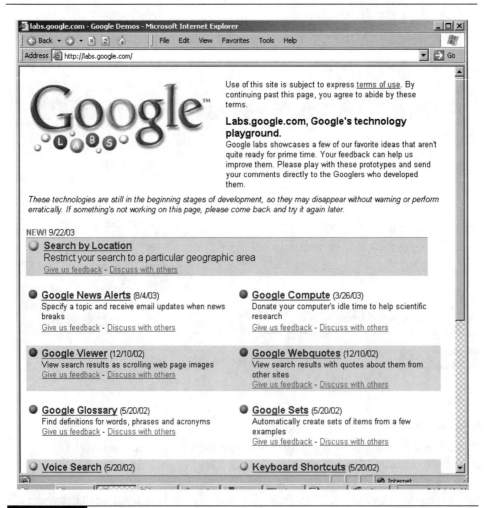

FIGURE 14-4   Google Labs is a place for Google employees to exhibit experiments and novelties.

 *Because Google Labs is a site for experimental features, it is not as well supported as other Google services. Thus, features on Labs are occasionally not available.*

Search by Location

Search by Location narrows a search to a particular area; search results will be focused on a geographic location, with a map showing the positions of each match. An example is shown in Figure 14-5.

Search by Location doesn't use the yellow pages to figure out where things are; it works by fishing for addresses and other hints of location in web pages. This means it can make mistakes, but it also means it is very flexible. For example, search for **hitchcock vertigo** in **san francisco, ca** to get a map of locations from the classic Alfred Hitchcock movie, *Vertigo*. You won't find those in the phone book!

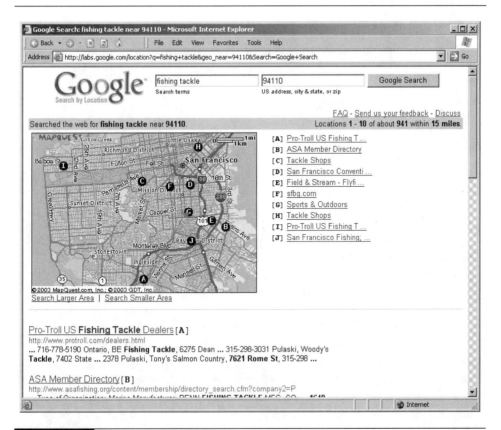

FIGURE 14-5 There's plenty of fishing tackle to be had in southeast San Francisco.

Google News Alerts

News Alerts is a service that e-mails you when new articles are published on Google News (see Chapter 8) about a topic of interest to you. You can choose to be alerted via e-mail each time a new article appears, or once per day with a list of new articles.

Signing up is easy: enter the search terms (just like in Google News), the frequency of alerts, and your e-mail address in the signup page (shown in Figure 14-6). You'll receive a confirmation e-mail containing a link you must follow to activate the alerts. In addition to the activation link, it contains a cancellation link, but you don't need to worry about saving this e-mail. Every alert email you receive includes a link to cancel that alert.

You can sign up for as many alerts as you'd like. You might find it useful to sign up for alerts about:

- The company you work for
- Competitors in your industry
- Companies you have invested in or are considering investing in
- Hobbies
- Sports teams or players
- Favorite celebrities
- Political figures

Origin of Google News Alerts

Google News Alerts started as a side project for Google engineer Naga Sridhar Kataru in February 2003. Naga became tired of repeatedly visiting Google News to check for developments in the imminent U.S. war with Iraq, and so decided to cook up his own application that would alert him when a new story broke.

Shortly after writing the first version of Google News Alerts, Naga demonstrated it for Google cofounder Sergey Brin, who liked it very much and signed up for a news alert for "google." A week later, with the encouragement of both Sergey and Marissa Mayer (Google's Director of Consumer Products), Naga began working full time on creating a full-blown product out of his pet project.

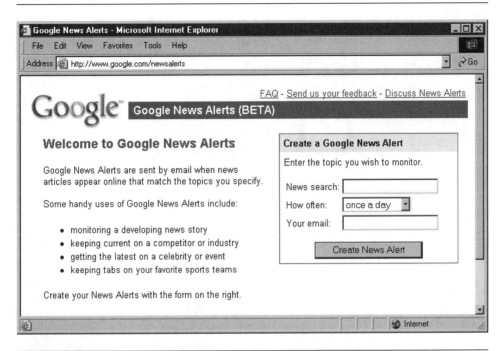

FIGURE 14-6   Use Google News Alerts to stay on top of current events.

- Developing news stories

- Areas of the world you're interested in

Depending on how you phrase your terms, you might get more information than you'd like. If so, you can use the Google News operators found in Chapter 8 to restrict your search to be more specific.

Google Sets

Google Sets (shown in Figure 14-7) is a novel service that generates a list of similar items in response to those you enter. For example, entering "apples," "bananas," and "grapes" displays a list of many different kinds of fruits. Similarly, suppose you'd forgotten the name of the fourth Beatle, you could list "Paul McCartney," "John Lennon," and "George Harrison" to reveal "Ringo Starr." (It also lists "The Rolling Stones", which may be part of the reason why Google Sets is hosted on Google Labs instead of on Google's main site.) The more items you enter, the more accurate the set typically is.

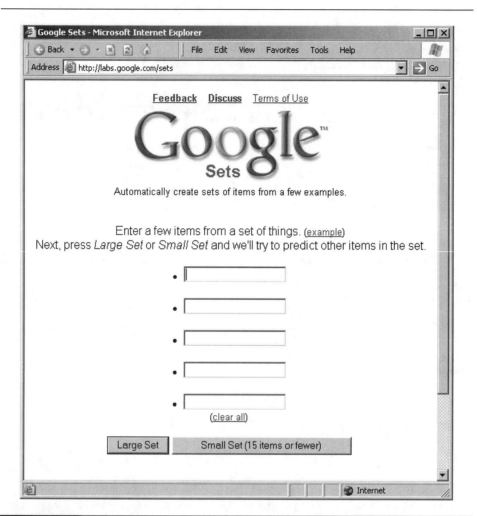

FIGURE 14-7 Given several similar items, Google Sets predicts a list of other items that are related.

You might be impressed by the sets Google can come up with. For example, if you enter "Golden Gate Bridge" "Palace of Fine Arts," and "Coit Tower," Google Sets suggests other tourist ,attractions in San Francisco. The set generated by entering the search engines "Excite," "Yahoo," and "Google" is shown in Figure 14-8.

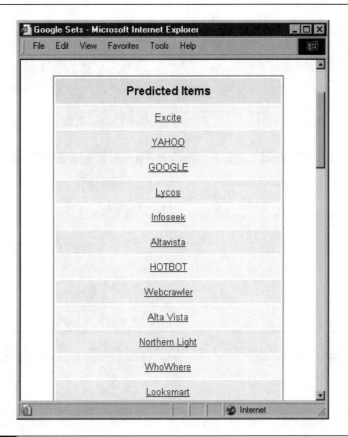

FIGURE 14-8   Part of the set generated by entering three search engines

The Google Glossary

Google mines the Web for word and acronym definitions and makes its findings available through the Google Glossary. You can enter a word or phrase and see a list of definitions extracted from web pages. The Glossary also shows a list of related phrases judged to be similar to your query.

The Google Glossary is useful for looking up definitions of words or acronyms you can't find in other sources, for example high-tech, slang, ethnic words, and other terms that haven't made it into mainstream usage. Figure 14-9 shows two definitions of the word "holi."

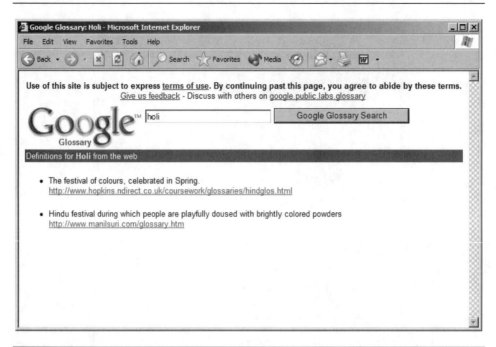

FIGURE 14-9   The Google Glossary is useful for terms with regional significance.

For more mainstream words, you'll probably get the best results by looking them up using online dictionaries. Conveniently, there are links to online directories on the Google Glossary results page, as well as on the result pages of normal searches (as we learned in Chapter 4).

Google WebQuotes

Google WebQuotes annotates a normal web search page with quotes describing each result. Whereas the snippets normally shown with search results (see Chapter 4) are excerpts of text from the page listed as a result, WebQuotes are snippets from pages talking *about* the page listed as a result. These quotes (three of them, by default) are mined from sites all over the Web, and so include all manner of comments.

Figure 14-10 shows a Google WebQuotes search for **harry potter**. Below the link to the first search result, you can see three quotes about the site and their sources, and the pages on which the quotes were found. Next to the result link, there is a link labeled 23 WebQuotes. Click this link to show you all the quotes about the site that Google found.

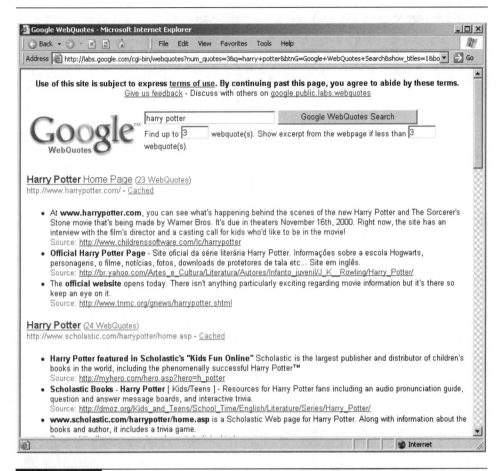

FIGURE 14-10 Google WebQuotes annotates search results with quotes about the site.

Keyboard Shortcuts

Keyboard Shortcuts (Figure 14-11) is an interface to Google Web Search that lets you navigate to search results without using your mouse. While you can do this in Internet Explorer using the TAB key on a regular results page, it's not very convenient. Keyboard Shortcuts lets you quickly skip from result to result and follow links, such as the cached and similar pages, by pressing a single key. For more information, see the Keyboard Shortcuts page itself.

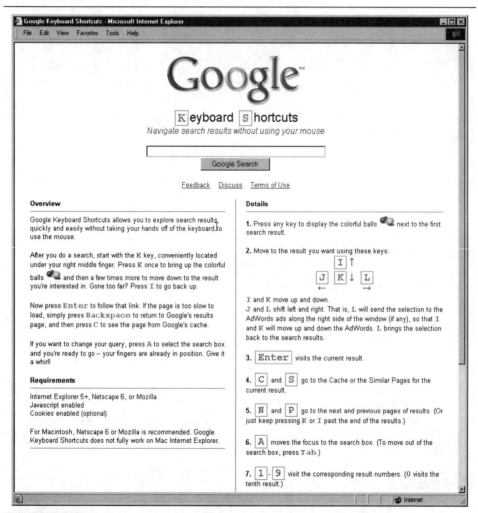

FIGURE 14-11   Keyboard Shortcuts enables keyboard-based navigation of search result pages.

The Google Viewer

The Google Viewer enables you to see a "slideshow" of the results for a query. Its search box is shown in Figure 14-12.

Enter a query into the Google Viewer to show you the page that is the first result for your search. Every five seconds the Viewer loads the page corresponding to the next search result. Each page is framed by a control panel that permits you to stop, start, rewind, and fast-forward the progression. You can also increase or

FIGURE 14-12   The Google Viewer will cycle through search result pages.

decrease the speed at which new pages are shown. Below the control panel the Viewer displays the search result for the currently showing page. All these features are shown in Figure 14-13 in which the Viewer is currently showing the third search result.

Google Compute

The term *distributed computing* refers to many computers in different places all working together to solve a particular problem. The problems tackled by distributed computing are typically very hard, for example, complex scientific calculations or sifting through masses of data looking for very rare pieces of information. Each computer that contributes to the effort solves only a very tiny portion of the problem, but when the progress of thousands of computers is combined together, the larger solution can be attainable.

There are a variety of distributed computing efforts underway on the Internet. Some of them perform complex biomedical simulations that help scientists understand the virus that causes AIDS or the effects of new drug therapies. Others search astronomical data for signs of intelligent life in other galaxies, or crack cryptographic codes for the sake of computer security research.

14

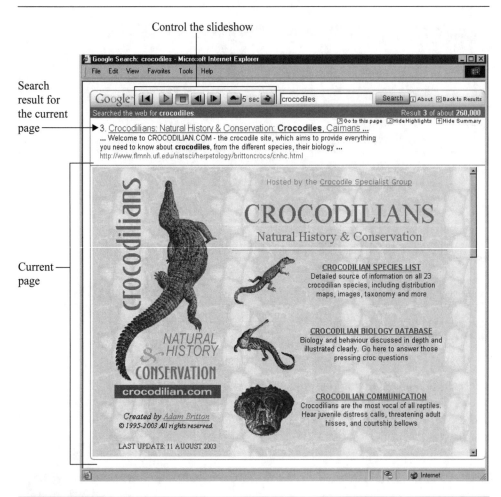

FIGURE 14-13 The Google Viewer slideshow displays the pages that are search results for your query.

Google Compute is a distributed computing utility built into the Google Toolbar (see Chapter 6) that can harness the idle cycles of your computer. That is, it can utilize the computer power that is wasted when your computer is turned on but not actively being used. When your computer isn't doing anything else, Google Compute can work on "protein folding" problems coordinated by Stanford University. The solutions to these problems contribute to researchers' understanding of diseases like Alzheimer's and cystic fibrosis.

Google Compute is not enabled by default. To enable it, go to the Google Compute page (Figure 14-14) and click the Install Google Compute button at the bottom.

Origins of Google Compute

Using the Google Toolbar to contribute to medical research was Google cofounder Sergey Brin's idea. He wanted the academic and research communities to benefit from Google's success, so he chose to team up with the Folding@Home project (**http://www.stanford.edu/group/pandegroup/folding/**) at his alma mater, Stanford University. Sergey worked closely with the engineers who developed the product, even implementing portions of the first sample application himself. Today, Google Compute users contribute more computing power to Folding@Home than any other single group.

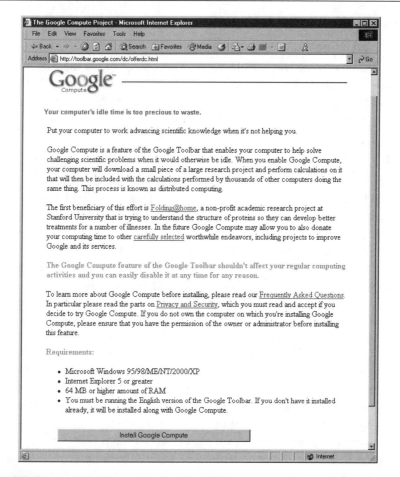

FIGURE 14-14   Google Compute uses your extra computing power for medical research.

Once installed, a small double-helix icon will appear on your Toolbar.

Click this icon to display a menu that allows you to configure aspects of Google Compute, for example, to make its resource usage more conservative.

Some users report that Google Compute negatively affects the performance of some applications, such as graphics-intensive games. If you notice sluggishness, switch to Conservative Mode through the menu accessed through the double-helix icon.

Fun Uses of Google Search

Google's popularity has spawned a subculture that puts Google's services to use in unexpected and amusing ways. Here, we've collected some of the most popular of these diversions, but there are many, many more. You can turn up others by... you guessed it... searching Google for them. For example, try **google tricks**, **google games**, or **google fun**.

Joke Pages

Perhaps the most popular Google amusements are prank pages accessed via I'm Feeling Lucky searches. For example, go to Google, enter **weapons of mass destruction**, and hit the I'm Feeling Lucky button. Be sure to read the fine print! For another example, go to Google, enter **french military victories**, and again hit the I'm Feeling Lucky button.

Not everything is as it seems. As much as the page you see for **french military victories** *looks* like a Google results page, it's not. Note the domain in your browser's address bar is not **google.com** and also the fine print at the bottom of the page. Take another look at the result for **weapons of mass destruction** as well. The URL shown in your browser's address bar for this page is *not* what an astute web user would expect from a browser error page.

What's happening here? Recall that using the I'm Feeling Lucky button takes you immediately to the first result for your search (see Chapter 2). So these pages are actually the first search results for the given queries; though they resemble "official" pages, they are just humorous simulations of them.

The **weapons of mass destruction** page simply became popular enough to be the first result for that query on its own merit, but the authors of the **french**

Joke Page Confusion

It's amazing how few people understand how joke pages accessed through I'm Feeling Lucky searches work. Whenever a new joke page becomes popular, Google is inundated with e-mails from users expressing all kinds of opinions. Commendations on Google's sense of humor are common, as are long rants accusing Google of conduct unbecoming of a search engine. Employees of Google receive an enormous number of e-mails from friends and family asking for explanations, so some create boilerplate replies because repeatedly responding to the same questions becomes tiresome.

Even *Time Magazine* mistakenly attributed a joke page to Google. The July 7–13, 2003 issue included a note about the **weapons of mass destruction** prank, and erroneously implicated Google as the source of the page. At the time of this writing, you can still find this citation online at **http://www.time.com/ time/verbatim/20030707/6.html**.

military victories page had to make a special effort; the humor value of their prank depends on it being the first result for that query, because that way it seems to be the result page of a Google Search. By coordinating the efforts of many people around the Web who were in on the joke, the pranksters managed to inflate the ranking of the page to the point where it became the first result for the query. At that point, any user performing an I'm Feeling Lucky search for **french military victories** would be taken directly to the page. You can verify this by searching for the terms without using the I'm Feeling Lucky button and observing the first result.

Googlism

Googlism (**www.googlism.com**, shown in Figure 14-15) uses Google to attempt to make statements about people, things, places, or dates you enter.

Figure 14-16 shows the results for **dizzy gillespie**. Most of the statements are incomplete, but you can tell that Dizzy Gillespie must have been a jazz musician.

NOTE *If you don't see an interface similar to Figure 14-15 when you visit Googlism, it's possible you accidentally typed **www.googleism.com** (there's no "e" in "Googlism").*

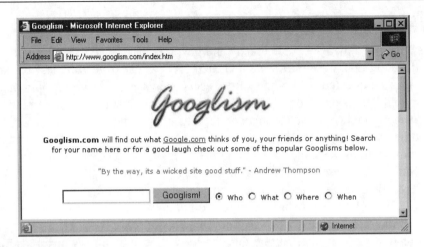

FIGURE 14-15   Googlism mines Google for statements about terms you enter.

Googlism extracts declaratives from Google by performing searches likely to turn up statements of fact. For example, when **dizzy gillespie** was entered, it probably searched Google with a query like **"dizzy gillespie is"** and extracted the sentence fragments shown in Figure 14-16 from the Google Search results page.

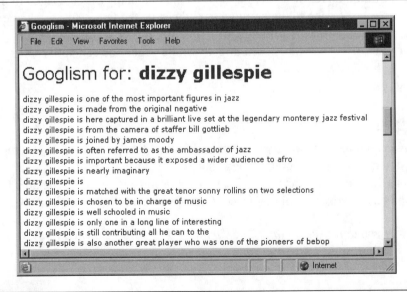

FIGURE 14-16   Statements about Dizzy Gillespie are extracted from web pages via Google.

The text returned by Googlism often appears to be nonsensical because it is taken out of context. However, the service is a diverting way to see what people on the Web are saying about you, your company, or something close to your heart. We discuss a better way to find information about people in the following section.

GooglePeople

GooglePeople extracts information from Google in ways similar to that of Googlism, but applies "text mining" techniques to achieve more reliable, better polished results. This service is run by AvaQuest, and is accessible through AvaQuest's website at **http://www.avaquest.com/**.

GooglePeople enables you to enter a question starting with "who," for example "Who is the prime minister of Canada?" It shows you its best guesses along with its confidence in each guess. Figure 14-17 shows the GooglePeople results for the question, "Who wrote The Star Spangled Banner?" (the national anthem of the United States).

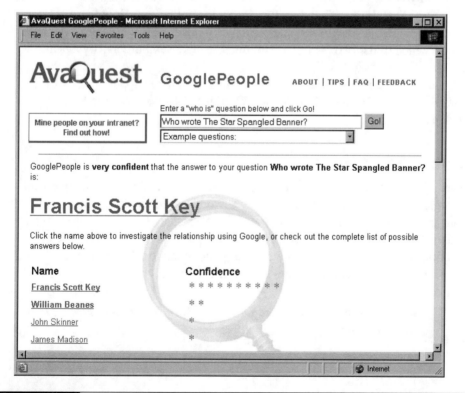

14

FIGURE 14-17   AvaQuest's GooglePeople service uses Google to answer questions about people.

You should really try this service; it can work amazingly well! However, you have to ask the right sort of question. Questions whose answers are a matter of opinion or speculation are hard for GooglePeople to answer. At the time of this writing, the question "Who is the most famous person alive?" turns up the answer "Lawrence Welk", who, sadly, is neither alive nor was ever quite *that* famous. See GooglePeople's drop-down list of example questions to get an idea of the sorts of questions that the site is good at answering.

 *AvaQuest also offers GoogleMovies, a service that extracts movie reviews from Google and presents you with an opinion of the movie based on what web sources are saying.*

Google Smackdown

Google Smackdown (**http://www.onfocus.com/googlesmack/down.asp** or just search for **google smackdown**) cleverly pits search terms against each other in a battle of website popularity. You simply enter two words or phrases, such as "hot dogs" and "hamburgers," and hit the Throw Down! button. Google Smackdown uses the number of results Google estimates it has for the two queries (Chapter 4) to see which of the two "wins." ("Hot dogs" beats "hamburgers" by a healthy margin, for example.)

Google Smackdown was built by an independent developer on top of the Google API (discussed in Chapter 7). Figure 14-18 shows **good** pitted against **evil**.

GoogleWhacking

Fans of Google have found a way to turn searching into a hobby: the quest for *GoogleWhacks*. A GoogleWhack is a two-word search with only one result: words that appear together only once on the entire Web (that Google knows about, at least). This includes such bizarre combinations as **tightfisted majorette** or **sandpapered ringmaster**. Many people spend much too much time searching for GoogleWhacks. But try it; it's harder than it looks!

 http://www.googlewhack.com/ takes the art of GoogleWhacking to a whole new level.

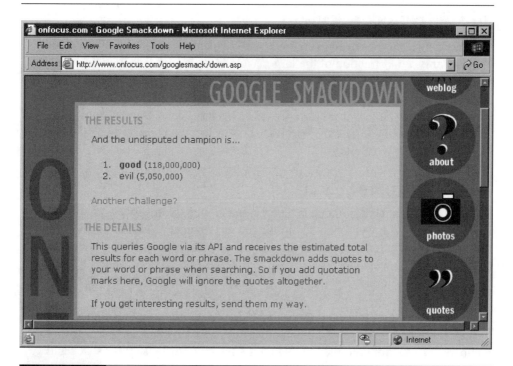

FIGURE 14-18   Whew!

Google Catalogs

Most of Google's services involve searching through pages that are already on the Web; Google's job is to find them for you. Google Catalogs (at **catalogs.google.com**) is an exception. Google has gathered thousands of printed catalogs, scanned them (that is, turned each page into a web-viewable image), and indexed the text on each page. You can use Google Catalogs to search through all these print catalogs, which is handy for finding specialty items from vendors that haven't made their wares available on the Internet.

Also, even vendors that are on the Web may have better pictures in their paper catalogs than on their website. It is actually easier to find a nice sweater from Land's End using Google Catalogs than it is to go to the **landsend.com** website, or to find that catalog you got in the mail last month.

Google Wireless Services

Wireless devices use a special version of the Web called the Mobile Web, which includes only a tiny fraction of the larger Web. Google Wireless Web Search searches not only the Mobile Web, but also the *entire* Web, and converts every web page on-the-fly to a version your device understands. For users with web-enabled wireless devices (phones or PDAs), Google Wireless is an essential service.

To learn how to use Google Wireless on your web-enabled wireless device, search for **google wireless**.

Google Number Search

Entering text on a mobile phone is tedious, but Google Number Search makes it easier for users with web-enabled mobile phones to enter search terms by pressing the button for each letter in the search just once; Google takes it from there and tries to determine what word you meant to enter. If you've ever tried to figure out what your phone number spells, that's just like what Google Number Search does. (For example, the phone number 555-2676 spells POPCORN.)

Point your microbrowser at **www.466453.com** to use Google Number Search. (Can you figure out what word the number 466453 spells?) Once there, press the numbers corresponding to the letters in your search terms. Use 0 for space and 1 for quote marks.

Other Ways to Search Using Google

There are a few other novel ways to search Google without using a web browser. If you think really hard and imagine some very unusual accessibility requirements, you can sometimes dream up situations where these services might be useful; but they are primarily a novelty, since you really need a browser to get much use out of the results they return.

You can search on Google through e-mail thanks to a service called CapeMail. To use it, just send an e-mail to **google@capeclear.com** with your search terms in the subject line. You will receive an e-mail response containing the search results. This service, built by CapeClear on the Google Web API, is further explained on **http://capescience.capeclear.com/google/** (or search for **google by e-mail**). As CapeClear's site admits, "It's not going to take the world by storm," but it's amusing to try.

A similar service, also built on the Google Web API, is Googlematic, which is a way to search Google using an instant messaging client like AOL Instant

Messenger. To use it, send an IM to the screen name "googlematic," and you will receive a message in response containing search results. Be warned, however, that this service is not consistently available. For more information, search for **googlematic**.

Finally, Google Voice Search (which can be found on **labs.google.com**) demonstrates technology which enables you to speak search terms into the phone rather than typing them on your keyboard. You will still need a browser to see the result pages. Search for **google voice search** to learn more about this feature.

14

Appendix

How Google Works

If you take a moment to think about it, the Google search engine is pretty amazing. Google answers thousands of queries per second, close to ten million queries per hour. Google servers around the world accept queries, find the most relevant pages on the requested topics, and return the results along with a number of targeted ads. To answer each query, Google sifts through more than three billion web pages, and it does so in less than one second! How did this Herculean task—so recently the stuff of science fiction—become a reality in just a few years?

The huge numbers of different web pages, not to mention the diversity of topics, and languages found within them, meant that no group of humans could ever hope to catalog it all by hand. There would be no way to keep up with the millions of web pages that change every day. Some kind of automated solution was required.

How Web Search Works

Google's computers do not check each page on the Web every time you search. Doing so would be far too slow. Given the size of the Web, any approach that requires sifting through billions of pages for each query is too slow to be useful.

Because of the vast amount of data that makes up the Web, Google must be doing something more clever. The answer is found every place you need to look up information quickly. Consider a library, for example. Libraries find books on any subject efficiently by keeping a card catalog, an index that allows you to quickly look up a topic and find a list of books related to it. The catalog is much smaller than the library itself, and is easily searched by hand or computer.

Similarly, one can find this technique applied in the indices of most textbooks and technical books like this one. This is exactly the concept that search engines

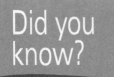

Where the Name Google Came From?

A googol is a math term for the number represented by a 1 followed by 100 zeros. A googolplex is the term for the number represented by a 1 followed by a googol of zeros. "The Googleplex" is what Google employees call Google's primary headquarters building.

like Google use. They create a giant index of the World Wide Web that permits them to quickly look up search terms and find the web pages to which they correspond. Instead of a list of words in a book and the corresponding page numbers, Google keeps a list of words on the Web and the corresponding web page addresses (URLs).

There are three steps involved to make the Web rapidly searchable:

1. Crawling

2. Indexing

3. Searching

The first two steps happen behind the scenes before your query is entered. The third step happens when you enter a query.

Crawling

To build their index, Google's computers must first download all the pages that Google suspects users might be interested in. This process is called *crawling* the Web.

Google determines which pages might be of interest based on several factors, most notably the number of incoming links and the content of the page. If a page has no incoming links, Google may not crawl it. It doesn't crawl some automatically generated pages, for example, older web-based newsgroup archives. Google also skips pages that require significant user interaction to download, for example, those accessed via form submission or those requiring browser technology like cookies.

The computers that crawl the Web are collectively known as the GoogleBot, and when Google starts a crawl these hundreds of computers start downloading pages all over the Web. Google conducts two types of crawls, *deep crawls* and *fresh crawls*, which we'll discuss in the following section.

The GoogleBot finds pages to download from three sources. Obviously, first it downloads any pages that it already knows about from previous crawls. Second, it downloads new pages submitted by webmasters through Google's website. And third, it downloads new pages when the GoogleBot finds a link to such a page in the course of the crawl. This permits the GoogleBot to automatically explore previously uncharted territory whenever a link to it exists anywhere Google knows about. In this way Google "follows" links all over the Web until it has downloaded every interesting page to which it can find a link.

A

Crawling three billion pages is a time-consuming task. Google allocates hundreds of machines to a crawl, but even so it takes days to complete. Some web servers might be down when the GoogleBot visits, so it may have to try again at a later time to download some pages when the website's servers are back up.

 GoogleBot downloads a snapshot of each page it crawls and caches (stores) that version. Google extracts snippets from the cached version that are included with most search results and displays the cached version when a user clicks on the Cached link. For further information about snippets and the Cached link, see Chapter 4.

Deep Crawl Versus Fresh Crawl

The crawl described in the previous section is known as the deep crawl because Google crawls "deeply" into the Web. It downloads all the pages it believes a user might want. It skips certain kinds of data, for example, huge message archives unlikely to contain much interesting information, but otherwise downloads any pages to which there are links. Because of the massive scale of the task, it happens periodically, typically once per month. Because a page might drastically change its content between deep crawls, the page that Google downloaded can become an increasingly inaccurate portrait of the current page.

Google's solution to this problem is to run a continuous fresh crawl in addition to the periodic deep crawl. The fresh crawl downloads a smaller number of frequently changing pages at a rate roughly proportional to how often they change. More popular pages are downloaded more often, which makes sense because Google strives to have an accurate idea of what's on popular pages. Google also takes this opportunity to download new pages it has recently become aware of, for example, submissions to Google by webmasters.

While the fresh crawl downloads fewer pages than the deep crawl, the combination of the two makes for a very effective approach. Google builds a large, solid base once per month using the deep crawl. Over the course of the following four weeks, it supplements this base with a continual series of small corrections and improvements that reflect any changes that occur in frequently updated sites.

Crawling explains why you can click a search result and get "Page Not Found." The page existed at the time of the crawl, but has since disappeared. The fresh crawl decreases the chances that this will happen for popular pages.

Indexing

Once Google has crawled all the pages of interest, it must build the index mentioned earlier in this chapter. Conceptually, this index is a list of words (possible queries) to each of which are attached the URLs of the web pages containing the word along with its locations on the web pages. Think of it as a humongous index for a book (the Internet), but instead of listing page numbers to which words correspond, the index lists web pages and word locations. Figure A-1 illustrates the concept. The index is created by the deep crawl and updated by each fresh crawl to keep the most fluid and popular parts up to date.

Searching

The final step occurs when a user enters a search. Google receives the query and checks its enormous index of words and corresponding web pages. It builds a list of pages the user might be interested in. Once Google has this list, it must decide which pages to show first for the query, as shown in Figure A-2.

This process is called *ranking*—when a search engine determines which pages to show first in its results. Primitive search engines employed simple ways to rank pages for a particular topic, for example, by the number of times the query terms appeared in the page. These types of techniques weren't that effective because they didn't do a good job of distinguishing pages with quality information from the rest.

Simplistic ranking techniques also fell victim to webmasters who began to cleverly craft their sites to get higher ranking. For example, to fool a search engine relying on word repetition, a webmaster might include popular search terms at the bottom of a page in white text on a white background. This text would be invisible to users, but a primitive search engine might find it appealing. The advent of such search engine "spammers" decreased the usefulness of the search engines to the point where results often had nothing at all to do with a user's query.

A

flowcharts - chartingtools.com, web1.acmepaper.com, ...
flowers - www.aflowercompany.com, petals-r-us.com, ...
floydpink - floyd.com, www.musicfanclub.org, ...
flu - www.cdc.gov, www.nih.gov, ...

FIGURE A-1 Google maintains an index of topics and web pages.

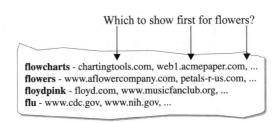

Which to show first for flowers?

flowcharts - chartingtools.com, web1.acmepaper.com, ...
flowers - www.aflowercompany.com, petals-r-us.com, ...
floydpink - floyd.com, www.musicfanclub.org, ...
flu - www.cdc.gov, www.nih.gov, ...

FIGURE A-2   Google must decide what order it will show these web pages.

In contrast to early search engines that relied on a single approach to determine ranking, Google combines many different approaches used by early search engines, as well as new techniques of its own.

Google's Rankings

In response to a query, Google assembles a list of candidate result pages. For example, for a one-word query, a list of pages returns in which the term is found. If a query contains multiple words, it looks up each of these words in its index and adds only those pages containing all the search terms to the list. For a quoted phrase, it finds all the pages containing the quoted words in consecutive locations and adds those pages to the list. Candidate pages are picked for other kinds of searches using similar logic.

For each candidate page, Google computes a *score*, a number indicating how likely Google believes the page will contain what the user is seeking. The higher the score, the more likely Google thinks the page is a good result. Pages receive lower scores if Google judges them less likely to be good results.

In order to compute the score for each page, Google considers more than 100 factors. These factors are often called *metrics*. A metric is simply a piece of information about a page, for example, the number of sites linked to it or whether or not the page contains the search terms in its title. Because these metrics are processed by computers, they are represented by numbers. For example, the metric indicating the number of sites linking to a page might be 10 if ten sites link to it. Similarly, depending upon whether a page contains the query terms in its title, the associated metric might be 1 (yes) or 0 (no). Representing metrics as numbers permits Google to combine them using a *scoring function* (or *scoring equation*), which we discuss in more detail in the following section. The concept is illustrated in Figure A-3.

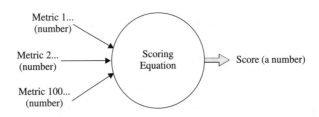

FIGURE A-3   For each page, metrics are combined by the scoring equation in order to determine rank.

Once Google has a score for each potential page, it is straightforward to determine rank. Because Google believes pages with higher scores are more likely to contain information matching the query, these pages are displayed in order of decreasing score. In other words, Google shows the pages deemed most likely to be relevant first. The page with the highest score is shown as the first result, the second-highest scoring page is shown second, and so forth.

In the following sections, we discuss some of the criteria Google considers when computing scores. Understanding this criteria will help you use Google more effectively.

PageRank

Google founders Sergey Brin and Larry Page, while graduate students at Stanford University, published a primary factor in Google's scoring computation. This factor treats the Web as a gigantic democracy, and is called PageRank.

NOTE   *Despite its name, PageRank is not the sole factor Google uses to determine rank. It is merely one metric among many. Other metrics Google uses are discussed in the following sections.*

A

The point of the Web is to provide an easy way to link to various sources of information. Larry and Sergey realized that they could use links on the Web to infer information about pages. They proposed that the quality of a page could be judged by the number of links to it. Furthermore, they reasoned that the more incoming links *to* a page, the more "important" links *from* that page should be.

These simple ideas turn out to be extremely powerful. They dictate a framework for determining what sites are likely to contain good information. If a page at **www.stanford.edu** has ten thousand high quality web pages linked to it, it is more likely to be an authority on a subject than, say, a site to which only two pages link.

In this way Google interprets each link as a "vote" for the link destination. The site's PageRank indicates roughly how popular a page is based of the number of "votes" for the page as well as the quality of the site casting each "vote." Those pages with many links by high-quality sites have high PageRank. Those pages with few quality links to them have low PageRank.

PageRank is not perfect, of course, since it is possible that a new site might have very useful information but hasn't yet been linked to because it hasn't been noticed. However, over time, PageRank has been shown to be a very effective tool for gauging relevance, and it is an important factor affecting the page rank shown by Google search.

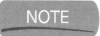

*Google ran the following "PigeonRank" parody of its search technology on April Fools Day, 2002: **http://www.google.com/technology/pigeonrank.html***

Simple Metrics

Google makes use of other sources of information about pages. Consider the typical web page shown in Figure A-4. Without reading the page carefully you can probably infer a good deal about its content. A page's title, any large headings it may contain, words or phrases that appear in bold or italics, and any specialized jargon appearing in the text all hint at the subject matter discussed in the page. Google's computers carefully examine each web page to extract this information. It is then used to compute metrics such as "does the term appear in a heading?", "does the term appear in italics?", and "does the term appear in the title?" These metrics could have value 1 if the answer is "yes" or 0 if the answer is "no."

The way links work provides another potentially useful bit of information. A link on a web page is composed of two parts: the link text and a link target. For example:

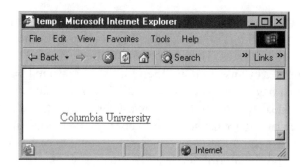

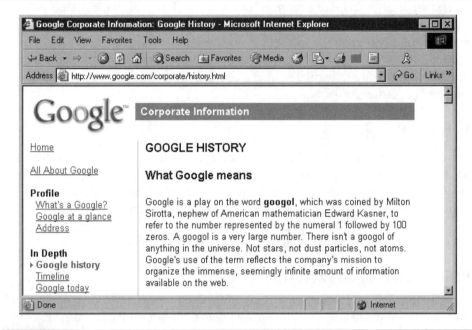

FIGURE A-4   Looking for meaning in a web page at Google.

The link text is the part that is visible to the user, in this case "Columbia University." The link target is typically not visible, and used by the author to tell the browser what page to load when the link is clicked. In this example, the link target might be **http://www.columbia.edu**.

One can think of a link as a piece of text (the link text) describing a web page (the link target). Doing so, you quickly realize that you can treat the billions of links that exist on the Web each as a small description of the site to which it links. This is an incredible database of human opinion! For example, one person might link to **www.columbia.edu** as "CU" another as "a university in New York" and perhaps yet another as "Columbia." Each of these links provides a small incremental amount of information that is fairly useless on its own. However, when combined with tens of billions of other links, the sum of these small things will quickly make a large pile! This information can be used in a variety of ways, for example, as a metric indicating how many links to the page contain the query terms.

Another factor that Google uses is *word proximity*. If you search for George Washington, for example, pages that contain these two words near each other in

A

the text are likely to receive a more favorable score. Pages for which "George" appears in one place and "Washington" appears several paragraphs later will be less favorably scored.

Google also harnesses users to improve ranking. It checks which results were clicked most often for a particular query, and infers that clicked results are the preferred pages for the query terms.

Arcane Metrics

There is more to determining what pages are about than examining cosmetics and links. Google brings scientists from a variety of specialized computer science fields to bear on the problem of web search. These experts apply advanced techniques—particularly from subfields of Artificial Intelligence—to extract information from the Web that can be useful for ranking and other related tasks. Some examples of the fields from which Google draws follow.

Natural-language Processing

Natural-language processing is the study of how to make computers understand, at least partially, human language. Since Web content is almost half human language, it should come as no surprise that advances in natural-language processing help Google in a number of ways, including determining the topic of a page. (The other half of the Web consists of images and other multimedia).

Machine Learning

Machine learning involves "training" computers to improve the way they carry out a specific task based on previous performance. For example, machine learning is often applied to automatically categorizing data, such as web pages. Google applies machine-learning techniques to a wide variety of problems, such as spelling correction and recognition of adult content for use with SafeSearch (as discussed in Chapter 7).

Data Mining

Researchers in this field come up with ways to analyze huge sets of data in order to discover unsuspected relationships among data. Google uses these relationships to improve search results by analyzing user behavior, to learn more about the Web by examining trends over time, and to provide services such as Google Sets (see Chapter 14).

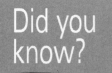

Google is a Brain Trust

Google employs over 60 Ph.D.s, most of them computer scientists. This is quite a lot of brainpower, especially in light of the fact that this is approximately the same number of Ph.D.-holding faculty members that make up the entire Computer Science department at UC Berkeley!

Information Retrieval

Information retrieval is the study of the most efficient ways to store, fetch, and analyze large sets of textual data. This is a tremendously important task for Google considering that by conservative estimates, the amount of information that must be processed during indexing is more than four million times as large as the complete works of Shakespeare.

The Scoring Equation

Given these metrics, how does Google use them to determine score? The answer is Google's scoring equation. You can think of a scoring equation as the recipe for computing scores. Google gives its equation the ingredients it needs—the metrics we just discussed—and the equation dictates how to compute a final score. This concept is illustrated in Figure A-5.

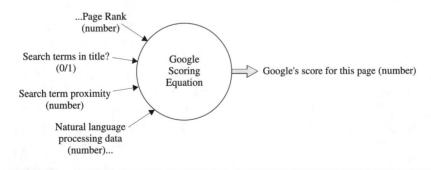

FIGURE A-5   To compute the score for a page, Google combines more than 100 metrics.

A

Different metrics have different weights, that is, different amounts of influence over the score. For example, because PageRank is a good indicator of the quality of information, PageRank might heavily influence the score. On the other hand, a metric such as the presence of query terms in the page title might carry less weight because page titles are often poor indicators of page content.

NOTE   *Because Google combines over a hundred different factors to determine score (and thus rank), it doesn't keep as simple an index as previously described. Rather, it maintains all the information necessary to efficiently compute its metrics. For example, to take word proximity into account, Google needs to maintain a database with the location of words on Web pages.*

The scoring function combines a large amount of diverse data in order to solve the problem of how to rank pages. Each one of the factors Google uses to determine rank is individually imperfect. There is nothing to keep someone from titling a page about bird watching as "The Life and Times of Joan of Arc," labeling a link to **www.stanford.edu** as "mashed potatoes," or filling a page purporting to be about UFOs with recipes for cheesecake. In fact, there are pages of this nature on the Web. However, by combining many different metrics and looking at them in their entirety, the impact of a few confusing, contradictory, or aberrant pieces of information is negated. The influence of the larger number of "good" indicators shines through.

For Technical Readers

Technically inclined readers might be interested in reading Larry Page and Sergey Brin's paper about creating Backrub, the research project at Stanford that turned into Google. It can be found at **http://www-db.stanford.edu/ ~backrub/google.html**.

Google's server architecture is described by engineers from the Google Systems Lab in a paper published in 2003 through the Institute of Electrical and Electronic Engineers (IEEE) called "Web Search for a Planet: The Google Cluster Architecture." It can be found at **http://www.computer.org/micro/ mi2003/m2022.pdf**.

Google's Engineering Principles

Have you wondered what engineering effort is required to make Google work? While a detailed discussion is clearly outside the scope of this book, we will enumerate some of the principles Google uses: parallelism, redundancy, low-cost hardware, and specialization.

Parallelism

A *serial task* is a task where each step can proceed only once the previous step has completed. Having a baby is a serial task. Only one woman can carry a pregnancy through to full term; you cannot add more women to the task in order to speed it along. A *parallel task* is a task where multiple steps can be executed at the same time. For example, making 100 pizzas is a parallel task. One cook with one oven could do it serially, but 100 cooks with 100 ovens could do it much faster.

Given the amount of data Google needs to sift through, it must take extreme care that it does so efficiently. For example, a task that required Google to operate on each of the pages on the Web, one after another (a serial task), for one second each, would take close to 100 years to complete. A similar task that could be run in parallel on 1,000 computers would complete in just over a month.

Finding parallel ways to do complicated things is one of the core competencies of a search engine like Google. Google achieves a lot of its speed by leveraging this principle. Since doing so requires a large number of simultaneously available computers, Google also maintains many backups.

Redundancy

Of all online services, Google has to be up there with the most reliable. It's a very rare day, indeed, that the Google site is down or inaccessible. Google's infrastructure was built to withstand not only the failure of a large number of its machines, but also the failure of entire datacenters, the locations where its machines connect to the Internet. Many people contend that if **www.google.com** doesn't respond, it's more likely that the entire Internet is down rather than Google's servers.

Google achieves this reliability not through a small number of very reliable machines, but through a massive number of low-cost machines. Google has more than 10,000 machines, which is more than ten computers per Google employee!

Low-cost Hardware

Google's entire infrastructure is built around large numbers of low-end, inexpensive PCs. Once Google figured out how to hook many computers together in a useful

A

way, a very powerful "distributed" computer made up of hundreds or thousands of cooperating machines was born. Instead of purchasing a few very powerful, very expensive machines, Google fashioned its own supercomputer-like system from a mass of cheap computers. This was likely an economical move, but imagine the day-to-day maintenance operations required for such a large number of computers!

Specialization

Google Web Search operates a bit like an assembly line. Instead of having one machine do everything required to answer a particular query, the task is broken up into many shorter steps that are carried out on many machines. Each machine specializes in just one task, so each machine can perform its duty very quickly. For example, one machine might receive a query from a user. This machine might pass the query terms to a machine that computes scores. The scoring machine might ask computers holding Google's index for potentially matching URLs and others for score-related data. While these machines carry out the tasks necessary to answer the search, the original machine that received the query is free to accept more.

Index

INTERNATIONAL CONTACT INFORMATION

AUSTRALIA
McGraw-Hill Book Company
Australia Pty. Ltd.
TEL +61-2-9900-1800
FAX +61-2-9878-8881
http://www.mcgraw-hill.com.au
books-it_sydney@mcgraw-hill.com

CANADA
McGraw-Hill Ryerson Ltd.
TEL +905-430-5000
FAX +905-430-5020
http://www.mcgraw-hill.ca

**GREECE, MIDDLE EAST, & AFRICA
(Excluding South Africa)**
McGraw-Hill Hellas
TEL +30-210-6560-990
TEL +30-210-6560-993
TEL +30-210-6560-994
FAX +30-210-6545-525

MEXICO (Also serving Latin America)
McGraw-Hill Interamericana Editores
S.A. de C.V.
TEL +525-1500-5108
FAX +525-117-1589
http://www.mcgraw-hill.com.mx
carlos_ruiz@mcgraw-hill.com

SINGAPORE (Serving Asia)
McGraw-Hill Book Company
TEL +65-6863-1580
FAX +65-6862-3354
http://www.mcgraw-hill.com.sg
mghasia@mcgraw-hill.com

SOUTH AFRICA
McGraw-Hill South Africa
TEL +27-11-622-7512
FAX +27-11-622-9045
robyn_swanepoel@mcgraw-hill.com

SPAIN
McGraw-Hill/
Interamericana de España, S.A.U.
TEL +34-91-180-3000
FAX +34-91-372-8513
http://www.mcgraw-hill.es
professional@mcgraw-hill.es

**UNITED KINGDOM, NORTHERN,
EASTERN, & CENTRAL EUROPE**
McGraw-Hill Education Europe
TEL +44-1-628-502500
FAX +44-1-628-770224
http://www.mcgraw-hill.co.uk
emea_queries@mcgraw-hill.com

ALL OTHER INQUIRIES Contact:
McGraw-Hill/Osborne
TEL +1-510-420-7700
FAX +1-510-420-7703
http://www.osborne.com
omg_international@mcgraw-hill.com

Know How

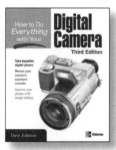

How to Do Everything with Your Digital Camera
Third Edition
ISBN: 0-07-223081-9

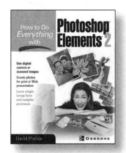

How to Do Everything with Photoshop Elements 2
ISBN: 0-07-222638-2

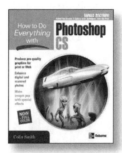

How to Do Everything with Photoshop CS
ISBN: 0-07-223143-2
4-color

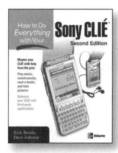

How to Do Everything with Your Sony CLIÉ
Second Edition
ISBN: 0-07-223074-6

How to Do Everything with Macromedia Contribute
0-07-222892-X

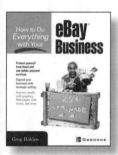

How to Do Everything with Your eBay Business
0-07-222948-9

How to Do Everything with Illustrator CS
ISBN: 0-07-223092-4
4-color

How to Do Everything with Your iPod
ISBN: 0-07-222700-1

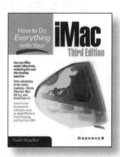

How to Do Everything with Your iMac,
Third Edition
ISBN: 0-07-213172-1

How to Do Everything with Your iPAQ Pocket PC
Second Edition
ISBN: 0-07-222950-0

Sound Off!

Visit us at **www.osborne.com/bookregistration** and let us know what you thought of this book. While you're online you'll have the opportunity to register for newsletters and special offers from McGraw-Hill/Osborne.

We want to hear from you!

Sneak Peek

Visit us today at **www.betabooks.com** and see what's coming from McGraw-Hill/Osborne tomorrow!

Based on the successful software paradigm, Bet@Books™ allows computing professionals to view partial and sometimes complete text versions of selected titles online. Bet@Books™ viewing is free, invites comments and feedback, and allows you to "test drive" books in progress on the subjects that interest you the most.